ISO 9000:200~ The Route to Registration

The Complete Guide to Implementation, Registration
And Profitability of Your Quality Management System

First Edition
Third Printing
2002

ISO 9000:2000
The Route to Registration

The Complete Guide to Implementation, Registration
And Profitability of Your Quality Management System

First Edition
Third Printing
2002

Edited by
Jason Hart
CEEM Inc.

Reston, Virginia

Other titles available through BSI CEEM...

- *The ISO 9000:2000 series of standards*
- *Quality Systems Update (monthly newsletter)*
- *ISO 14000 Questions and Answers*
- *ISO 14000 Case Studies: Models for Implementation*
- *International Environmental Systems Update (monthly newsletter)*

To obtain a free copy of BSI CEEM's latest training and publications catalog, call 800-745-5565, or visit our virtual library on the Internet: www.ceem.com.

Table of Contents

Module 2: Introducing ISO 9000:2000 to Employees

Module 3: Understanding the ISO 9001:2000 clauses

Module 4: Developing the Quality Manual

Module 5: Developing Appropriate Documentation

Module 6: Implementing the System

Module 7: Measurement

Module 8: Auditing

Module 9: Management Review

Module 10: Registration the BSI Way

The Future: Today and Tomorrow

Annexes

Utilization Chart

> **"***A great society is a place where men are
> more concerned with
> the quality of their goods
> than the quantity of their goods.***"**
>
> —*Lyndon B. Johnson*
> *May 22, 1964*

Foreword...

No matter what business you're in, leadership takes courage and vision. We've heard or read that a thousand times, from dozens of self-help books to the barrage of "inspirational" infomercials on television.

But few people actually put those words into action—or understand them, for that matter. Many believe that leadership is simply a personality trait—most of us probably know at least one or two "born leaders," regardless of their trade.

The fact is, however, being a leader takes a lot of continuous hard work, and although personality has something to do with it, diligence is really the key to success. I guarantee that any good leader will tell you that any chance he or she gets.

At BSI, we believe that diligence and leadership are the fundamental ingredients for success at all levels for every organization, and since 1901, we've been helping businesses around the world realize their own potential for controlled growth and a sustainable future. As the world's oldest national standards organization, however, we understand that being leaders and "doing things right" aren't easy. In fact, the opposite is quite often the case.

That's precisely why we've developed this book—to help organizations improve and quite frankly, *do things right* in the business world. That doesn't mean the tasks at hand (ISO 9001:2000 implementation and registration) will be easy or guarantee perfection by any means. But by operating to a set of refined international standards and continually improving your organization's performance—leadership, quality and success will be much easier to achieve.

Indeed, President Johnson's words ring truer today than ever before. And at a time when the competition moves faster than the picture on the cover of this book, the highest quality of products and services will propel all of us into the leadership realm that we've worked so hard to attain.

This book will help you take that first step toward better quality, and indeed, becoming a leader in your industry. After reading it, you'll understand that the new ISO 9001:2000 and the BSI Way are not just about getting a "Badge on the Wall"—both are about the diligence and leadership it takes to attain excellence. We hope you enjoy *The Route to Registration*, utilize its guidance and achieve all of the objectives that you are about to set. And of course, if there's anything we can do to help you with your quality journey, please contact us. We're here to help.

Robert Perry   Joseph C. Lissenden
President, BSI Inc.   General Manager, CEEM Inc.

Reston, Virginia — July 2001

About BSI Inc...

BSI Inc. is the North and South American hub of the British Standards Institution, the world's leading international standards, testing, registration and certification organization with offices in more than 100 countries.

The BSI Inc. corporate office is located in Reston, Va., with additional offices in 16 locations throughout North and South America. BSI provides local service with a global reach to a range of clients, including small-, medium- and large-sized corporations, public and private firms and government entities.

BSI has been helping organizations improve their operating activities for 100 years. Established in 1901, BSI was the world's first national standards body, and in the 1980s, the BSI Standards Development Team managed the creation of BS 5750, which was later adopted as ISO 9000.

BSI has registered more than 35,500 locations to ISO 9000, and now offers registration to many management systems, including:
- ISO 9001:2000—Quality Management Systems
- QS-9000/ISO/TS 16949/VDA 6.1—Quality Management for the Automotive Supply Industry
- AS 9100/TL 9000—Quality Management for the Aerospace and Telecommunications industries, respectively
- ISO 14001—Environmental Management Systems
- OHSAS 18001—Occupational Health and Safety
- BS 7799—Information Security Management

Indeed, the need for management systems registration today is as strong as ever. Profitability, competitiveness, globalization, adaptability, growth, technology and speed of change are all challenges of doing business in the 21st century. BSI recognizes that meeting these challenges is a tall order for any organization. We believe the good organization will have processes/procedures and standards of performance to meet these challenges—but the great organizations will have management systems registration.

Management systems registration helps organizations achieve continuous performance improvement. A proven management system, combined with ongoing validation, enables an organization to continually identify areas to increase profits, reduce cost, improve time and resource management, enhance communications, improve product/service consistency and deliver superior customer satisfaction, while managing risk.

Management systems registration means:
- verifying practice vs. process
- objective third-party validation
- benchmarking performance

As the world's largest and most experienced registrar, BSI has:
- experience across all industries, manufacturing, process and service related.
- worked with organizations of all sizes from 2 to 200,000 employees.
- teams of assessors, working from home, geographically positioned for easy contact with you.
- experienced assessors who recognize that every business is different and act accordingly.

Our registration of your management system is backed up by our own accreditation by an independent body. Our accreditation provides assurances to you that BSI Inc. continues to operate according to internationally accepted criteria. We have accreditation from RAB (USA) for QMS and EMS and from InMetro (Brazil) and SCC (Canada) for QMS.

Please contact us if you have any questions concerning the topics covered in this book.

About CEEM Inc...

With the 21st century now officially here, today's businesses face more challenges than ever to be effective, efficient and sustainable for a profitable future. Issues such as globalization, competition, profitability, quality, the environment, information security and health and safety affect not only the business performance of today's products and services, but also the job performance of millions of professionals.

At CEEM Inc., helping businesses manage those issues proactively is our mantra. Since 1979, CEEM has hosted scores of seminars, workshops and courses, and also has created dozens of publications and products to assist companies around the world to enhance business performance.

To further our global reach, CEEM became a member of the BSI group in July 1998 after enjoying a decade-long training relationship with BSI. The combination of these talents offers state-of-the-art courses, enhanced training materials, excellent training facilities, premium trainers and consultants and a variety of products to assist clients with business performance needs.

Relevant CEEM courses to ISO 9001:2000 include:
- Understanding ISO 9001:2000
- Quality Systems Documentation
- ISO 9001:2000 Auditor Transition
- Implementing ISO 9001:2000
- ISO 9001:2000 Lead Auditor
- ISO 9001:2000 Internal Quality Systems Auditor
- ISO 9001:2000 Management Briefing
- ISO 9001:2000 Essentials for Registrars

Through KEMA Registered Quality Inc., CEEM was one of the first companies in the world to register to the ISO 9001:2000 standard—just five days after it was published.

For more information about CEEM or our products and services, call 800-745-5565, or visit our Web site: www.ceem.com.

Our Mission

CEEM's mission is to create long-term national and international customers by providing the finest training, consulting and information tools in the field of specialty management.

Further, CEEM's mission is to provide these products and services in the most profitable and sustainable manner.

Acknowledgments...

Several experts from around the world contributed to the development of this book, and naming them all would be an impossible task. But the following quality professionals made significant contributions to the vision, content and release of this product. They deserve recognition and thanks from the staff.

Mark B. Baker
Vice President of Sales and Marketing, CEEM Inc.
Mark Baker is vice president of Sales and Marketing for CEEM Inc. Mark began his tenure with CEEM in 1995, after teaching English Literature and nonfiction writing for the Fairfax County Virginia Public Schools for 10 years. Since that time, he has been a full-time CEEM employee, developing several products such as *The ISO 14000 Handbook*, *The ISO 14000 Case Studies* book and the *Trained Eye* newsletter.

Reg Blake
Vice President of Corporate Development, BSI Inc.
Reg Blake currently serves as Vice President of Corporate Development for BSI Inc. in Reston, Va. He also was one of the "founding members" of BSI Inc. when the company was established in the United States in 1992. Reg also is well-established within the ISO community, serving as a member of the RAB QMS Advisory Council; director of the Independent Association of Accredited Registrars; member of the American Aerospace Quality Group; and committee member for the development of the TL 9000 standard for telecommunications suppliers.

John W. (Jay) Fisher
Trainer/Consultant, CEEM Inc.
Jay Fisher is an RAB lead auditor, an IRCA certified lead auditor and has assisted numerous companies (in the areas of plastics, aircraft engine repair, textile, kaolin and chemicals) prepare to implement ISO 9000. Jay also performs certification audits primarily in the Standard Industrial Codes (SIC's) relating to the computer, chemical plastics, aerospace, communications and general manufacturing industries. Jay teaches ISO 9000 overview, implementation, documentation and auditing courses and specializes in the service industries.

John Guzik
Trainer/Consultant, CEEM Inc.
Prior to joining CEEM Inc., John Guzik served as a consultant with an Atlanta-based firm, and throughout his career, has guided some 50 client companies through the various phases of preparation/implementation for ISO 9001 and QS-9000 registration. In the quality management arena, John was the first Quality Manager in Georgia-Pacific Corp.'s Container Division to successfully pilot a box plant through ISO 9001 registration. Later, he was instrumental in repeating this

success with four other sister plants within one year. John also was appointed the Quality Systems Manager for Oxford Container Co. of Tim-Bar Corp., where he acted as corporate director of ISO systems. John has a deep background in quality management, production/manufacturing, journalism and consulting.

Bill Hoellrich
Vice President of Operations, BSI Inc.
Bill Hoellrich joined BSI in 1990 and now runs the operations division and systems assessment team for BSI Inc., offering a wealth of experience in the quality and environmental arenas. Prior to joining BSI, Bill's expertise has included work in the following areas: aerospace components, mechanical, electronics, chemicals, rubber and plastics, semiconductor, telecommunications, service industries and petrochemical.

Diane Hunt
Trainer/Consultant, CEEM Inc.
Diane Hunt has been an RAB-certified ISO 9000 assessor since 1996, and has audited more than two dozen organizations as a lead auditor or audit team member. Additionally, Diane has taught courses about ISO 9000 and quality management for more than seven years, and has a wealth of experience as a trainer and consultant.

Matthew A. Kreib
Assistant Editor, CEEM Inc.
Matthew Kreib is an Assistant Editor at CEEM Inc. Matthew writes on a variety of topics related to CEEM's core business. His primary responsibility is to produce CEEM's flagship publication *International Environmental Systems Update*, a monthly publication that offers the latest information on developments in the ISO 14000 standards arena as well as breaking news from the global EMS community. Matthew is a member of the U.S. Technical Advisory Group to ISO Technical Committee 207 on environmental management systems.

Art Lewis
Trainer/Consultant, CEEM Inc.
Art Lewis has worked with CEEM since 1998 and has more than 26 years of experience implementing management systems. Art has assisted more than 30 organizations achieve ISO/QS registration. Art is an IRCA certified lead assessor, IATCA senior auditor and an AIAG certified QS-9000 lead assessor. He is also a certified management accountant.

Kevin Linden
BSI Inc. Auditor
Kevin Linden has conducted ISO 9000 assessments in 38 states, amassing more than 1,600 audit days of experience. Kevin has taught numerous courses for CEEM, including the Internal Quality Systems Auditor, Lead Auditor, ISO 9001:2000 Revisions, the Process Assessment Workshop and many more. He also has assisted several companies as a consultant in the implementation of ISO 9001

and eventual successful registration. Kevin is a certified BSI auditor and has trained dozens of BSI auditors. He has performed more than 160 days of auditing for over 10 years at BSI. Kevin also held the position of manufacturing quality manager at Bardex Plastics, which successfully implementing ISO 9001, and was the research plant manager for ICI Research. His experience includes plastic technology, thermodynamics, hydraulics, electrical engineering and project design.

Joseph C. Lissenden
General Manager, CEEM Inc.
Joe Lissenden is General Manager of CEEM Inc., responsible for the company's continuing performance in the areas of training, consulting and information services. With Joe's leadership, CEEM became one of the first companies in the world to register to the new ISO 9001:2000, just five days after the standard was published. Joe has been in the ISO 9000 industry for nine years, conducting extensive market research, developing and managing training programs, consulting to ISO 9001/2 and ISO 9001:2000 and lecturing on management systems nationwide.

Dick Mascis
Trainer/Consultant, CEEM Inc.
Dick Mascis has been a quality management consultant and instructor for nine years and has more than 35 years of professional experience in the quality arena. He is an RAB certified lead auditor and past president of the Northern Virginia ASQ Chapter. He has conducted program management on major programs such as Trident I and II Weapon System development and production—the largest successful defense acquisition project ever conducted. Dick is qualified to instruct all CEEM ISO 9000 programs including all four RAB accredited courses for quality management systems.

Ronald D. Mathis, CMS
Vice President of Marketing and Sales, BSI Inc.
Ron Mathis joined BSI Inc. in January 2001 as Vice President of Marketing and Sales. Ron brings with him extensive skills in the Sales and Sales Management arena, along with a well-versed ISO 9000 knowledge base. Before joining BSI, Ron served for three years as Vice President of Marketing and Sales for another registrar in the Washington, D.C., area. In addition to his ISO 9000 background, Ron's repertoire of skills also includes telemarketing and telesales management, professional sales training, technical training and guest lecturing; all gained through his previous career experiences. With GTE, Ron held several senior management positions including Vice President of Sales, Vice President of Marketing & Sales, Director of Operations and Director of Sales.

Mike Murphy
Operations Manager, BSI Inc.
With more than 20 years of experience in quality and environmental control, regulatory, safety and quality auditing, Mike Murphy has worked with major *Fortune 100* clients in the development of quality and environmental programs. His expert-

ise also includes statistical process control, programming, graphs, training personnel and the interpretation and evaluation of data. Mike is a certified RAB, EARA and IRCA lead quality auditor and EMS assessor.

Martin Puetz
Trainer/Consultant, CEEM Inc.
Martin Puetz conducts training and consulting services for CEEM and has broad experience and expertise in the areas of operations management, internal consulting, strategic planning, staff training and development, enterprise resource planning (SAP), Lean manufacturing/Six Sigma, regulatory compliance assessment, quality and environmental auditing, project management and EHS systems management. Martin is an IRCA QMS Lead Auditor and an EMS Lead Auditor and has spent the past 18 years in the defense and aerospace industry. Martin was a quality engineer at Boeing, a quality program manager and a procurement quality engineer while at Lockheed Martin Tactical Aircraft Systems. Martin is also a specialist at integrating management systems.

Gary D. Scalise
Trainer/Consultant, CEEM Inc.
Gary is an independent quality professional, a senior associate with CEEM and has been a manager and director of quality assurance functions with several *Fortune* 500 firms, including 10 years with GTE. He has been a corporate staff instructor with the Eaton Quality Institute, and continues to develop and deliver courses in Quality Systems, Process Improvement, Quality Engineering, DOE, SPC and auditing. His industrial, academic and professional experience has brought management assignments ranging from experimental design to reform of business culture. Gary is knowledgeable in plastics and rubber, printing and publishing, lighting and sound, medical devices, electrical and automotive components, audio, testing laboratories and textiles. He has been an ASQ Certified Quality Engineer since 1979 and a CQE instructor for more than 15 years.

Paul Scicchitano
Publisher, Quality Systems Publishing
Paul Scicchitano is publisher of QSU Publishing Co., the producer of *Quality Systems Update*, a monthly newsletter devoted to ISO 9000 issues and the ISO 9000 Registered Company Directory North America, which collects data on more than 45,000 third-party registration certificates in the United States, Canada and Mexico. Paul regularly attends meetings of the international body charged with drafting the ISO 9000 family of standards and he recently oversaw a comprehensive study of ISO 9000 certificate holders, which examined the potential costs and benefits associated with registration in a 300-page analysis published by The McGraw-Hill Companies. QSU Publishing Co. is headquartered at 3975 University Drive, Suite 230, Fairfax, Virginia 22030; Tel: 866-225-3122; Web: www.qsuonline.com.

Tom Shelley
Marketing Manager, BSI Inc.
Tom Shelley joined BSI in December 1997, as a graduate management trainee. He has worked on a number of projects in the international arena, focusing on BSI international development in Asia and the Americas. He has worked as International Marketing Manager and as Brand Marketing Manager for BSI in the United Kingdom, where he gained a CIM Post Graduate Diploma in Marketing. Tom joined BSI Inc. as Marketing Manager in April 2001, utilizing his expertise in management systems marketing.

Sean Victor
Trainer/Consultant, CEEM Inc.
Sean Victor is a management consultant who uses his strong background in quality management to guide organizations implementing quality, environment, hazard analysis critical control point systems and total business improvement. His career experience involved management positions in strategic quality management, where he facilitated organizational improvements resulting in profitable gains and product quality enhancements. Sean is a trainer and facilitator with CEEM and has successfully led many companies to achieve international quality system registration with particular application in the credit counseling industry. a graduate of Phillip Crosby Associates Quality Management College, he is a certified quality improvement facilitator, a registered Lead Auditor with the International Register of Certificated Auditors, a senior member of the American Society for Quality, a Certified Quality Manager and a Certified Quality Auditor. He speaks at quality conferences and has been a resource quality consultant for the University of West Indies.

Larry Whittington
President, Whittington & Associates
Larry Whittington is president of Whittington & Associates, LLC, a consulting company located in Marietta, Ga. His broad experience includes strategic planning, technical education, management consulting, systems engineering, software development, quality auditing and project leadership. Larry is an IRCA and RAB certified ISO 9000 Lead Auditor, is a trained TickIT lead assessor for software systems and an AIAG certified QS-9000 lead auditor for the automotive industry. Larry is also an ASQ certified quality auditor and ASQ certified software quality engineer.

Jim Wilson
Trainer/Consultant, CEEM Inc.
Jim Wilson is registered as an IRCA ISO 9000 lead auditor and has led the implementation of ISO 9000 and for many other organizations including manufacturing and service companies. He has extensive experience in the design, development, implementation and assessment of change projects in military, government and private sector organizations.

Introduction...

As one of the world's foremost registrars, BSI receives constant feedback from clients regarding the ISO 9001 registration process. Since the inception of ISO 9000 in 1987, BSI has registered more than 35,500 organizations worldwide, and the wealth of information generated in working with these clients has enabled BSI to refine the route to registration to one that is efficient, easy to manage and supported by expert Client Managers.

The purpose of this book is to share with you the most helpful information gathered from thousands of organizations, hundreds of thousands of client meetings and millions of hours spent auditing companies. Once you've read *The Route to Registration*, you'll feel comfortable with what lies ahead as you embark upon the ISO 9001:2000 registration process.

As you will become aware through this book and through personal experience, the relationship between a Client Manager and client is extremely important. If you have any questions upon completing *The Route to Registration*, you may want to contact BSI at 800-862-4977 and begin your own quality journey.

How to use this book...

The ISO 9000:2000 Route to Registration is the complete guide for any organization to implement, register and/or transition a quality management system to the requirements of the ISO 9001:2000 standard. This book takes you through the typical implementation process, from gaining management approval and interpreting the new standard to understanding the registration process and maintaining your system.

The primary focus of the book is on the new ISO 9001:2000 and its requirements. However, *The Route to Registration* also answers 100 of the most frequently asked questions regarding the new ISO 9000:2000 series, with user-friendly language that business people can understand.

This book also includes several resources to aid an organization's registration process, most notably, the entire content of British Standard (European Norm) ISO 9001:2000. It also includes a clause-by-clause interpretation by some of the world's finest experts in quality management. Additional resources in *The Route to Registration* include examples of procedures, quality objectives, quality policies, a quality manual and other tools to assist organizations through their continuous quality management journey.

At the end of several sections, you'll also notice specific guidance for organizations transitioning to ISO 9001:2000 from the 1994 version, called "**Transition Tips.**" These pointers help organizations through some of the more complex interpretations of the new standard, but they should not be considered the only interpretations that exist in the marketplace. Also, at the end of each module, a special "Notes" section has been established so that readers can keep a record of ideas and interpretations that can aid with their own implementation efforts.

Indeed, as many companies worldwide experience the implementation process, there likely will be as many interpretations. To avoid any ambiguity, *The Route to Registration* uses language like "the intent of the standard" or "auditor's expectations." This language is used not to confuse the reader in any way, only to show that varied interpretations will develop in many areas of the new standard.

To that end, this book is a continuous joint project for BSI and CEEM. As auditors become more comfortable conducting audits to the new guidelines and best practices evolve, *The Route to Registration* will be revised with new case studies and additional guidance to assist organizations with ISO 9001:2000.

Of course, if you have additional questions after reading this book, please feel free to contact CEEM by telephone at 800-745-5565 or by e-mail: solutions@ceem.com. Your comments and suggestions can help us create an even better Second Edition!

module
1

Introducing ISO 9000:2000
To Management

 ## What is ISO?

Before we get started with all the details concerning the world's most popular and widely used standards for quality management systems, it's a good idea to know a little about "ISO" and what it's all about. This information can be used as background when explaining your registration plans to the management team.

ISO refers to the International Organization for Standardization, a worldwide federation of national standards bodies from more than 130 countries. Founded in Geneva, Switzerland, in 1946, ISO was created to develop a common set of manufacturing, trade and communication standards for a growing international community.

According to ISO officials, ISO comes from the Greek word *isos*, which means "equal." From "equal" to "standard," the line of thinking that led to the choice of "ISO" as the name of the organization was easy to follow. Additionally, the name "ISO" is used around the world to denote the organization, thus avoiding the plethora of acronyms resulting from the translation of "International Organization for Standardization" into the different national languages of members.

The mission of ISO is to promote the development of standardization and related activities in the world to facilitate the international exchange of goods and services, and to develop cooperation in the spheres of intellectual, scientific, technological and economic activity. ISO's work results in international agreements, which are published as International Standards.

The technical work of ISO is highly decentralized, carried out in a hierarchy of some 2,850 technical committees, subcommittees and working groups. In these committees, qualified representatives of industry, research institutes, government authorities, consumer bodies and international organizations from around the world come together as equal partners in the resolution of global standardization problems. Some 30,000 experts participate in meetings each year to develop standards for everyday life.[1]

Indeed, ISO standards are a part of our lives in many ways. Some examples of ISO's work include:

- The *ISO film speed code*, among many other photographic equipment standards, has been adopted worldwide making things simpler for the general user.
- Standardization of the format of *telephone and banking cards* means the cards can be used worldwide.
- The *internationally standardized freight container* enables all components of a transport system—air and seaport facilities, railways, highways and packages—to interface efficiently. This, combined with standardized documents to identify sensitive or dangerous cargoes, makes international trade cheaper, faster and safer.
- *Paper sizes.* The original standard was published by DIN in 1922. Now used worldwide as ISO 216, standard paper sizes allow economies of scale with cost benefits to both producers and consumers.
- The *ISO international codes for country names, currencies and languages* help to eliminate duplication and incompatibilities in the collection, processing and dissemination of information. As resource-saving tools, universally understandable codes play an important role in both automated and manual documentation.
- The diversity of screw threads for identical applications used to represent an important technical obstacle to trade. It caused maintenance problems, and lost or damaged nuts or bolts could not easily be replaced. A global solution is supplied in the ISO standards for *ISO metric screw threads*.
- And, of course, more than 400,000 organizations have implemented and registered to *ISO 9000:1994*, which provides a framework for quality management and quality assurance. The *ISO 14000* series provides a similar framework for environmental management.

 What is the development process of an international standard like ISO 9000:2000?

A proposal to begin work in a new field of technical activity usually comes from ISO itself, but on occasion, it may originate from an outside international organization. All new proposals for standardization are submitted to ISO for consideration, and if accepted, ISO's Technical Management Board—the governing body of ISO—will designate a "technical committee" (TC) to begin the work. In the case of ISO 9000, TC 176 was created in 1987 to develop the series of standards.

The development of an international standard is sometimes an arduous process, but one based on consensus from the TC's membership. The process has numerous stages, but often follows this structure:

---

[1] *ISO Web site—www.iso.ch*

- A new work item proposal with an initial draft is submitted for consideration and circulated to committee members for a three-month letter ballot.
- If approved, the item is assigned to the appropriate group for development and a project leader is chosen.
- The initial draft will then progress through the following stages:
  1. A final Working Draft
  2. A Committee Draft (CD—subjected to a three-month letter ballot review)
  3. A Draft International Standard (DIS—five-month letter ballot review)
  4. Final Draft International Standard (FDIS—two-month yes/no vote, no comment period)
  5. International Standard is published

The entire process can take three to eight years, although some standards, such as ISO 17799 on Information Security Management Systems, can be fast-tracked. When that happens, a standard begins at the DIS level and can be approved in less than a year.

When voting takes place within technical committees, each member country of ISO has one member body and one vote, similar to the way the United Nations operates. In the United States, the American National Standards Institute (ANSI) is the representative body to ISO. In the United Kingdom, BSI is the representative body to ISO. For a complete listing of other ISO representatives, visit the ISO Web page at www.iso.ch.

But don't think that the "experts" of TC 176 aren't people just like you. Each country has a Technical Advisory Group (TAG) that supports each TC. In fact, you can get involved in the development process by becoming a TAG representative and attending the TC meetings. This can allow you to voice your implementation experience and provide feedback to the ISO committee(s).

Just remember that ISO standards are based on a consensus process, which means that not everyone will get what they want on every issue. This eliminates the extremes but does, on occasion, help to explain why a certain clause in the standard might be diluted from an intent that may be ideal. Always keep in mind that international standards represent the minimum of what needs to be done—they do not prevent any organization from going beyond the minimum requirements.

What is Quality?

A 19th-century Irish novelist coined the phrase, *"Beauty is altogether in the eye of the beholder."*

There's no doubt about that statement's validity then and now, but if you stop and think about it, the same can be said about "quality." It can mean a million different things to a million different people. For example, a quality car to a 40-year-old executive could mean a dependable, safe and well-engineered Cadillac Seville with a beautiful leather interior. But to an 18-year-old college freshman, it could mean a cherry red Ford Mustang with alloy wheels and a loud stereo. Both cars meet the needs and expectations of the user, but they are defined quite differently.

In terms of a quality management system and ISO 9000, however, the term "quality" has a clear and succinct definition. In the new ISO 9000:2000 standard, it is defined in this way:

> *"The degree to which a set of inherent characteristics fulfills requirements."*

Of course, the concept can be much more complex than that, depending on your organization and your expectations for quality, but it doesn't have to be. In a nutshell, "quality" is all about *customer satisfaction*, a term with which you'll become more familiar as you read this book. The simple fact is, customers require products and services with special characteristics that satisfy their stated or implied needs and expectations, which can be expressed in contracts, agreements, product specifications or just by your customers telling you what they want. And, of course, that's exactly the point—the customer *always* determines the acceptable parameters, and it's up to you to meet and/or exceed those expectations.

The issue for business, however, is that those quality parameters are changing constantly. The teen-ager who loves that red Mustang may not have the same "quality" expectations 20 years from now—in fact, that beautiful Cadillac may not seem so bad! On the other hand, the Mustang may be a better fit for that executive in 20 years as well.

I think you get the point. Quality is, indeed, in the eye of the beholder, and the beholders are you, your organization's top management, your stakeholders, interested parties and, of course, your customers. Let's drill down a little deeper about quality and a quality management system...

 ## What is ISO 9000?

ISO 9000 is a series of generic, internationally recognized standards for quality management. These standards should be viewed simply as a tool, based on common-sense principles that representatives from industry have developed and that help you manage and control your business. These principles can be applied to any type or size of business in any industry wishing to meet and satisfy customers' needs and expectations.

ISO 9000 is a model or framework that can improve any business or organization. It places significant emphasis on understanding the importance of processes and their improvement. It is important to understand that the ISO 9000 series of standards addresses quality management systems and, on its own, cannot guarantee the quality of the delivered product or service. These standards are complementary to the technical (product) standards, and the two frequently are used in combination for product certification purposes, i.e., when obtaining the BSI Kitemark or other product certifications. The conceptual diagram in both ISO 9001:2000 and ISO 9004:2000 clearly shows the relationship between the realization process, quality management system and the final product or service delivered to the customer.

Indeed, the requirements of ISO 9000 don't tell you how to run your business. That's up to you. The requirements do, however, describe "what" needs to be achieved to reach an internationally recognized standard of performance, i.e., a quality performance. All you need to do is:

• Understand the process approach.
• Plan your processes.
• Implement your processes.
• Check the processes to ensure they are effective.
• If they are not, consider both corrective and preventive action.
• Seek opportunities for continual improvement.

Module 3 of this book describes all of the clauses of the standard in a user-friendly manner. If you have any questions, don't hesitate to contact CEEM. It is advised that you discuss larger interpretation issues with BSI (or whomever your registrar might be) at any time in the process. Information to do so is located on the inside cover of this book.

 ## How did the ISO 9000 standards come about?

As the old proverb says, "Necessity is the mother of invention."

With ISO 9000, this was truly the case. But you may be interested to know that the international standard for quality didn't begin with business at all.

During World War II, Great Britain and the European Allies were under extreme pressure to manufacture the tools of war, while simultaneously under the constant threat of German aerial attacks. So to avoid being completely devastated by the constant bombing, the British had a fantastic idea—they spread their manufacturing facilities across the entire country like a spider's web. Certain engine parts would be manufactured in the North, while other vital parts and weapons would be built in other regions. Then, once all of the parts were completed, they would be brought together for assembly. That way, if one plant was destroyed by the enemy, another could quickly fill in.

Of course, in those days, there wasn't much time for product testing to make sure everything fit and worked together. So the U.K. Ministry of Defense quickly learned that setting standards and specifications was the only way to ensure everything was compatible the first time. In the end, more than 400 emergency standards were created during WWII, helping the Allies streamline operations and save vital resources at a crucial time in the world's history.

After the war, the concept of standardization quickly spread to the private sector to rebuild Britain's devastated cities. During the 1950s and 1960s, more standards were created than in the entire 50 years before. But it soon became apparent that standardization to ensure quality of all products and services was needed on a much higher level.

To that end, BSI facilitated the writing of the first national quality management system standard for businesses in 1979. It was called *British Standard (BS) 5750*, and it provided a generic framework for quality assurance for British industry. Based on NATO's Allied Quality Assurance Procedures, a U.S. Department of Defense quality program—Mil-Q-9858A—and a number of U.K. industry standards, BS 5750 was developed, quickly becoming the norm for quality systems in the United Kingdom.

Simultaneously, during the last half of the 20th century, the economy began to become truly global. Industry, particularly companies in Europe, needed harmonized requirements to ensure consistent levels of quality in operations—no matter where those operations were located. At the same time, multinational corporations saw significant value in leveling the playing field and raising the bar for quality assurance for their operations and their supply chains.

So in the mid-1980s, ISO saw an opportunity to prevent national proliferation of similar standards and sought to supercede all quality management systems standards. ISO believed that doing so would reduce cost to industry by having one set of standards that apply to organizations worldwide in any industry. To that end, ISO created Technical Committee (TC) 176, a group of quality experts from more than 160 countries, to develop ISO 9000. TC 176 got to work and used BS 5750 as a core document to create the first version of the ISO 9000 family in 1987. The standards were a huge success on a global scale and have since become the most popular and widely used standards for the global marketplace. Globally, companies have saved billions of dollars on nonquality costs, improved their productivity and product quality, and customer satisfaction and expectations have experienced significant gains.

But like all things in life, there is always room for improvement. With that in mind, TC 176 began a revision process of the ISO 9000 family—a process that is required by ISO procedures every five years to improve standards if needed. And in 1994, a slightly modified version of the ISO 9000 family was released to the marketplace.

But by 1997, the ISO 9000 family had grown to a cumbersome bunch—a dozen standards with 20 required elements, with more on the way from specific industries.

So TC 176 went back to work. The result was ISO 9000:2000—a greatly reduced series that consists of only three standards, six requirements and an auditing document (ISO 19011) that will allow integration of other management systems standards with ISO 9001.

 ## Why ISO 9000:2000?

In today's competitive marketplace, businesses must move at the speed of light to stay alive. From General Motors to your neighborhood dry cleaner, companies are facing greater demands from their customers and stakeholders, who will go elsewhere in a heartbeat if their needs or requirements are not being met.

Indeed, customers have more choices than ever before when it comes to products and services, and few will tolerate poor quality (or variation from their needs and expectations as a business). Of course, consumers and stakeholders are also more prepared to complain if they're not satisfied, or they'll simply seek other organizations to supply the goods and services they need—without a word to you about their dissatisfaction. Studies show that 90 percent of unhappy customers will not proactively tell you their problems, but the one who is upset will tell 10 others of the dissatisfaction! This emphasizes the damage poor quality can cause your organization in a short amount of time.

Additionally, customers are demanding that their suppliers operate to a recognized standard and often seek to minimize the number of external parties with which they do business. As you've just read, the standard adopted by these customers since 1987 has often been ISO 9000, the world's only internationally recognized standard for quality management systems. Businesses have found that registration to ISO 9000 not only helps them to maintain existing customers, but also to attract new ones. Registration also assists them internally and many other ways by driving out failure, error, needless rework and unnecessary expense across the business. (The registration process will be discussed in greater detail later in this book, but essentially the process involves an independent third-party verification, or operational audit of the system, to assess its effectiveness.)

To date, more than 400,000 companies have registered to ISO 9000 because they recognize registration as the most efficient way to obtain competitive advantage, exceed customer satisfaction and raise the level of quality of their products and services. In fact, in many parts of the world, registration has become a mandatory part of doing business, and because of this phenomenon, the ISO 9000 standards have transformed world trading practices by eliminating barriers and leveling the playing field for all.

Why were the standards revised again with the current requirements?

Centuries ago, someone, somewhere, said three prophetic words:

"Keep it simple."

Who knows what that person was talking about at the time. The truth is, it doesn't really matter. The adage is timeless.

Indeed, today's world is anything but simple, yet we strive for simplicity every day in our complicated lives. Can you imagine a world without cell phones, e-mail, microwave ovens and, of course, *"Dummy Guides"*? Difficult, to say the least. The fact is, however, being "user friendly" is the model for success today, simply because no one has the time for complicated products or services anymore.

With that in mind, TC 176 went to work again in 1997, studying the extensive surveys that have been performed on a worldwide basis to understand the needs of all users of the management system standards. The new revisions take into account previous experience with management system standards (1987 and 1994 editions) and emerging insights into generic management systems.

Why did they take on such an onerous task that took more than three years and millions of dollars to complete? The answer is quite simple: They believe in the concept of *continual improvement*—something you'll find embedded in every aspect of the new ISO 9001:2000.

Other major reasons for the year 2000 revisions of the standards include:
- emphasizing the need to monitor customer satisfaction;
- meeting the need for more user-friendly documents;
- assuring consistency between management system requirements and guidelines; and
- promoting the use of generic management principles by organizations.

 ### What exactly has been revised?

As mentioned previously, TC 176 needed to make the ISO 9000 family "simpler" during its last revision cycle. Without question, its mission was accomplished.

Prior to ISO 9000:2000, the ISO 9000 family consisted of 27 standards, which included these core documents:

1. ISO 8402: Quality vocabulary
2. ISO 9000: Quality management and quality assurance standards
    Part 1: Guidelines for selection and use
    Part 2: Generic guidelines for the application of ISO 9001, 9002 and 9003
    Part 3: Guidelines for the application of ISO 9001 to the development,
        supply and maintenance of software
    Part 4: Application for dependability management
3. ISO 9001: Quality systems-model for quality assurance in design,
    development, production, installation and servicing
4. ISO 9002: Quality systems-model for quality assurance in production,
    installation and servicing
5. ISO 9003: Model for quality assurance in final inspection and testing
6. ISO 9004: Quality management and quality system elements
    Part 1: Guidelines
    Part 2: Guidelines for services
    Part 3: Guidelines for processed materials
    Part 4: Guidelines for quality improvement
7. ISO 10005: Quality management-guidelines for quality plans
8. ISO 10007: Guidelines for configuration management
9. ISO 10011: Guidelines for auditing quality systems
    Part 1: Auditing
    Part 2: Qualification criteria for quality systems auditors
    Part 3: Management of audit programs
10. ISO 10012: Quality assurance requirements for measuring equipment
11. ISO 10013: Guidelines for developing quality manuals

Ugh.

You can see why a little housecleaning was necessary. So in December 2000, TC 176 released the new and improved ISO 9000 family:

1. ISO 9000:2000—Quality management systems—Fundamentals and vocabulary
2. ISO 9001:2000—Quality management systems—Requirements
3. ISO 9004:2000—Quality management—Guidelines for performance improvements
4. ISO 19011 (to be published in 2002)—Guidelines on quality and/or environmental management systems auditing

Before the ISO 9000:2000 series was released and depending on the scope of the system and/or the organization, a company could become registered to:
- ISO 9001, (where the organization has a product/service design function, not including process design);
- ISO 9002 (where the organization undertakes no design); or
- ISO 9003 (companies with inspection and test only).

Now, there is only one "requirements document" for registration purposes:
ISO 9001:2000. However, it is recommended that when purchasing or using the standards for implementation or registration, be sure to use all three documents and the auditing document when it becomes available. TC 176 wrote these standards to be used together, and they are often intertwined and referenced with one another. For more information on how to obtain standards, turn to the last section of this book.

 ## What is ISO 9004:2000?

ISO 9001:2000 and ISO 9004:2000 were developed together by TC 176 to be a "consistent pair" of quality management system standards. They are designed to be complementary—but they also can be used independently.

ISO 9001:2000 is the document that gets the most attention, because it is the only standard in the new series that specifies the requirements of a quality management system. Those requirements can be used for internal implementation, contractual purposes or for third-party registration.

ISO 9004:2000 is a much broader document, offering guidance on a range of objectives that are not required by ISO 9001:2000 but are definitely good ideas for your organization to consider. For example, ISO 9004:2000 takes the concepts outlined in ISO 9001:2000, such as continual improvement and overall organizational performance, to another level. It is designed to take an organization beyond the requirements of ISO 9001:2000. It is not designed, however, for registration purposes.

This guide for performance improvement also might be seen as a tool for best practice, or one possible way to meet the requirements for ISO 9001:2000 (although it is not an implementation guide). ISO 9004:2000 discusses ISO 9001:2000 in a way that says a company, "might," "could," "should" or "really ought to consider" meeting the requirements document by doing what is detailed in the guide. It is written as a "forward-looking" standard in order to accommodate those organizations that subscribe to self-assessment. The latter parts of the document detail this opportunity.

However, ISO 9004:2000 is not *essential*, but highly recommended reading to review and understand its concepts when implementing ISO 9001:2000. Registrars should not audit against ISO 9004:2000 as if it were a requirements document, but could undertake assessments based on individual client needs.

ISO 9004:2000 also has a number of other benefits, utilizing the eight "Quality Management Principles" that are listed on p. 42. If the system is implemented appropriately, all interested parties can benefit in the following ways[2]:

---

[2]*Information obtained from the International Organization for Standardization.*

Customers and users will benefit by receiving products that are:
- conforming to international requirements;
- dependable and reliable;
- available when needed; and
- maintainable.

People within an organization will benefit by:
- better working conditions;
- increased job satisfaction;
- improved health and safety;
- improved morale; and
- improved stability of employment.

Owners and investors will benefit by:
- increased return on investment;
- improved operational results;
- increased market share; and
- increased profits.

Suppliers and partners will benefit by:
- stability;
- growth; and
- partnership and mutual understanding.

Society will benefit by:
- fulfillment of legal and regulatory requirements;
- improved health and safety;
- reduced environmental impact; and
- increased security.

More will be said about the "consistent pair" concept and ISO 9004:2000 throughout this book.

 ## What will happen to all of the other standards in the ISO 9000 family?

Most of the standards listed on Page 9 have been integrated into the new ISO 9000 family. Others that haven't will be withdrawn, transferred to other technical committees within ISO or replaced by technical reports, technical specifications or brochures. There is one exception, however—ISO 10012 will remain an international standard because of its specificity for measurement. TC 176 will carefully review each document in the years ahead to determine their retention or withdrawal.

What are the differences between the 1994 and 2000 versions of ISO 9000?

The ISO 9000:1994 family contained 27 standards and ancillary documents. Many users found that just too many to be useful. With the Year 2000 revision, there are now just four new primary standards. The new standards are simply and clearly written—designed not to impose bureaucracy, but rather to afford structure based on well-proven systems and, thus, to bring solid business benefits. They take the best of the famous "Plan-Do-Check-Act" model and integrate process management. They now call for establishment of objectives, linking these to performance measures and, in doing so, paving a path for successful business management.

Of course, the most noticeable change is in the new format. Whereas the 1994 version had 20 core elements (clauses), the new ISO 9001 has just five. They are:
- Clause 4—Quality Management System
- Clause 5—Management Responsibility
- Clause 6—Resource Management
- Clause 7—Product Realization
- Clause 8—Measurement, Analysis and Improvement

That said, there are considerably fewer "mandated" documented procedures in the ISO 9000:2000 series—but that is not to imply documentation is frowned upon. The clauses will be discussed in detail in Module 3 of this book; Documentation will be discussed in Module 5.

But in short, the ISO 9000:2000 standards are based on a process model using eight quality management principles that reflect current best practices and facilitate continual improvement of the business. They are:
1. Customer Focus
2. Leadership
3. Involvement of People
4. Process Approach
5. System Approach to Management
6. Continual Improvement
7. Factual Approach to Decision-Making
8. Mutually Beneficial Supplier Relationships

Putting these principles into practice in an organization should stimulate overall efficiency, thus improving response to customers' needs and, in turn, raising the competitive advantage. Application of these principles will demonstrate management's commitment to drive consistency in process outputs as well as lead to strategies for deployment and definitive actions. An auditor will look for objective evidence of the application of these principles together with the establishment of quality-related objectives and evidence showing achievement and positive improvement trends.

The quality management principles are discussed in detail on p. 42.

Is the ISO 9000:2000 series more prescriptive than the 1994 standards?

No, in fact, the opposite is true. The ISO 9000:2000 series is *less* prescriptive than its predecessors.

As mentioned previously in this Module, the 1994 series had 20 clauses and 27 documents—which turned out to be a lot of documentation to track while running a business. So TC 176 revised the standards for the 2000 release with the user in mind, making the ISO 9000:2000 series easier to understand and easier to use. There are only five clauses in the new ISO 9001:2000 standard—the only standard used for registration purposes.

When you get to Module 3 of this book and begin to examine the clauses of ISO 9001:2000, you'll see that those five sections specify activities that need to be considered when you implement your system. They also define what you should do consistently to provide products that meet customer and applicable statutory or regulatory requirements, as well as enhance customer satisfaction by improving your quality management system.

But the requirements section of ISO 9001:2000 isn't the only improvement that TC 176 made—all of the documents now are harmonized in structure and terminology to assist you to move smoothly from one to the other, and they all use a process approach, something you'll learn more about in Module 3.

What are some tangible benefits that can be extracted from registration?

One thing you'll discover quickly during the implementation of any management system is that it generates a lot of useful data for business improvement. Internal audits, management reviews, customer feedback, corrective and preventive actions and measurement information all will become part of your daily life, but it can be overwhelming if you don't manage the data effectively.

When done correctly, however, an effective management system will give you valuable information so that you can draw conclusions, make sound decisions and take action to improve the business—no matter what it is you do.

A quality system with ISO 9001:2000 can do even more. In fact, the bottom line is, it can affect the *bottom line*—and the top line as well. Here are some specific examples, according to companies that have registered to ISO 9001 with BSI:

Case Study 1
Garden State Consumer Credit Counseling
Location: Freehold, N.J.

No. of employees: 95

Business scope: A nonprofit agency that provides consumer credit counseling and education.

Garden State Consumer Credit Counseling is the first credit agency that achieved ISO 9001 registration.

The primary driver for Garden State Consumer Credit Counseling to seek registration was to concentrate on a high level of quality and service to not only clients, but also creditors. Additionally, it wanted to have a structured system for quality management and to have an approach to control and monitor the system.

The ISO 9000 standards provided the structure for the quality management system. Another advantage of ISO 9000 was that it supplied an approach about what needed to be followed, rather than a strict system that said what needed to be done.

Garden State Credit Consumer Credit Counseling already had 70 percent of the ISO 9001 system covered with its existing quality management system. However, the additional 30 percent gained by the ISO 9000 standards made a significant difference in terms of better structure, control and monitoring. Furthermore, it improved what was already in place.

Specifically, using ISO 9000 standards led to the development of a matrix form for the organization, now used monthly to record and monitor every problem. If a trend occurs, then re-training is introduced. Every six months, all of the matrix forms are analyzed and a report is written. This process resulted in the re-writing of procedures. It is believed that without ISO 9001 registration, this structured process might not have occurred.

Since the implementation of ISO 9001, Garden State Consumer Credit Counseling has received 19 percent more client inquiries, and, of those inquiries received, 16 percent more have been completed each month. In addition, the organization has reinstated 21 percent more clients and is able to help 20 percent more of its new callers.

Using ISO 9000 standards also has led to the development of documented procedures for customer satisfaction. For example, the organization now has documented client surveys and feedback/complaints processes in place. Feedback forms are taken to the vice president of administration for review, resulting in the implementation of 50 percent of the suggestions generated by this process.

Case Study 2
Sun Chemicals General Printing Ink (GPI)
<u>Location:</u> Cleveland, Tenn.
<u>Headquarters:</u> North Lake, Ill.
<u>No. of employees:</u> 14,000 worldwide
<u>Business scope:</u> The world's largest manufacturer of high-quality printing inks and coatings and high-performance organic pigments.

Sun Chemicals GPI is the world's largest manufacturer of high-quality printing inks and coatings and high-performance organic pigments. In 2000, the company had sales of approximately $3.3 billion.

The branch in Cleveland, Tenn., employs 26 people and produces packaging ink. All branches are independently ISO 9000 registered, but the Cleveland branch started ISO 9001 preparations with another registrar in 1994 and achieved registration in 1997. It then transferred to BSI, and the company is working diligently to transfer its registration to the requirements of ISO 9001:2000.

The main driver for registration at Sun Chemicals is that key customers required the company to get registered. A second motivation is that the company that previously owned the branch was registered as well and recommended registration. Since 1997, Sun Chemical has secured $6 million in sales from key customers, which is directly linked to registration.

Additionally, registration also has resulted in customers having more confidence in consistent quality. Customer complaints have decreased 75 percent between 1997 and 2001, with none received in 2000.

At the beginning of the registration process, staff's views of the new ISO 9000 quality management system varied, with some viewing it as additional work. This has changed significantly, and now, most perceive the system as helpful in avoiding mistakes through clear procedures and direction. Better documentation of procedures resulted in fewer employee mistakes, fewer customer complaints and improved operational effectiveness in day-to-day work.

Employee training also has improved due to improved training material. Employees now have the training and documentation they need to more efficiently perform their job functions. Moreover, the system increased employee awareness of the relationship between their job functions and the quality of the final product.

Overall, the ISO 9000 quality management system provides consistency in operations and overall quality at Sun Chemical, which resulted in increased knowledge of job responsibilities and increased knowledge of customer requirements across the organization. Also, increased knowledge of procedures has lowered quality costs due to reduced errors in manufacturing, quality control and shipping.

Other customers have had similar results from registration to ISO 9001. Here are some basic facts and figures from BSI clients concerning their registration experience[3]:

- Approximate total one-time savings (United States and Canada) associated with implementing an ISO 9000 system: **$104,500**
- Approximate total annual/ongoing savings (United States and Canada) associated with implementing an ISO 9000 system: **$93,076.92**

Regarding external market conditions, the most significant benefits companies experienced as a result of achieving registration:

Higher perceived quality	48.6%
Competitive advantage	21.6%
Reduced customer quality audits	16.2%
Increased market share	5.4%
Improved customer demand	2.7%
Quicker time to market	2.7%
Other	2.7%

Regarding internal operations, the most significant benefits companies experienced as a result of achieving registration:

---

[3]*Data provided by Quality Systems Update Publishing. ISO 9000 Survey '99.*

Improved documentation	40.5%
Resulted in greater quality awareness by employees	29.7%
Resulted in greater operational efficiency/productivity	21.6%
Enhanced inter-company communications	5.4%
Reduces scrap/rework expenses	2.8%

Of companies surveyed that have registered to ISO 9000 with BSI, **89.2 percent** said that registration resulted in a marketing tool that the company previously did not have.

Of companies surveyed that have registered to ISO 9000 with BSI, **45.9 percent** said that registration resulted in additional outside contracts.

So as you can see, a quality system based on ISO 9000 can have a significant positive impact on an organization, regardless of size or scope. For more information on savings and benefits, contact CEEM or BSI. Contact information is provided inside the front cover of this book.

 14

How can I convince management to register to ISO 9001:2000?

While implementation and registration to ISO 9001:2000 needs attention and resources, most management teams today recognize the value of a systems approach to business and a process approach to operations. That's why more than 400,000 ISO 9000 registrations have been issued worldwide and more than 50 percent of the *Fortune 100* companies embrace the standard. It simply makes good sense for business.

Still, there are critics out there who may not see the benefits of ISO 9001:2000 implementation and registration. Indeed, if you look at the data on Page 16 of this Module, you'll see that not all of the companies surveyed stated that registration added significant value to the organization—the majority had and continue to have excellent results, while the minority didn't have as much to cheer about.

The fact is, however, if your organization has a *commitment* from top management to continually improve operations, cut costs, increase customer satisfaction and add value to the organization in myriad ways, there is virtually *zero chance* of failure. You'll learn more about management commitment in Module 3—which is really the fundamental cornerstone needed by any organization to achieve quality and enjoy success.

Of course, if you need to show management hard data on the results of registration, just show them the information provided in this Module. That should do the trick!

How can ISO 9001:2000 address the needs of specific business sectors?

The standards are applicable to all types of organizations—that was TC 176's prime directive when setting out to revise the ISO 9000 series. The language in the revised standards is simpler, user-friendly and with less manufacturing bias. Additionally, the new standards are appropriate to all sectors, including service providers.

Still, some industries have evaluated the ISO 9000 documents in pilot studies, with some recognizing that sector-specific initiatives are in order. To date, the principles and requirements generated by TC 176 have been used by four sectors for more precise language and guidance concerning quality management:

- **Aerospace**—Industry experts developed and released AS 9100 in March 2001, with alignment to the ISO 9000:2000 requirements expected by mid-2001.
- **Automotive**—Experts published QS-9000 in the late 1990s, then took the principles of ISO 9000:2000 and translated them into a technical specification called TS 16949. This document is expected to be completely aligned to ISO 9000:2000 in mid-2001.
- **Finance**—This concept is just under way in 2001, with some members of the financial services sector expressing a desire to create "FS 9000." The group had met only once, however, as of April 2001. But the meeting is an indication that TC 176 has succeeded in creating guidance that can be used by the service sector.
- **Telecommunications**—Experts developed TL 9000 in 2000, with alignment to the ISO 9000:2000 requirements—called version 3.0—published in March 2001.

But as mentioned previously in this book, there are more than 400,000 registrations to ISO 9000 in circulation, with more certificates issued every day. It's safe to say that out of all those organizations, every type of organization, large and small, can benefit from registering its quality management system.

 Are the new standards flexible for small businesses?

Yes, in fact, as mentioned earlier in this Module, flexibility was a key ingredient that TC 176 incorporated into the new ISO 9000:2000 for all organizations—especially small businesses.

But, as we all know, no two organizations are alike. With that in mind for small businesses, there is guidance on excluding certain requirements for specific processes (such as design activities) that are not performed by the organization. Provisions have been made to exclude non-applicable requirements in ISO 9001:2000 through Clause 1.2, *Application*. (**Note:** Exclusions can only be applied to Clause 7 of ISO 9001:2000, and only if they do not affect your organization's ability to provide conforming product or service.)

For example, if the nature of your products does not require you to perform design activities, or if your product is provided on the basis of established design, you will need to discuss and justify the exclusion of these requirements with an auditor or registration body.

It will, however, be up to the individual organization to determine the complexity of the system needed to demonstrate its capability to meet customer and applicable statutory/regulatory requirements for its products. For more information on permissible exclusions, see Module 3 p. 56, or visit this Web site: www.abcb.demon.co.uk.

 ## Will the new ISO 9000:2000 series affect my organization's current registration?

Organizations are encouraged to make the transition to ISO 9001:2000 registration as soon as possible to maximize the standard's potential for all organizations.

ISO 9002 and ISO 9003 will become obsolete after the transition period (December 2003). Certificates issued to the 1994 editions of ISO 9001, ISO 9002 or ISO 9003 shall have a maximum validity of three years from the date of publication of ISO 9001:2000. You will need to evaluate which specific requirements of ISO 9001:2000 are applicable to the nature of your business and the extent to which your present quality management system meets those requirements.

One of the best ways to transition to the year 2000 revisions for a stress-free experience is to conduct a "Health Check" or gap analysis between your current ISO system and the revised standards.

BSI's intention is to convert the majority of its client registrations to ISO 9001:2000 by December 2002. Any organization not converted after three years (December 2003) will have its registration withdrawn.

But don't be discouraged! Remember, the new standards are designed to be flexible and easy to use. Once the system has been converted to ISO 9001:2000, it will be more responsive to your customers, and your business will be clearly distinguished from those that haven't taken the big step toward continual improvement.

 ## How will my organization deal with the transition to the ISO 9000:2000 standards?

You've taken the first step by reading this book, which explains the transition process from experts who helped develop the ISO 9000:2000 series.

The next thing you should consider is obtaining a copy of the ISO 9000:2000 series, which is available from your national standards body or its distributors. For a list of companies that distribute or sell standards, turn to the back of this book.

Once you receive the standards, give them a thorough review so that you fully understand any new terminology, new requirements and the "consistent pair" concept between ISO 9001 and ISO 9004. You also might want to consider additional training for your organization from qualified ISO 9000 professionals. With that in mind, CEEM offers several RAB-accredited courses that can help, such as:
- Understanding ISO 9001:2000
- Implementing ISO 9001:2000
- ISO 9001:2000 Auditor Transition
- ISO 9001:2000 Internal Quality Systems Auditor
- ISO 9001:2000 Lead Auditor
- Quality Systems Documentation

It's also a good idea to contact your registrar and ask about their transition policy for ISO 9000:2000, because if you already have registration, there is a good chance that you can be updated to the new standard during your continuous assessment visits. As mentioned previously, BSI plans to convert the majority of its clients to ISO 9001:2000 by the end of 2002. This will be accomplished by the evaluation of four main sections of ISO 9001:2000 during four continuing assessment visits that the majority of clients will receive during that period. On each visit, one section of ISO 9001:2000 will be discussed with the client and an action plan put into place for the next visit in six months.

The order that the ISO 9001:2000 sections will be addressed can either be agreed with the client or will be assessed in the following order:
- Quality management system and product realization
- Measurement, analysis and improvement
- Management responsibility
- Resource management

The BSI ISO 9001:2000 Transition Process

Define Processes

The process flow to the left is the arrangement that BSI auditors will follow throughout the transition. It is not in the same sequence as ISO 9001:2000.

1st Assessment Visit: Review Quality Management System and Product Realization

Following discussions with clients, we decided to start the transition process from the 1994 standard with the Quality Management System and Product Realization sections. These sections address the majority of the clauses in ISO 9001/2:1994.

2nd Assessment Visit: Review Measurement, Analysis and Improvement

This process provides the opportunity to transfer gradually from the old standard to the new over two years, at no extra cost through your scheduled continual assessments.

3rd Assessment Visit: Review Management Responsibility

After the first Continual Assessment Visit, the focus will move onto Measurement, Analysis and Improvement. This will provide the Management Representative with information to report to their Top Management and ready the organization for the next visit, which will cover Management Responsibility.

4th Assessment Visit: Review Resource Management

The final visit will cover Resource Management. It is at this final visit that registration to ISO 9001:2000 will be reviewed, and if appropriate, recommended.

If you already have the standard, you may notice that the order listed above is not the same order that the standard outlines. This is because the majority of firms that already have registered to ISO 9001:1994 have the part of their organization covering product realization registered, so it seems sensible to begin the transition process with this section.

TC 176 also has released Transition Guidance and Planning documents to help organizations understand the issues and new requirements of the ISO 9000:2000 series. Organizations are encouraged to download and review these documents free of charge from the ISO Web site: www.iso.ch.

Of course, if you have specific questions, contact a BSI client manager, or contact BSI headquarters at the information listed on the inside front cover of this book.

 ### How will the ISO 9000:2000 series help my organization improve its efficiency and gain competitive advantage?

The ISO 9000:2000 standards should be thought of as a basis for good business management. By applying well-thought-out processes and proactively pursuing continual improvement and customer satisfaction, success is almost guaranteed.

Working together, these standards effectively manage the issues of any organization, including:
- Quality control
- Quality assurance
- Training
- Process management
- Resource management
- Supplier management
- Customer satisfaction
- Continual improvement of the business
- Consistency across the organization
- Connection of management systems to organizational processes
- Compatibility with other management systems such as ISO 14000
- Significant reduction in the amount of required documentation
- Consideration of the needs of and benefits to all interested parties
- Communication within the organization and to customers and suppliers should improve

The last point is crucial, because at the end of the day, your organization isn't just about you and the management system—it's about products, people, customers, the community and much more. That's important, because as you "drill down" on the benefits of ISO 9001:2000, you'll see how it all fits together in the global marketplace. In fact, think of these proven facts while considering implementation of ISO 9001:2000:
- Customers and end-users will benefit by receiving products that are more likely to meet requirements, more consistent, more dependable and reliable, available when needed and more maintainable.
- People within the organization will benefit from better work conditions, increased job understanding and job satisfaction, improved safety, improved morale and stability.
- Owners and investors will benefit from increased return on investment, improved operational results, increased market share and increased profits.

- <u>Suppliers and partners</u> will benefit from stability, growth and mutually beneficial supplier partnerships.
- <u>Society as a whole</u> will benefit from fulfillment of statutory and regulatory requirements, improved safety, reduced environmental impacts and increased security.

Of course, by achieving the expectations of the interested parties listed above, ISO 9001:2000 also can provide a marketing edge with new customers. Think about how customers feel about organizations that follow international guidelines to improve quality in every respect! And, again, if you need hard facts and figures on the benefits of implementation, turn to p. 16 of this Module.

 ## Should my organization seek registration to the new standard?

To focus your attention on the reasons why you should seek registration, complete the first column of Figure 1 at the end of this Module. If you can't, or find it difficult to identify why you should seek registration, then contact BSI.

As you've already read in this book, more than 400,000 organizations have benefited from registration to ISO 9001 and more than 50 percent of *Fortune 100* companies have embraced the standard's third-party scheme to ensure quality standards are met around the globe. In fact, in some industries, such as the automotive, aerospace and telecommunications sectors, registration is often a requirement to do business. That's because it is one of the most cost-effective ways to ensure suppliers meet specific quality requirements—no matter where your organization is on the supply chain.

But while considering you decision about registration, remember one thing: *A registrar is there to help your business improve.* It is a value-added service designed to assess your system and show where improvements can be made to the organization as a whole.

Having registered so many businesses, BSI has developed an effective method to achieve registration. But, inevitably, you will need to carry out some work on your own. The Modules in this book have been designed to walk you through these activities and are the result of reviewing and assessing different quality systems developed and implemented in numerous companies and organizations.

 ## How much is the transition to the new standards going to cost?

One of the goals of TC 176 was to produce standards that will minimize any potential costs to ensure a smooth transition to ISO 9000:2000. Any additional costs may be considered as a value-added investment.

The cost of implementing any necessary changes to meet the new requirements of ISO 9001:2000 will vary from one organization to another, depending on various factors such as the actual state of implementation of the quality management system, the size and complexity of the organization, the attitude and commitment of the top management, etc. It is expected, however, that the benefits to all organizations will outweigh eventual costs associated with the transition.

If you need rough estimates, however, the following information could be used as a guide. The information was obtained from *Quality Systems Update*, a newsletter on ISO 9000 and QS-9000, which produced the *ISO 9000 Survey* in 1999:
- Average costs associated with registration in North America—**$156,000**
- Average savings associated with registration in North America—**$187,000**
- Overall savings to cost ratio associated with registration in North America—**1.2**

To get specific quote information for your organization, contact BSI. Information to do so is on the inside cover of this book.

Where can we go for clarification or interpretation of the new standards?

TC 176 developed specific transition guidance that can be downloaded from the Internet at the following address: www.iso.ch.

If you have specific questions, contact either CEEM or BSI. Both organizations have many experts and years of experience in perfecting quality management systems. Information to do so is on the inside cover of this book.

Briefing the management team

Now that you've gained an outline of what ISO 9000 is, how registration can work for you and the steps to take, the next stage is to brief the management team. Depending upon the size of the organization, the management team could consist of only you, or it could represent a much larger group. Either way, you need to ensure that the whole team is committed to working toward and achieving registration.

The best possible way to get buy-in and ownership of your quality system is to involve everyone in the design, development and implementation phases. This is the key to having a meaningful, effective and efficient system. This also will ensure that the system is relevant and will be maintained in the future. Systems designed without top-down commitment and bottom-up involvement are difficult to implement and maintain and tend to fall quickly into disrepair. Involvement starts with the management team, which can be briefed in a number of ways. For example, you may brief your management team at a formal meeting with a prepared presentation. Whichever method you choose, the following information should be included:

- what ISO 9000 is;
- what ISO 9000 is NOT;
- clarification of the role each organization plays (accreditation/registration/consulting/training, etc.)
- agreement to use BSI to support you toward registration;
- agreement on why you are seeking registration and its benefits;
- agreement on the plan, including timeframe;
- agreement to review the project's progress periodically; and
- agreement on the individual who will champion the project.

Also, complete Figure 1-1 on p. 26 and use the information to help you prepare for the management meeting. Some potential concerns that may be expressed are exhibited in Module 2.

The management meeting is an important first step toward registration; therefore, if you need or would like an ISO 9000:2000 expert to attend the meeting with you, CEEM or BSI can assist you.

Don't forget to make a record of the agreements reached. The record should be dated, show who attended and include brief details of all agreements struck. File these notes at the conclusion of this Module.

The next stage is to brief your employees, which is covered in Module 2.

Figure 1-1

Why Do We Want to Achieve Registration?	What Are the Benefits To Us?
Date Completed:	Date Completed:

Notes:

Notes:

module 2

Introducing ISO 9000:2000 To Employees

 23 Why does management need to brief employees before starting?

Although outlining the way your business operates is management's responsibility, it is the employees who undertake many of the tasks allocated to them to satisfy customer needs.

As you've read in Module 1, the eight quality management principles are essential to your business and registration success. One of those principles is *Involvement of People*, and an ISO 9001:2000 program is doomed to fail if a team approach isn't utilized throughout the implementation process. Indeed, there is an implicit level of group planning, implementation and control that is vital to the program's success.

Explaining the project to employees will ensure they are involved from the start and are aware of their involvement as the project progresses. Achieving this level of involvement has a number of benefits that will help you gain registration, including:

- **Implementation**—which is made easier if employees have been involved, as there is less resistance to any necessary changes;
- **Employees having a stake in achieving registration**—remember, management isn't the only stakeholder;
- **The business as one big team**—nobody is excluded and everyone generates ideas and solutions;
- **Improved morale and motivation**—employees feel they have a say in product output and business operations, and their responsibilities and level of accountability are better defined;
- **Design of documentation made easier and quicker**—employees know what they do best and what they require;
- **Transparency**—management can show they are sincere and open with nothing to hide;

- **Changing the way work is completed**—willfully accepting new ideas, particularly when these have been introduced by the employees themselves; and
- **Ownership of what has been produced**—again, if employees have a stake in the system that can improve their jobs as well as the business, the chances of success increase severalfold.

Additionally, new employees should have a firm understanding of how the business operates before embarking on this implementation. All other items being equal, team members who understand your business process are imperative to the success of the implementation team and, ultimately, registration.

 TRANSITION TIPS: Be sure to let the organization know what is planned with the implementation process—why it is happening, the benefit to them, who is involved and the schedule of key activities. If employees are kept in the dark about the project, they will be less supportive when you need their help to implement the required practices. However, don't announce the project and then never communicate the status. Keep them informed of progress and how they can contribute or help. Making the project visible (with plans for regular progress updates) will help confirm management support and encourage the team to stick to the schedule.

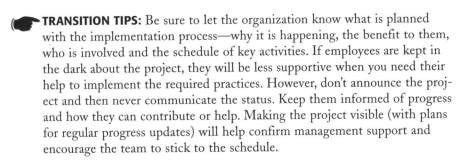 Have the training requirements changed in the new standard?

ISO 9001:2000 presents considerably broader training requirements than its 1994 predecessor. Most of Clause 6 (Resource Management) is devoted to these issues. In addition to previous requirements in ISO 9001:1994 for identifying training needs, providing training, assigning qualified personnel and maintaining records, ISO 9001:2000 now requires evaluation of training effectiveness and establishment of employee awareness programs. (See Figure 2-1.)

Organizations also must keep records of education, skills and experience. These records were not specifically mentioned in the 1994 version.

There also are new requirements in Clause 5 on internal communication. Though not explicitly linked to training, it would make good sense for companies to look for integration of training with employee awareness and communication.

In terms of when to provide training to achieve maximum efficiency and expedite implementation, you should consider doing a training-needs analysis early in the process. A suggested path to follow here is to first train personnel responsible for implementation, then develop operational control procedures, complete the needs analysis and, finally, conduct the remaining appropriate training.

The following clauses contain pertinent new requirements in ISO 9001:2000:

- Clause 5.1 requires top managers to demonstrate their commitment to creating an awareness of the importance of meeting requirements;
- Clause 5.5.2 requires the management representative to ensure promotion of awareness of customer requirements throughout the organization;
- Clause 5.5.3 requires the organization to establish communication processes within the organization, regarding the quality system; and
- Clause 6.2.2c/d requires evaluation of effectiveness of actions taken, and a means to ensure employee awareness of how they contribute to the achievement of the quality objectives.

The Six "R's" of Evaluating Training Effectiveness

The following are some excellent questions you can use to evaluate the effectiveness of your training programs, no matter what the training might be.

REACTION

What was the reaction of the participants?
This measure is an assessment of the student satisfaction as expressed on an evaluation form at the end of the training session.

RETENTION

What learning has taken place?
This measure can be determined through a pre-test and post-test to indicate how much information has been retained by the students. It can show what skills, knowledge or attitudes have changed, and by how much.

RELEVANCE

Have the participants applied what they learned?
Students assess the relevance of the training through a follow-up evaluation a few months after they return to their jobs.

RATING

Has their job performance improved?
This rating summary of the participants is extracted from their performance appraisals while maintaining strict confidentiality of personal information.

RESULTS

Did the application of the learning produce the desired results?
This measure focuses on the business results achieved after the training objectives have been met.

RETURN

Did the monetary value of the results exceed the cost of the training?
This measure of return on investment compares the monetary benefit of the training to its costs.

Use of these 6-R's may give new insights on how to comply with the standard, meet your training needs and justify your training investments.

Figure 2-1

Module 3 has more information on these clauses and how they can be interpreted by any organization and its employees.

 If my organization is transitioning to the new standard, how should I re-train my auditors?

Without question, auditors will need to be re-trained to the new requirements of ISO 9001:2000, but the level of training is up to you and top management.

For internal purposes, a great start to understanding the new requirements of ISO 9001:2000 is reading this book. It answers some of the most frequently asked questions and interprets each clause of the new standard for implementation and registration endeavors.

However, you and your organization should consider formalized, accredited training to ISO 9001:2000 as well. A number of organizations specializing in the quality management arena provide accredited training courses. Those organizations must follow specific guidelines established by the Registrar Accreditation Board (RAB), the U.S. accreditation body recognized by the American National Standards Institute and ISO. The primary focus of any training to the new standard encompasses the process approach to plan and conduct audits as described in ISO 9001:2000. Other benefits of formalized training can include understanding the:

- purpose of a quality management system and its role in helping an organization operate with increased effectiveness, efficiency, consistency and enhanced customer satisfaction;
- changes to audit methodology in areas such as continual improvement, top management commitment and responsibility and the process approach.
- eight quality management principles described in ISO 9000 and ISO 9004;
- requirements of the new ISO 9001:2000 and the objective evidence needed to show conformance and effectiveness of the quality management system; and
- differences between ISO 9001:1994 and ISO 9001:2000.

For more information about accredited training courses, visit the RAB Web site: www.rabnet.com. If you need training information from a specific country, its accreditation body and its requirements, visit the ISO Web site: www.iso.ch.

If you have specific questions concerning ISO 9001:2000 training, contact CEEM. Information to do so can be found on the inside cover of this book.

 How do I get employees involved?

There are a number of ways that employees can become involved, and it is important that they do so from the start. Listed on the next page are a number of ideas, some or all of which may be adopted, and you may know others:

- discussing the content and intent of the standards;
- identifying the business processes and interrelationships;
- undertaking internal training;
- contributing to the content of procedures;
- deciding how to simplify and improve the way procedures work;
- changing bad work practices;
- suggesting new ways of working;
- acting as internal auditors;
- reducing the level of complaints;
- finding better ways to satisfy customers (internal and external); and
- improving working practices.

When introducing any change, from altering the way people work to moving locations to buying a new machine, employees will have concerns and will want to ask questions about what is being proposed. These concerns usually manifest themselves in resistance and anxiety from employees. Seeking registration to ISO 9001:2000 is no different; therefore, these concerns need to be dealt with before the project starts so employees can effectively take part.

An informational briefing is an opportunity for the employees to voice concerns and for management to deal with them. Listed below are a number of concerns frequently raised, together with possible answers:

CONCERN: *The business/company located down the road has ISO 9000; it's painful!*
POSSIBLE ANSWER: "Badly designed systems and documentation can cause problems. Since we will be involved, it's up to each and every one of us to get it right. If it's painful, then it's our fault. Set realistic goals and expectations. We should seek to have a balance of documentation—minimal to prevent bureaucracy and confusion but enough to ensure/maintain operational control of the business."

CONCERN: *I don't see why I should write down what I do. I know what I've been doing.*
POSSIBLE ANSWER: "Good point, but businesses often go through change, and saying that, we need to record what you do so that we can handle any changes that may affect your job. In addition, you do not need to document every little detail—that again is up to us. Once documented, processes can be better understood and improved."

CONCERN: *ISO 9000 will create more management bureaucracy.*
POSSIBLE ANSWER: "Generally, all we will be doing is describing what we already do. If we have to add something, then you will be involved in deciding how that will be achieved. The standard only consists of good, common-sense business rules. If we ever feel we are doing something unnecessary for our business because of ISO 9001, then we are probably misinterpreting its requirements.

But rest assured, we all will be involved in the project; the level of bureaucracy is up to us. If there is too much, then it's our fault. The standard describes what we need to do, not how we do it. It is important to get the balance right on the content and amount of documentation. We should always ask if we need a procedure or is there a better way of expressing the intent by pictures, diagrams, flowcharts or just better training."

CONCERN: *Will we be using a consultant?*
POSSIBLE ANSWER: "That is up to us. CEEM can provide guidance notes and examples of what we need to achieve and also can offer consultant services. They also can offer support throughout the implementation process, which can help us keep track of our own progress. If we use a consultant, we will select one with consulting experience in our industry and with the skills we need to supplement our activities. Our consultant should be our mentor and guide but not the person who documents our processes. We best understand our processes and hence we should be the scribes. The fee for a consultant should save us time and money in the long run. However, we will want to become self-sufficient as soon as possible. But we need to understand that BSI Inc. (or any registrar) cannot be both our consultant and registrar, since this would create a conflict of interest."

As preparation for briefing employees, spend a few minutes thinking about the possible concerns and questions that might arise. Write these down in the first column of Figure 2-2 at the end of this Module. Once you have a list, then write what your answers might be in the second column. If you have identified a concern or question to which you do not have an answer, then contact BSI for assistance. Information to do so can be found on the inside cover of this book.

How might employees benefit?

Just as there are benefits to the business in achieving registration, there are also benefits to the employees. This is spelled out more than ever in the new ISO 9000:2000 series. Benefits include:
- increased job satisfaction;
- improved motivation and training;
- less frustration and waste;
- involvement in the resolution of problems;
- seeing the business continually improve;
- being an essential part of a successful and profitable business;
- having a clear understanding of what is expected; and
- worker safety.

For a successful implementation of a quality management system, employees need to understand its value to them. The better they understand what is in it for them and how the organization also benefits, the more receptive they will be to the changes and work involved to make it happen.

Employees will benefit from the improved internal communication and top management support. Conformance with ISO 9001 will mean suitable and well-
maintained equipment, along with the training needed to perform their jobs.
Work instructions, where necessary, will be available to guide them in their activities. They will have a better understanding of their role in the system and their
contributions to meeting objectives.

Additionally, there will be a sense of order and control, which will carry over into clean
and well-organized work areas. Since the organization wants to continually improve the
system, employees will be encouraged to report problems and suggest improvements.

Briefing the employees

The first step is to identify who will present the briefing. Although the project
leader could do this and often does, it is best presented by senior management for
the following reasons:
- It demonstrates commitment from the top (we are all involved) and that the
  project will happen.
- It shows that management is serious about quality.
- It allows management to answer any questions and explain what the business
  hopes to achieve.

The agenda for the briefing should include:

AGENDA ITEM: *What is ISO 9000:2000?*
CONTENT: See p. 4 of Module 1 for information to this item.

AGENDA ITEM: *Why is the business seeking registration?*
CONTENT: See p. 13 of Module 1 for information to this item.

AGENDA ITEM: *How will registration be achieved?*
CONTENT: The plan

AGENDA ITEM: *How will employees be involved?*
CONTENT: See p. 32 for comments made earlier in this Module.

AGENDA ITEM: *How might employees benefit?*
CONTENT: See p. 34 for comments made earlier in this Module.

AGENDA ITEM: *Issues and concerns*
CONTENT: Open session that allows employees to voice any concerns and ask questions about the process.

AGENDA ITEM: *Next steps*

CONTENT: Indicate when the documentation will be written and in what form. In addition, explain that before any writing takes place, everyone will be advised of his or her involvement. Give assurance that contributors will be a fundamental element of the interactive feedback process.

The communication process now is completed, and everyone is aware of what the project is about and what, in outline, needs to be achieved. The next step in the process is to gain an understanding of the standard and the clauses it contains. This material is covered in Module 3. It will help you understand the standard, complete your quality manual correctly and provide valuable information when writing the supporting documentation.

Figure 2-1 (from p. 34)

Concerns and Questions	Possible Answers

Notes:

module
3

Understanding the
ISO 9001:2000 clauses

 How do I get started?

This Module details the clauses and requirements of the new ISO 9001:2000 standard, which is a great way to get started on your route to registration. Each clause is outlined and describes what needs to be in place if you are to meet the requirements of the new standard.

However, some industry sectors have additional guidelines for quality management systems (such as aerospace, automotive, telecommunications, healthcare and medical devices). This is the time to identify those if any exist in your sector. If you need assistance, contact BSI. Information to do so is on the front inside cover of this book.

After reading each clause and each Module of this book, you will be able to identify the work that needs to be completed, i.e., the gap. In addition, the information you generate will be very useful when you begin to prepare your documentation in Module 5.

Guidelines on terminology used in Module 3:

Shall	*Must*—it is mandatory.
Standard	BS EN ISO 9001:2000—Each country has its own version of ISO 9001:2000. For example, in the United States, it is called Q9001-2000. In the United Kingdom, BS EN stands for "British Standard, European Norm" ISO 9001:2000. For information on the standard's official name in your country, visit ISO's Web page: www.iso.ch.
Organization	Generally, this is the organization implementing ISO 9001:2000. It is officially defined in ISO 9000:2000 as a "group of people and facilities with an arrangement of responsibilities, authorities and relationships."

Supplier   Someone who supplies you, (your company), with a product, material or service that you use, directly or indirectly, to develop your product(s) or service(s). This was called a "subcontractor" in the 1994 standard.

Product   The result of a process; (i.e., what your business is offering; it could be a service or object.)

Customer   Organization or person that receives a product.

Remember: In understanding the standard, it is imperative that you accept that everyone who works in the company, either directly or indirectly, has an effect on the quality of the product or service you supply. If you don't already know this, you'll understand why it's important later in this Module....

 ## What is the Plan-Do-Check-Act (PDCA) model?

The ISO 9001:2000 requirements document follows a concept called the Plan-Do-Check-Act model—a process that is designed for continual improvement of any management system. This cycle is critical to understand the new standard and its requirements. Keep this in mind as you read ISO 9001:2000 and ISO 9004:2000 because you'll see some, if not all parts, of the PDCA cycle in nearly every clause.

TC 176 used this concept after great success by its sister technical committee on environmental management systems (TC 207). That committee used the approach while developing its ISO 14000 series to continually improve the environmental performance of an organization. Organizations soon found out that the same concepts can be applied to a quality system as well because the goal is the same—*continual improvement* (which is described later in this Module).

The basic concepts of the PDCA cycle are pretty straightforward:

Plan—This is a critical stage, and ISO 9001:2000 is riddled with proper planning requirements and suggestions in nearly every clause. But the basic concept is simple—formulate a plan to fulfill your quality policy and the objectives of the system. Planning is addressed in detail later in this Module. But just remember the old adage—*if you fail to plan, plan to fail*. It is certainly applicable with ISO 9001:2000.

Do—This is a fairly simple concept as well. It means implement the processes you've laid out in your plan.

Check—This means monitor and measure what you're doing so that you have data to evaluate and improve the processes and overall system.

Act—After you have data, you must do something with it to improve, and, of course, plan for the improvement (which begins the cycle again). The "act" usually stems from management reviews, internal audits, customer audits, data gathering or even third-party assessments. More information on all of these items is discussed later in this Module.

What is Continual Improvement?

Continual improvement is a fairly simple concept to grasp—whatever you do in your business, implement a process to ensure it is done better the next time.

In ISO 9000:2000, "continual improvement" is defined this way: "Recurring activity to increase the ability to fulfill requirements." However, the definition has a specific note attached to it to add clarity. It states that the process "of establishing objectives and finding opportunities for improvement is a continual process through the use of audit findings and audit conclusions, analysis of data, management reviews or other means and generally leads to corrective or preventive action."

Figure 3-1: Model of a process-based quality management system. (Note: This graphic is sometimes called the PDCA cycle.)

In terms of requirements to the quality system, think of continual improvement as the common thread woven throughout ISO 9001:2000. It really is the stitch that holds it all together, because it requires a commitment from top management to improve the system and the business holistically. From the planning phase to management reviews, continual improvement affects all aspects of everything you do, because at the end of the day, improving the business will enhance customer satisfaction and increase the business' bottom line.

The concept of improvement is somewhat new to ISO 9001:2000 and it even has its own section to ensure it occurs at every level (clause 8.5). In the old standard, it was implied but never explicitly required.

In short, management should proactively seek to improve process effectiveness rather than wait for problems to reveal opportunities for improvement. When a problem does occur, the cause must be determined and a corrective action taken to prevent its recurrence. The management system includes a formal way to trigger this action and see it to closure. The standard requires a trend analysis of those business problems.

The new standard emphasizes planning for the system, its resources, its processes and the measurements necessary to evaluate performance. Part of the planning is to anticipate what might go wrong and try to prevent the occurrence of these potential problems.

Even when processes are producing compliant products (to regulatory and customer requirements), the processes could be more efficient and effective. The aim of a continual improvement program is to increase the odds of satisfying customers by identifying areas needing improvement. After setting improvement objectives, the organization searches for possible solutions, selects and implements the appropriate one and evaluates results to confirm objectives are met.

The documented quality policy statement must include a commitment to continual improvement. To ensure this focus, the management representative must report to top management on the need for any improvements. In fact, recommendations for improvement must be among the management review inputs and any actions or decisions regarding improvements must be recorded.

For more information on continual improvement, see p. 131 in this Module.

31 What are the eight quality management principles and why are they important?*

TC 176 developed all standards in the ISO 9000:2000 series with the eight quality management principles in mind, which provide the foundation of a sound quality management system. However, the principles are listed only in ISO 9000 and ISO 9004 and are not requirements of the system; therefore, they are not a direct part of ISO 9001. But they crucial to understand and follow for your system's improved performance and ultimate success—which is really what this is all about. Here they are:

1. **Customer Focus**—If you understand the continual improvement model on p. 41, customer focus is a fairly simple concept to grasp. On the left hand side of the model, customer requirements are considered as inputs to the system, and on the right hand side we have customer satisfaction. ISO 9001:2000 is about meeting customer needs, understanding their expectations, getting their feedback and adding value with an aim of enhancing their satisfaction level with your products and services.

---

*Language of the eight quality management principles provided by BS EN ISO 9000:2000

2. Leadership—You and top management need to demonstrate and practice sound leadership skills within your organization, that is to say "Lead by example."

3. Involvement of People—In almost every business, people are the most valuable resource, and it is therefore of vital importance that they are party to any decisions and activities affecting the Quality Management System.

4. The Process Approach—Your daily business activity consists of many processes and sub-processes. You need to identify your processes and ensure that everyone is aware of their various actions and interactions. The process approach simply means desired results are achieved more efficiently when activities and related resources are managed as a process. Remember that some processes extend beyond the boundary of your organization, e.g., outsourcing. When such activities are undertaken, the process still has to be managed.

5. A Systems Approach to Management—Being aware of what systems are in place and improving your systems is a sure way of enhancing your products and services, and ultimately, the satisfaction levels of both internal and external customers. Identifying, understanding and managing interrelated processes as a system contributes to the organization's effectiveness and efficiency in achieving its objectives.

6. Continual Improvement—By knowing what your organization does and how well it does it, you can identify ways to improve both your systems and your processes.

7. Factual Approach to Decision Making—By analyzing data and conducting internal audits and management reviews, you can improve business performance and the quality of your products and services.

8. Mutually Beneficial Supplier Relationship—By communicating with your suppliers, you can ensure that in the process of satisfying your needs, they also gain benefits in terms of decreased cost and improved performance.

Although third-party auditors are not likely to audit these principles explicitly, the intent of the ISO 9000:2000 series is clear in this regard.

Again, these eight principles are important because they are the fundamentals your organization will need for quality management system success and, more important, business improvement. As you read more in this book, you'll see exactly how those fundamentals fit with your organization's system, its requirements and beyond.

What is the process approach?

A "process" is a system of activities that uses resources to transform inputs into outputs. As the fourth quality management principle, the "process approach" promoted by ISO 9001:2000 systematically identifies and manages these processes and their interaction within a quality management system. Understanding the process approach is critical to implementing and registering an ISO 9001:2000 quality management system, and it is the first substantive item addressed in the standard (Clause 0.2).

When writing ISO 9001:2000, TC 176 developed the *process model* (shown on p. 41), which illustrates the linkage of ISO 9001:2000 clauses (4-8) based on the Plan-Do-Check-Act model. This PDCA methodology can be applied to all processes, and when used within a quality management system in conjunction with the process approach, it emphasizes the importance of:
- Understanding and meeting requirements;
- The need to consider processes in terms of added value;
- Obtaining results of process performance and effectiveness; and
- Continual improvement of processes based on objective measurement.

As you can see, the process model and PDCA go hand in hand. In the Plan step, you establish the objectives and processes necessary to deliver results in accordance with customer requirements and organization policies. These processes are implemented in the Do step. Then you monitor and measure the processes in the Check step and report the results. The Act step takes the actions needed to continually improve process performance.

An advantage of the process approach is the ongoing control it provides over the linkage between individual processes within a system of processes, as well as their combination and interaction. According to clause 4.2.2 (Quality Manual) in ISO 9001:2000, the quality manual must describe the interaction of the processes within the quality management system. (See p. 67 for more information on 4.2.2.)

In short, the process approach outlined in the introduction of ISO 9001:2000 is TC 176's attempt to show that organizations can operate effectively using this model. However, it is not the only model for success and it is not a requirement of ISO 9001:2000. It is simply one way to manage business processes to meet customer requirements and continually improve the organization.

 What's the best way to transition my organization to a "process approach"?

While there is no "best way," a common and effective method is using flowcharts to map out how your organization operates. This can be as easy as drawing some flowcharts on a piece of paper or as complex as using specific software to analyze your business processes. Regardless of how you choose to do it, the fact is, an organization that understands and controls its processes can manage process changes better for greater overall efficiency and improvement.

There are several software tools available in the marketplace that vary in complexity. CEEM evaluated all of the major software products and has endorsed and agreed to distribute a tool called Process Expert Professional™ (PEP). This product is considered to be an all-inclusive tool to implement and maintain management systems that use the process approach, which include ISO 9001, ISO 14001 for environmental management and OHSAS 18001 for occupational safety and health management.
In short, PEP is a flexible software program that enables an organization to:
- Develop dynamic and integrated process maps through state-of-the-art technology;
- Attach existing documentation to process activities;
- Measure and analyze every business process and activity;
- Identify waste and duplication of activities and processes;
- Identify staff responsibilities and process owners;
- Use "what if" analysis to measure impact of change; and
- Post all maps, processes and documentation electronically in a secure environment.

PEP also includes features such as document version control, multi-lingual support and the ability to link all of the clauses of the new ISO 9001:2000 and ISO 14001:1996 as well. Additionally, it is easy enough to learn and use with only a day of training.

For more information or a free demonstration of PEP's functionality, visit the CEEM Web site: www.ceem.com.

34 How can I enhance the satisfaction of my customers with the new standards?

It's important to realize that ISO 9000:2000 is not just about "standards." Each and every day, it's about *customer satisfaction*, because without happy customers, you'll likely experience the same fate as the dinosaurs.

Customer satisfaction is defined in ISO 9000:2000 as a "customer's perception of the degree to which the customer's requirements have been fulfilled." As will be discussed later in this Module, Clause 8.2 (Measurement and Monitoring) requires the organization to monitor that perception.

Indeed, quality management systems can assist organizations in enhancing customer satisfaction on a continual basis.

Customers require products and/or services with characteristics that meet their needs and expectations. Such needs are expressed as product specifications or service requirements, and collectively referred to as "customer requirements." These may be specified contractually by the purchaser or may be determined by the organization itself—or both. In any case, the customer ultimately determines the acceptability of the product and/or service, and because needs and expectations change, organizations are driven to continually improve their products and services.

The quality management system approach encourages organizations to analyze customer requirements, define processes that contribute to meeting customer requirements (including product technical performance) and to keep processes under control. A quality management system can provide the framework for continual improvement to enhance customer satisfaction.

It also provides confidence to the organization and its customers that it is able to provide products and/or services that consistently fulfill requirements. And don't forget, ISO 9000:2000 is the most successful and recognizable set of standards that ISO has ever produced. People all over the world associate ISO 9001 registration with quality products and services because the fundamentals are flexible enough for any organization to manage. The fact is, if your customers know that you have a sound management system in place based on international standards to manage and improve quality, they'll sleep better at night—and so will you.

 TRANSITION TIPS: Organizations should review Clauses 1, 2 and 3 of ISO 9001:2000 for further explanation of scope, application and terms and definitions. Those clauses begin on p. 50.

How do I choose a team to help me implement ISO 9001:2000?

Choosing the right team to implement and audit to the ISO 9001:2000 standard is key to any successful quality program, but it's not the easiest thing to do. There is no right or wrong way to choose a team because organizations vary on size, scope and complexity. But it is optimal to have people on the team with different skill sets from cross-functional parts of the business that can provide valuable input to the implementation process. This allows business synergies and communication to occur across the business.

Team members for implementation and audits should be identified early in the process, but make sure you have people who represent all relevant departments. Some examples of departments or divisions that will be profoundly affected by the quality system include:
- Engineering
- Purchasing
- Quality

- Operations
- Sales and/or marketing
- Administration
- Customer service
- Shipping, receiving and fulfillment

However, the above list should not be considered to be exhaustive, as the process approach may well include other departments not shown above. In a process environment, few departments are excluded.

Additionally, it is a good idea to consider personality traits for the members of the team. For example, because there will likely be a lot of meetings in the beginning for implementation planning, setting objectives and the quality policy, you should consider personnel who work well together in groups. Group decisions can provide a lot of creative feedback, which is often cyclical in providing more employee ownership and buy-in to the project. Other personality traits you should consider could include:

- **Action-oriented**—The team needs to be ready to act and implement change.
- **Experienced**—It's a good idea to have team members who know the business of the organization. People who have been around a while and know how things operate can be invaluable to your team.
- **Detail-driven**—Documentation and implementation means dotting the "i's" and crossing the "t's", and deadlines are often absolute.
- **Holistic thinkers**—When implementing ISO 9001:2000 for an organization, team members must be able to see the "Big Picture."
- **Good communicators**—Once the system begins, awareness and understanding is crucial. This is where a strong team becomes essential, because spreading the word about quality can only be a good thing. Just make sure that the information that is communicated is consistent and relevant.

You may recognize some of these qualities in yourself—which is a good thing. These traits often translate into leadership fundamentals. But remember that these personality types often define strong people as well, who may not always agree. That's OK. It's healthy for groups to disagree from time to time. That's one of the great benefits of consensus building and good decision-making.

However, don't get caught up in consensus process too much, or you'll never get the job done! The team also needs to have a leader who can ultimately make the decision and make sure it is carried out. This role is often that of the management representative, which is discussed in detail later in this Module.

One more thing: An important issue to consider with the team is to reward them somehow when the organization achieves its registration goals. It is an excellent accomplishment, and one that is worth rejoicing. But this issue will be discussed later in Module 10.

How do I begin the process of implementation?

The way forward is to treat the implementation process as a project, which means appointing a project team with a project manager (as discussed previously), preparing a project plan and evaluating and monitoring progress according to the plan. This demands certain prerequisites, including top management commitment, good communications at all levels and ownership of the quality system by all.

ISO 9001:2000 implementation will be discussed further in Module 6, but to provide a quick overview, here are some basic steps that can get your organization started toward registration. In fact, you may want to consider these steps as your own personal **12-step program** to improve your business and its bottom line:

1. Determine needs and expectations of customer
2. Establish quality policy and quality objectives
3. Define necessary processes and responsibilities
4. Establish measures for process effectiveness
5. Determine current effectiveness of processes
6. Search for process improvement opportunities
7. Prioritize improvements for optimal results
8. Plan strategies, processes and resources
9. Implement the plan
10. Monitor the effects of the improvements
11. Assess the results against expected outcomes
12. Review activities to identify follow-up actions

As you can see, these steps are surrounded by the concept of *action*, which if done effectively and continuously, will lead to improvement.

But before you begin Step 1, there is an important preface that must take place. Indeed, understanding the ISO 9001:2000 standard is essential in your route to registration. So let's get started with the requirements and clauses of ISO 9001:2000, and more importantly, how they will affect your organization and its quality management system.

Getting Started

This part of Module 3 is key in helping you understand the clauses and requirements of ISO 9001:2000. Each clause is outlined and describes what needs to be in place if you are to meet the requirements of the standard. Some industry sectors, such as the aerospace, automotive and telecommunications fields, have additional guidelines, so if you haven't done so yet, this is the time to identify those items, if any exist.

After completing each Clause, you will be able to identify the gaps that remain. Additionally, the information you generate will be useful when you begin to prepare documentation in Module 5.

NOTE: In understanding the standard and the system you're about to implement, it will be useful if you accept that everyone who works in the company, either directly or indirectly, including suppliers, has an effect on the quality of the product or service you supply. Also, if you have difficulty understanding some of the terminology in the clauses, please consult the Glossary at the back of the book for some of the definitions from the ISO 9000:2000 series.

0-Introduction

0.1 General

The adoption of a quality management system should be a strategic decision of an organization. The design and implementation of an organization's quality management system is influenced by varying needs, particular objectives, the products provided, the processes employed and the size and structure of the organization. It is not the intent of this International Standard to imply uniformity in the structure of quality management systems or uniformity of documentation.

The quality management system requirements specified in this International Standard are complementary to requirements for products. Information marked "NOTE" is for guidance in understanding or clarifying the associated requirement.

This International Standard can be used by internal and external parties, including certification bodies, to assess the organization's ability to meet customer, regulatory and the organization's own requirements.

The quality management principles stated in ISO 9000 and ISO 9004 have been taken into consideration during the development of this International Standard.

Source: BS EN ISO 9001:2000

Although vital to understanding the ISO 9001:2000, Clause 0 is not a requirements clause of the standard. It simply is an informative introduction to provide background on the standard, its requirements, use and flexibility.

However, Clause 0.1 is important for all organizations beginning the implementation or transition process to review and understand. Particular attention should be paid to the notation regarding the eight quality management principles, which can be found on Page 42. These principles will help you develop the foundation of your quality management system, and they appear in both ISO 9000 and ISO 9004.

0.2 Process Approach

This International Standard promotes the adoption of a process approach when developing, implementing and improving the effectiveness of a quality management system, to enhance customer satisfaction by meeting customer requirements.

For an organization to function effectively, it has to identify and manage numerous linked activities. An activity using resources, and managed in order to enable the transformation of inputs into outputs, can be considered as a process. Often the output from one process directly forms the input to the next.

The application of a system of processes within an organization, together with the identification and interactions of these processes, and their management, can be referred to as the "process approach."

An advantage of the process approach is the ongoing control that it provides over the linkage between the individual processes within the systems of processes, as well as over their combination an interaction.

When used within a quality management system, such an approach emphasizes the importance of

a) understanding and meeting requirements,
b) the need to consider processes in terms of added value,
c) obtaining results of process performance and effectiveness, and
d) continual improvement of processes based on objective measurement.

The model of a process-based quality management system shown in Figure 1 illustrates the process linkages presented in clauses 4 to 8. This illustration shows that customers play a significant role in defining requirements as inputs. Monitoring of customer satisfaction requires the evaluation of information relating to customer perception as to whether the organization has met the customer requirements. The model shown in Figure 1 covers all the requirements of this International Standard, but does not show processes at a detailed level.

Source: BS EN ISO 9001:2000

0.2 Process Approach cont...

NOTE In addition, the methodology known as "Plan-Do-Check-Act" (PDCA) can be applied to all processes. PDCA can be briefly described as follows.

Plan: establish the objectives and processes necessary to deliver results in accordance with customer requirements and the organization's policies.

Do: implement the processes.

Check: monitor and measure processes and product against policies, objectives and requirements for the product and report the results.

Act: take actions to continually improve performance.

Source: BS EN ISO 9001:2000

Figure 1—Model of a process-based quality management system. (Note: This graphic is sometimes called the PDCA cycle.)

Like the clause before it, Clause 0.2 is not a requirement. However, organizations should definitely consider it when implementing a quality management system.

The process approach is the fourth quality management principle, which can help an organization systematically identify and manage processes and their interaction within a quality management system. Understanding the process approach is critical to implementing and registering an ISO 9001:2000, and perhaps more importantly, aids improvement.

Turn to Page 44 in this Module to review the process approach if necessary. Also, Figure 1 should help you understand the process and its interactions within a business. Organizations should note, however, that this graphic is only one example of the process approach and is not required. But the intent of the standard's development is quite clear. The process approach is strongly encouraged.

0.3 Relationship with ISO 9004

The present editions of ISO 9001 and ISO 9004 have been developed as a consistent pair of quality management system standards which have been designed to complement each other, but can also be used independently. Although the two International Standards have different scopes, they have similar structures in order to assist their application as a consistent pair.

ISO 9001 specifies requirements for a quality management system that can be used for internal application by organizations, or for certification, or for contractual purposes. It focuses on the effectiveness of the quality management system in meeting customer requirements.

ISO 9004 gives guidance on a wider range of objectives of a quality management system than does ISO 9001, particularly for the continual improvement of an organization's overall performance and efficiency, as well as its effectiveness. ISO 9004 is recommended as a guide for organizations whose top management wishes to move beyond the requirements of ISO 9001, in pursuit of continual improvement of performance. However, it is not intended for certification or for contractual purposes.

Source: BS EN ISO 9001:2000

As mentioned in Module 1, ISO 9001 and ISO 9004 are different standards and have different scopes, but share a unique relationship within the new series, called the "consistent pair" concept. Clause 0.3 simply describes the important role that ISO 9004 has regarding an organization's quality management system, with emphasis on ISO 9004's guidance on continual improvement.

Turn to Module 1 Page 10 for more information on ISO 9004:2000 and an explanation of the "consistent pair" concept.

0.4 Compatibility with other management systems

This International Standard has been aligned with ISO 14001:1996 in order to enhance the compatibility of the two standards for the benefit of the user community.

This International Standard does not include requirements specific to other management systems, such as those particular to environmental management, occupational health and safety management, financial management or risk management. However, this International Standard enables an organization to align or integrate its own quality management system with related management system requirements. It is possible for an organization to adapt its existing management system(s) in order to establish a quality management system that complies with the requirements of this International Standard.

Source: BS EN ISO 9001:2000

When TC 176 began the revision process for the ISO 9000 series a few years ago, compatibility with other management systems, such as ISO 14001 for environmental management, was an important consideration. This clause simply explains that standards developers went to great lengths to ensure compatibility.

Additionally, TC 207—the committee charged with revising ISO 14001—also is considering the compatibility issue as it begins its own revision process. Both standards will be harmonized even more when the new ISO 14001 is released, sometime in 2003.

Compatibility will be addressed more in Module 8—*Auditing*.

1-Scope

Source: BS EN ISO 9001:2000

1.1 General

This International Standard specifies requirement for a quality management system where an organization

a)　needs to demonstrate its ability to consistently provide product that meets customer and applicable regulatory requirements, and

b)　aims to enhance customer satisfaction through the effective application of the system, including processes for continual improvement of the system and assurance of conformity to customer and applicable regulatory requirements.

NOTE In this International Standard, the term "product" applies only to the product intended for, or required by, a customer.

SCOPE

This clause is straightforward, describing the scope or intent of ISO 9001:2000. In a nutshell, it basically says that the standard is flexible and can be used in any type of industry or organization where customer satisfaction is a key performance indicator. Organizations should understand, however, that the scope provided in this clause refers to the standard—not the scope of the quality management system. The QMS scope will be discussed later in this Module, and Module 4 as well.

1.2 Application

All requirements of this International Standard are generic and are intended to be applicable to all organizations, regardless of type, size and product provided.

Where any requirement(s) of this International Standard cannot be applied due to the nature of an organization and its product, this can be considered for exclusion.

Where exclusions are made, claims of conformity to this International Standard are not acceptable unless these exclusions are limited to requirements within clause 7, and such exclusions do not affect the organization's ability, or responsibility, to provide product that meets customer and applicable regulatory requirements.

Source: BS EN ISO 9001:2000

Clause 1.2 *Application* probably will be one of the most controversial sections of the new ISO 9001:2000 as organizations begin implementing the standard and registrars begin conducting third-party audits.

It is intended that organizations seeking to implement ISO 9001:2000 will comply with all the requirements of the standard that are applicable to the products within the scope of the quality management system.

However, even when an organization includes all its products in the scope of its system, it may be found that some of the requirements of ISO 9001:2000 clause 7 *Product realization* cannot be applied. This could be due to the nature of the organization, and that of its products or realization processes. In such circumstances, the organization may limit the application of the requirements of ISO 9001:2000, in accordance with clause 1.2.

It should be noted that Clause 1.2 applies to specific requirements of this International Standard. There may be circumstances, however, where an entire clause or subclause can be excluded. An example would be clause 7.3 *Design and development*, which could be excluded in its entirety if no part of the design and development process is performed by the organization and it has no responsibility for this process.

Where an organization finds that it cannot apply certain requirements of ISO 9001:2000, this must be defined and justified in the organization's Quality Manual. Any publicly available documents, such as certification/registration documents or marketing materials, should be carefully phrased in order to avoid confusing or misleading customers and end users regarding the application of ISO 9001:2000 requirements within the organization's quality management system.

If an organization excludes from its quality management system requirements that do not meet the criteria established in clause 1.2 *Application*, then conformity to ISO 9001:2000 may not be claimed or implied. This includes the following situations:
- Where an organization fails to comply with the requirement in clause 4.2.2(a) *Quality manual* to provide justification for the exclusion of specific clause 7 *Product realization* requirements.
- Where requirements in clause 7 have been excluded because they are not required by regulatory bodies, but the requirements affect the organization's ability to meet customer requirements.
- Where an organization decides not to apply a requirement in clause 7 based only on the justification that this was not a requirement of either ISO 9001:1994, ISO 9002:1994 or ISO 9003:1994, and had not been previously included in the organization's QMS.

Organizations are encouraged to consult a registrar prior to a third-party audit if they believe that exclusions might occur within the system. Additional guidance also is available on the TC 176 Web site: http://isotc176sc2.elysium-ltd.net. You should download *Document #524R2* for further information.

2-Normative Reference

The following normative document contains provisions which, through reference in this text, constitute provisions of this International Standard. For dated references, subsequent amendments to, or revisions of, any of these publications do not apply. However, parties to agreements based on this International Standard are encouraged to investigate the possibility of applying the most recent edition of the normative document indicated below. For undated reference, the latest edition of the normative document referred to applies. Members of ISO and IEC maintain registers of currently valid International Standards.

ISO 9000:2000, Quality management systems—Fundamentals and vocabulary.

Source: BS EN ISO 9001:2000

This clause simply states that the only normative document in the standard is ISO 9000:2000, which contains terms and definitions used in the ISO 9000:2000 series.

3-Terms and Definitions

For the purposes of this International Standard, the terms and definitions given in ISO 9000 apply.

The following terms, used in this edition of ISO 9001 to describe the supply chain, have changed to reflect the vocabulary currently used:

Supplier ⟶ Organization ⟶ Customer

The term "organization" replaces the term "supplier" used in ISO 9001:1994, and refers to the unit to which this International Standard applies. Also, the term "supplier" now replaces the term "subcontractor."

Throughout the text of this International Standard, wherever the term "product" occurs, it can also mean "service."

Source: BS EN ISO 9001:2000

TERMS AND DEFINITIONS

This clause notes some language changes from the 1994 version of ISO 9001. Organizations should note these changes throughout the remaining portions of ISO 9001:2000.

4-Quality Management System

Clause 4 is really where the requirements of ISO 9001:2000 begin, so from this point, you should really try to understand the meaning and intent of the standard, and how it will fit with your organization.

But before getting started, let's imagine it's a cold, winter night, and you're settling in for a long weekend with your favorite author's new bestseller. What's the first thing you do? Well, hopefully you won't turn to the last page and see what happens at the end of the book first—what a waste of time that would be!

No, the first thing you do is turn to Chapter 1 and start from the beginning, hoping it's a real page-turner.

The same is true for ISO 9001:2000. In fact, the authors have made it an easy-to-read document using the Plan-Do-Check-Act (PDCA) approach from start to finish. This was explained more earlier in this Module, but it really becomes important now as we begin to understand the standard's requirements. From now on, in each clause, the PDCA approach will be used in some way. Let's take a look...

4.1 General Requirements (1994 clause, 4.2.1)

The organization shall establish, document, implement and maintain a quality management system and continually improve its effectiveness in accordance with the requirements of this International Standard.

The organization shall

a) identify the processes needed for the quality management system and their application throughout the organization (see 1.2),
b) determine the sequence and interaction of these processes,
c) determine criteria and methods needed to ensure that both the operation and control of these processes are effective,
d) ensure the availability of resources and information necessary to support the operation and monitoring of these processes,
e) monitor, measure and analyze these processes, and
f) implement actions necessary to achieve planned results and continual improvement of these processes.

These processes shall be managed by the organization in accordance with the requirements of this International Standard.

Where an organization chooses to outsource any process that affects product conformity with requirements, the organization shall ensure control over such processes. Control of such outsourced processes shall be identified within the quality management system.

NOTE Processes needed for the quality management system referred to above should include processes for management activities, provision of resources, product realization and management.

Source: BS EN ISO 9001:2000

QUALITY MANAGEMENT SYSTEM

This section is a perfect example of a well-written Chapter 1, just like that bestseller you're reading. It sets up exactly (without all the details) what needs to happen for you to get to the end successfully.

In a nutshell, this section says that you must "establish, document, implement and maintain a quality management system and continually improve its effectiveness." Additionally, as you'll understand later, Clause 5.4.2 requires system planning that will meet the requirements of clause 4.1. How do you do that? By following these steps:

a. Identify the processes needed for the quality management system and their application throughout the organization; (Planning and Doing)
b. Determine the sequence and interaction of these processes; (Planning and Doing)
c. Determine criteria and methods needed to ensure that both the operation and control of these processes are effective; (Planning, Doing and Checking)
d. Ensure the availability of resources and information necessary to support the operation and monitoring of these processes; (Checking and Doing)
e. Monitor, measure and analyze these processes; (Doing and Checking)
f. Implement actions necessary to achieve planned results and continual improvement of these processes. (Acting)

Of course, the majority of the "doing" is applying these steps to your business processes in everything you do, including any time your organization chooses a process that affects product conformity with requirements.

Sounds easy, right?

OK, let's get out the microscope.

Getting back to that favorite book of yours, let's imagine you're our hero in a story about going to war. Picture yourself in the War Room at the Pentagon, with lots of people, computers and big TV screens telling you exactly what's going on at every moment around the globe. Generals are telling you what forces you have, where they are, what their specialties are, how they can be used together to defend or attack, etc. You get the picture.

Now, think of your business or organization in the same way. Get your team together (including top management representation) and go to the War Room. (See p. 46 in this Module on how to choose a team.) Ask yourself some very basic questions about your business and what you're trying to accomplish, and be sure to review, and if necessary, update your mission statement. Begin looking at exactly how your business operates, and by all means, if you already have procedures, work instructions and other documentation on how your business operates, use them. You don't want to re-invent the wheel while mapping out the processes of your business. Consider using flowcharting methods and tools to achieve a holistic approach of the business and integrate any existing documentation. (See Module 3 regarding Process Expert Professional™.)

Once all the generals on your team have told you what they do and how they do it, begin looking at ways to connect the functional parts of your business. You'll start to find out that many parts of the organization are using the same general processes and sub-processes, but they may be doing them a little differently. Some generic examples of processes in many organizations include, but are not limited to:
- calibration
- complaint handling
- purchasing

QUALITY MANAGEMENT SYSTEM

- communication
- production planning
- sales and marketing

This is where a quality management system under ISO 9001:2000 becomes your best tool, because at its heart, the standard's basic requirement is to identify and manage all of those processes you and your team have just laid out in the War Room. It's the *managing* of these processes using a "process approach" that makes the difference. This is the critical first step of your journey, and if you need more insight on that concept, now would be a good time to re-visit it. (See p. 44.)

So, here are some examples of what you should be asking your team members and what they should be asking themselves:
- What is it we do and how do we do it?
- How do the things we do interact with one another?
- Are these processes already documented? (i.e., procedures, work instructions, flowcharts, etc.)
- Does the team have the resources to do these processes efficiently and effectively? (i.e., funds, management support, time, people, information, etc.)
- Does the organization have processes in place to measure performance results?
- Can we improve our performance with these processes?

Once you've answered these and other questions effectively, you've officially begun the engineering of your management system.

TRANSITION TIPS: When transitioning your system to ISO 9001:2000, remember that the new standard insists that you take a Big Picture approach. In the 1994 version of ISO 9001, documentation and procedures were needed everywhere, but in the new standard, flexibility has been built in for management to decide how to address the requirements. The whole mindset that your organization needs to have mountains of procedures is now gone. The significant reduction of documentation requirements shifts the emphasis from "creating paper" to "understanding processes."

Additionally, you need to consider that the new standard goes beyond the 1994 version, which focused largely on the compliance-related details. Now, you need to focus on conformance and consider all interested parties—employees, shareholders, suppliers, the community and, of course, your customers, internally and externally.

One more thing, and it's very important...

Everything you do with ISO 9001:2000 should consider the concept of **continual improvement**. If you don't focus your entire system around this concept, you're wasting time and resources. What that means is, the status quo is no longer acceptable to any of your organization's "interested parties," so it can be no longer acceptable to you and your organization.

4.2 Documentation Requirements
(1994 clauses, 4.2.1, 4.2.2, 4.5.1, 4.5.2, 4.5.3, 4.16)

4.2.1 General

The quality management system documentation shall include:
a) documented statement of a quality policy and quality objectives,
b) a quality manual,
c) documented procedures required by this International Standard,
d) documents needed by the organization to ensure the effective planning, operation and control of its processes, and
e) record required by this International Standard (see 4.2.4)

NOTE 1 Where the term "documented procedure" appears within this International Standard, this means that the procedure is established, documented, implemented and maintained.

NOTE 2 The extent of the quality management systems documentation can differ from one organization to another due to:
a) the size of organization and type of activities,
b) the complexity of processes and their interactions, and
c) the competence of personnel.

NOTE 3 The documentation can be in any form or type of medium.

Source: BS EN ISO 9001:2000

Albeit brief, this clause is critical and must be applied to the rest of the standard and your management system. In fact, think of it as the umbrella clause of the entire system.

Right from the start, there's a new emphasis on your organization's *quality policy*, which simply stated, means the overall intentions and direction of your organization—in terms of quality—as formally expressed by top management.

In the 1994 version of ISO 9001, there was a requirement for a quality policy with stated quality objectives. But frankly, that policy was something that often was simply placed on the lobby wall of an organization, without much meaning to interested parties. It was audited against, but it wasn't a *living* document.

QUALITY MANAGEMENT SYSTEM

The new standard focuses on the objectives of the quality management system and its policy, and more importantly, how it aligns with the overall objectives of your *business* and the objectives of your *customers*. This also aligns more with the language of ISO 9001:2000's sister standard, ISO 14001, on environmental management systems. (See Module 8 for more information on ISO 14001.)

In short, this clause lays out very clearly exactly what needs to be documented:
   a. Documented statements of a quality policy (5.3) and quality objectives (5.4.1)
   b. A quality manual (4.2.2)
   c. Documented procedures that are required by ISO 9001:2000

Figure 3-2

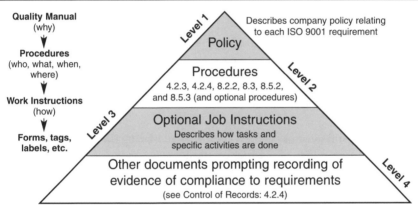

Level 1—Quality Manual
Overview of the company and its products and services; agreement to comply with applicable ISO 9001 requirements; quality policy; system scope; exclusions; organization and responsibilities; sequence and interaction of processes; documented procedures or reference to them.

Level 2—Quality Procedures
Describes the who, what, when and where of quality processes and interdepartmental controls that address the ISO 9001 requirements; may be in ISO 9001 order or process order; references lower–level documentation. ISO 9001 mandates six specific procedures.

Level 3—Work Instructions
Explains details of specific tasks or activities: the how of performing a specific task, making or verifying product. This level may include quality plans, work instructions, drawings, flowcharts, workmanship standards, product specifications, machine manuals, etc.

Level 4—Other Documents
Forms, tags, labels and other documents that prompt the recording of evidence (per levels 1, 2 and 3 documentation) of compliance to requirements. Records may be mandatory or implied for each ISO 9001 clause.

d. Documents needed by the organization to ensure the effective planning, operation and control of its processes

e. Records required by ISO 9001:2000

The first two subclauses are explained with examples later in this book. As for documented procedures, the new standard has six that must be included in your management system. Those six documented procedures are:

- 4.2.3—Control of Documents
- 4.2.4—Control of Records
- 8.2.2—Internal Audit
- 8.3—Control of Nonconforming Product
- 8.5.2—Corrective Action
- 8.5.3—Preventive Action

Although the requirements above are key, these six documented procedures are the *minimum*, and it may be necessary to retain or write other procedures to ensure effective operation of the quality management system. For example, you may wish to look at design, control of monitoring and measurement devices, and other areas, depending on the organization.

Of course, there still must be "defined" processes addressing the other requirements. These other processes may or may not be documented, depending on whether the organization needs the documents for effective planning, operation and control of its quality management system. (Organizations should note subclause 4.2.1.d concerning other necessary documents.)

There are other issues that you should consider during the documentation phase as well. For example, ISO 9004:2000 suggests that you should satisfy the "contractual, statutory and regulatory requirements, and the needs and expectations of customers and other interested parties" concerning the nature and extent of the documentation. This means that items such as contracts, standards used by the organization, applicable regulations and other information regarding the needs of your stakeholders should be considered.

But remember that the ISO 9001:2000 standard is designed to be *flexible* and it encourages innovation. It stresses that there is no "correct" way regarding documentation. Rather, it notes that the extent of the documentation will vary between organizations, depending on the size and scope of the organization, the complexity of the processes and their interactions and the competency of the personnel. Concerning the last point, for example, if you have an employee who has been doing the same job very well for the past 30 years, that person doesn't need a lot of paperwork explaining his or her daily activities.

However, when an organization chooses to include documentation, it should write the documentation based on the defined competency levels for that job. Other people who perform the job in the absence of the experienced person might need more documentation, even though they are competent to do the work.

In other words, be precise—not burdensome—with what you document.

TRANSITION TIPS: Because of the flexibility built into Clause 4.2.1 concerning what is required with documentation, you may want to consider combining some areas that are similar, such as the corrective and preventive action requirements. Also, although it is not a requirement, most organizations will have at least one design procedure and another for purchasing. If you have difficulty evaluating what needs to be documented, consider this as a rule of thumb: *If it's a critical process, complicated or a lot of people are involved, it's a good idea to have it documented.*

One more thing... Please keep in mind that the management system isn't just for managers or operations, and it's not just something that affects the shop floor. The management system and the documentation encompass every level of the organization. This is an important concept as you consider the processes of your business.

> ### 4.2.2 Quality Manual (1994 clause, 4.2.1)
>
> The organization shall establish and maintain a quality manual that includes:
> a) the scope of the quality management system, including details of and justification for any exclusion (see 1.2)
> b) the documented procedures established for the quality management system, or reference to them, and
> c) a description of the interaction between the processes of quality management system.
>
> *Source: BS EN ISO 9001:2000*

You should read this clause now and understand it as best as you can. But because this clause is so important, we have developed an entire Module devoted to it. Please turn to Module 4, Page 139, when you have completed Module 3.

4.2.3 Control of Documents (1994 clause, 4.5)

Documents required by the quality management system shall be controlled. Records are a special type of document and shall be controlled according to the requirements given in 4.2.4.

A documented procedure shall be established to define the controls needed:
 a) to approve documents for adequacy prior to issue,
 b) to review and update as necessary and re-approve documents,
 c) to ensure that changes and the current revision status of documents are identified,
 d) to ensure that relevant versions of applicable documents are available at point of use,
 e) to ensure documents remain legible and readily identifiable,
 f) to ensure that documents of external origin are identified and their distribution controlled, and
 g) to prevent the unintended use of obsolete documents, and to apply suitable identification to them if they are retained for any purpose.

Source: BS EN ISO 9001:2000

This clause is a significant improvement from the 1994 version because the new language takes out any ambiguity of what needs to be controlled. It also is the first place in ISO 9001:2000 where you'll need to have a documented procedure, which means the control of documents must be established, documented, implemented and maintained. This comes first because it is one of the first steps you should do during implementation. (**Note:** Corrective and preventive action should come before this when documenting. Turn to p. 132 for more information on corrective and preventive action.)

Try to remember that there is no need to *over-document!* The language of this section is clear concerning what needs to be documented. Some organizations (particularly larger organizations or those with complex processes) may need additional documented procedures to implement an effective system. Others may need additional procedures as well, but the size and/or culture of the organization could enable these to be effectively implemented without necessarily being documented.

In a nutshell, to meet the requirements of this clause, you must have a documented procedure for identifying, collecting, indexing, accessing, filing, maintaining and the disposing of documents.

TRANSITION TIPS: Although the language has been streamlined and improved in this clause, much of the intent remains the same as the 1994 standard. Organizations should review the language carefully here and note the slight differences from the 1994 version. Basically, the standard states that relevant documents need to be adequate to the task, available at points of use, up-to-date and legible. But if you change a process at any time, make sure you also change the procedure. The change also should be discussed in management review.

Additionally, one new section of the standard (4.2.3.f) says that external documents must be identified and their distribution controlled. The intention here is to have some kind of register or database that provides an up-to-date (and dated) copy of a document from the outside. A customer drawing or specification would be a good example of an external document that needs to be controlled. (So is the ISO 9000:2000 series of standards.)

Some companies have spent years creating a culture using mounds of procedures and documenting everything, and if that works for them, that's OK. There is no need to "re-invent the wheel" when it comes to documentation. But adhering to the new standard gives you an opportunity to "clean house" and make the wheel roll a little smoother.

4.2.4 Control of Records (1994 clause, 4.16)

Records shall be established and maintained to provide evidence of conformity to requirements and of the effective operation of the quality management system. Records shall remain legible, readily identifiable and retrievable. A documented procedure shall be established to define the controls needed for the identification, storage, protection, retrieval, retention time and disposition of records.

Source: BS EN ISO 9001:2000

Not a lot has changed from the 1994 version of ISO 9000 in this clause. In short, quality records are the evidence that shows you have, in fact, followed your system. Some good examples of records are purchase orders, sales records, contracts, internal audits, meeting minutes, test data and anywhere ISO 9001:2000 states "see 4.2.4."

Records must be legible and retrievable in a reasonable timeframe. (You decide what is reasonable to your organization.) These records should be thought of as long-term documents and must be stored where they cannot be damaged. It might be a good idea to get your legal and IT departments involved when making decisions about records—what should be kept, how long you should keep them, how they should be stored and how they should be disposed.

TRANSITION TIPS: There are several places in ISO 9001:2000 that require records. Any time the standard states "See 4.2.4," a record is required.

QUALITY MANAGEMENT SYSTEM

However, other records not specifically mentioned will be necessary to show conformance with requirements and demonstrate effective operation of the system.

If you're transitioning to the new standard and already have a lot of records to deal with, you may want to consider using your organization's Intranet to post and store records. Today, most companies tend to store their records in one area that has been deemed safe for storage. It's a good idea to have a central, physical area for documentation, whether it's in your building or cyberspace.

Also, if you're going to dispose of records, consider shredding them if it's paper copy. Paper shredders are relatively inexpensive, and the leftover product can be recycled in a number of ways. If you store records electronically, as many organizations now do, consult your technology department to ensure proprietary documents don't fall into the wrong hands.

Figure 3-3: Comparison of Requirements for Documented Procedures

ISO 9001 (year 2000 issue)		ISO 9001 1994	
Clause	Documented Procedures Required	Clause	Documented Procedures Required
		4.3.1	Contract Review
		4.4.1	Design Control
4.2.3	Control of documents	4.5.6	Document and Data Control
		4.6.1	Purchasing
		4.7	Customer Supplied Product
		4.8	Product ID and Traceability
		4.9	Process Control
		4.10.1	Inspection and Testing
		4.11.1	Control of I-M-T Equipment
		4.12	Inspection and Test Status
8.3	Control of nonconforming product	4.13.1	Control of Nonconforming Product
8.5.2	Corrective action	4.14.1	Corrective and Preventive Action
8.5.3	Preventive action		
		4.15.1	Handling, Storage, Packaging, Preservation and Delivery.
4.2.4	Control of records	4.16	Control of Quality Records
8.2.2	Internal audit	4.17	Internal Quality Audits
		4.18	Training
		4.19	Servicing, as applicable
		4.20	Statistical Techniques

QUALITY MANAGEMENT SYSTEM

Figure 3–4: Requirements for Documentation Other Than Procedures

ISO 9001 2000	Specific Documentation Requirement	ISO 9001 1994
4.1	"Organization shall establish, document...a quality management system..."	4.2.1
–	Documentation of the responsibility and authority and interrelation of personnel..."	4.1.2.1
4.2	"...documentation shall include:	4.2.1
	a) Statement of quality policy & objectives b) A quality manual c) Documented procedures d) Documents needed by the organization to ensure effective planning, operation and control	4.1.1 4.2.2a 4.9
–	"Quality manual shall...outline the structure of the documentation used in the quality system."	4.2.1
7.1b *	"...the output of the planning shall be documented..."	4.2.3
4.2.2	"The quality manual shall be controlled."	4.2.1
7.1*	"...Planning of the product realization shall be consistent with the requirements of the other processes of the QMS...The output shall be in a form suitable for the organization's method of operation."	4.9a
7.3.2**	"...\<Design\> inputs relating to product requirements shall be defined and documented..."	4.4.4
7.3.3**	"outputs of design/development shall be in a form that enables verification..."	4.4.5
7.3.7	"Design and development changes shall be identified and records maintained..."	4.4.9
7.3.7**	"Records of the results of review the of changes..."	–
7.4.2*	"Purchasing documents shall contain information \<to\> ensure the adequacy of...purchasing documents prior to their release." (1994)	4.6.3
*	Author's note: only the need to determine what documentation is needed is actually stated in the standard, and then in whatever form is suitable.	
**	Author's note: the standard now refers to the required documentation as being "records," as opposed to documents, or requires them to be in some "suitable form."	

QUALITY MANAGEMENT SYSTEM

Figure 3-5: Comparison of Record Requirements

ISO 9001:2000		ISO 9001:1994	
Clause	Documented Procedures Required	Clause	Documented Procedures Required
5.6.1	Management review	4.1.3	Management review
6.2.2e	Education, training, skills and experience	4.18	Training records
7.1d	Records needed to provide evidence that...product fulfills requirements	4.16	Records to demonstrate conformance to requirements and effective operation of the system
		4.2.3h	Records during quality planning
		4.10.1	Records to be established in quality plan or procedures
		4.10.5	Evidence of product inspection/test
7.2.2	Review of product requirements	4.3.4	Contract review
7.3.2	Records of design/development input		
7.3.4	Results of design/development review	4.4.6	Records of design review
7.3.5	Results of design/development verification and follow-up action	4.4.7	Design verification measures shall be recorded
7.3.6	Results of design/development validation and follow-up actions	4.4.8	Design validation
7.3.7	Results of review of design changes	4.4.9	Design changes
7.4.1	Evaluations of suppliers	4.6.2c	Records of acceptable subcontractors
		4.10.2.3	Urgent release of incoming material
7.5.3	Unique identification of product, where traceability is a requirement	4.8	Unique identification of individual product, where traceability is rqrmt.
7.5.4	Occurrence of customer property lost, damaged or otherwise unsuitable	4.7	Customer or supplier product lost, damaged or unsuitable
7.5.2d	Process validation records	4.9	Qualified processes, equipment and personnel as appropriate
7.6a	The basis used for calibration	4.11.1	Calibration checks
7.6	Validity of previous (suspect) results	4.11.2f	Validity of previous results...
7.6	Results of calibration & verification	4.11.2e	Calibration records for I-M-T-E
		4.11.2d	Calibration status indication
8.2.2	Records of audit results	4.17	Results of audits
8.2.2 *	Note: Follow-up verifications of corrective actions must be reported, but does not specify a record.	4.17	Follow-up audit records as related to corrective action taken
8.2.4	Evidence of conformity to acceptance criteria and records to indicate authority for release of product	4.10.5	Records to identify the inspection authority responsible for release of product
8.3	Records of the nature of nonconformities and any subsequent actions taken	4.13.2	Description of nonconformity accepted, and of repairs
		4.14.1	Changes to documented procedures as result of corrective action
8.5.2e	Results of corrective action taken	4.14.2b	Results of investigation into cause of nonconformity
8.5.3d	Results of preventive action taken	4.16	Quality records in general to demonstrate conformance to requirements, and retention times
4.2.1e and 4.2.4	Records required by the Standard Records shall be maintained to provide evidence of conformance to requirements		
		4.19	Servicing reports, where a contract requirement
*	Editor's Note: "Reporting" may not necessarily require a written record, where an oral report is sufficient.		

QUALITY MANAGEMENT SYSTEM

5-Management Responsibility

As you already know from previous modules in this book, ISO 9001:2000 has a new emphasis on top management's commitment and ongoing role with the quality management system. In fact, top management should be involved in myriad areas, from the design and development of the system—including setting objectives that align with your organization's strategic business plan—to ensuring that the system is continually improving.

Clause 5.1, *Management Commitment*, kicks off with that language in its first sentence. The authors (TC 176) wanted to set a strong tone from the beginning, because without active participation and action from your organization's leaders throughout the PDCA cycle (process approach) and the management system itself, it is doomed to fail. This has been somewhat of a failure of the 1994 standard.

Why? Because without top management's commitment for identifying all of the relevant requirements of the business, communicating the organization's policy and goals and providing resources to ensure implementation and maintenance of the system, continual improvement *cannot and will not happen*. And in today's competitive marketplace, a business that is not in a constant state of improvement ultimately will fail.

5.1 Management Commitment (1994 clause, 4.1.1)

Top management shall provide evidence of its commitment to the development and implementation of the quality management system and continually improving its effectiveness by

  a) communicating to the organization the importance of meeting customer as well as statutory and regulatory requirements,
  b) establishing the quality policy,
  c) ensuring that quality objectives are established,
  d) conducting management reviews, and
  e) ensuring the availability of resources.

Source: BS EN ISO 9001:2000

This clause makes the "top 5 list" of new changes in ISO 9001:2000.

To begin, the phrase "top management" is used in ISO 9001:2000 instead of the old phrase, "executive management." The change occurred for two reasons: First, "executive management" didn't translate well into other languages, such as French and Russian. Second, and perhaps more important, there is a much stronger emphasis concerning the involvement of an organization's top leaders as active participants to ensure the PDCA cycle works properly.

Of course, there's still room for interpretation concerning how "top management" is defined in your organization—and that's up to you (and top management) to decide.

In ISO 9000:2000, top management is defined simply as a "person or group of people who directs and controls an organization at the highest level." That could mean the person or group might be located across the hall from you or they might be at headquarters on the other side of the world. However you define it, this must be established early in your journey for your organization to have success with implementation and registration.

Another major change with ISO 9001:2000 appears in Clause 5.1.a, which states that top management must communicate to the organization "the importance of meeting customer as well as statutory and regulatory requirements." Although the standard says little to explain what that means, this is very important to the business and the management system from every perspective.

Think of it this way: Your company makes automotive parts for all of the major manufacturers, and you've just discovered that your products (which were shipped to the client last Thursday) failed to meet the industry's baseline safety standards. Additionally, you just found out that while manufacturing these products, your company violated 11 national and state regulations, which range from violations concerning the environment to transportation and distribution statutes in four states.

This situation is obviously not good for anyone. Your company has violated laws and failed industry standards, which will cost the organization significantly in areas such as fines and penalties, lost product, bad value for the long term and bad press—not to mention that nasty shareholder meeting the CEO is going to have to deal with next quarter.

All of this might have been avoided, however, if top management had communicated those regulations and standards effectively throughout the organization. At the end of each day, a company needs to make sure it's following all applicable laws so that potential infractions don't prevent it from doing business.

The new standard also stresses management's commitment and involvement with establishing the organization's quality policy and quality objectives. This commitment was similar in the 1994 version, but there is a new emphasis and intended requirement with ISO 9001:2000 to align the quality policy and quality objectives with the organization's overall business plan. Doing so can ensure that everyone in the business is reading from the same book—chapter and verse. Turn to page 76 in this Module for more information on setting a sound quality policy and objectives.

TRANSITION TIPS: When revising your quality policy to ISO 9001:2000, be sure to consider the eight quality management principles that were discussed earlier in this module and peppered throughout the ISO 9000:2000 series. This isn't a requirement—just a good idea.

Also, when establishing quality objectives, make sure they're quantitative. You need to be able to measure the objectives effectively to ensure continual improvement for the system.

And don't forget... One quality objective should be customer satisfaction. Again, this isn't a requirement, but it's certainly implied in the standard. And, of course, doing so makes good business sense.

Here are some examples of quality objectives to consider:
Customer satisfaction—strive for a 100 percent net satisfaction index from all customers each year.
Sales—provide sales quotations for new business before the proposal due date and conduct quality calls after each sales visit.
The quality management system—close all corrective and preventive actions raised during assessments by the date projected.
Products—Ship all inventoried products within two business days of the customer order.

As you can see, quality objectives don't have to be long, drawn-out promises of what the business will do. They simply need to be quantitative measures of important objectives of your business.

5.2 Customer Focus

Top management shall ensure that customer requirements are determined and are met with the aim of enhancing customer satisfaction (see 7.2.1 and 8.2.1).

Source: BS EN ISO 9001:2000

This clause is completely new in ISO 9001:2000 and packs quite a punch in one sentence: "Top management shall ensure that customer requirements are *determined* and are *met* with the aim of enhancing customer satisfaction."

That means top management must help set the framework concerning what the organization's customers require—it doesn't mean top management must be in constant contact with the customers. Management's responsibility is to ensure that

MANAGEMENT RESPONSIBILITY

resources flow accordingly for continual improvement and customer satisfaction to happen effectively. In short, contracts define what the customer wants, and management takes that contract to the people who are going to take care of it.

As simple as that may seem, it doesn't happen as effectively as it should in many companies. Customers often have special needs, and those needs must be communicated from the highest level. A good way to make sure those needs are determined and met is to conduct internal audits and follow through on any findings. Internal audits can help enhance customer satisfaction, because the auditors will be talking with lots of people in the organization to make sure those customer needs are being communicated effectively. If those needs aren't being discussed, distributed and met, the auditors will certainly raise a red flag during a management review to fix it.

Organizations also should review Clause 7.2 regarding determining and reviewing customer requirements and Clause 8.2.1 regarding customer satisfaction. For more information on internal audits, turn to Module 8.

> **5.3 Quality Policy** (1994 clause, 4.1.1)
>
> Top management shall ensure that the quality policy
>
> a) is appropriate to the purpose of the organization
> b) includes a commitment to comply with requirements and continually improve the effectiveness of the quality management system,
> c) provides a framework for establishing and reviewing quality objectives,
> d) is communicated and understood within the organization, and
> e) is reviewed for continuing suitability.
>
> *Source: BS EN ISO 9001:2000*

Although it was implied in the 1994 version that top management was responsible for setting the quality policy, it really wasn't driven from that level in many organizations. The language in the new standard, however, gets down to business with five requirements, which ensure that the quality policy:
- is appropriate to the purpose of the organization;
- includes a commitment to comply with requirements and continually improve the effectiveness of the quality management system;
- provides a framework for establishing and reviewing quality objectives;
- is communicated and understood within the organization; and
- is reviewed for continuing suitability.

In basic terms, the quality policy is a single statement of commitment from the highest-level members of the organization that articulates their visions of how they will meet their business objectives and satisfy their customers. As you can see from above, the language of the five requirements is clear: The first three address the requirements of the policy, and the remaining two address how the policy will be communicated throughout the organization and how it will be reviewed for its "suitability" to the business.

But remember that ISO 9001:2000's language in this clause is designed for flexibility, stating up front that the policy must be "appropriate to the purpose of the organization." That means two things: First, it means that every quality policy out there will be different because every organization in the marketplace is different. Indeed, organizations shouldn't use a "cookie cutter approach" when designing the quality policy—it should be relevant to what the organization does. Second, make sure the policy is appropriate for the organization and its No. 1 priority—the *customer!* If you write an eloquent policy but the organization can't meet its expectations, then the system is doomed to fail right out of the starting blocks.

The policy also should create "a framework" for the organization's quality objectives, meaning that every goal you establish for the business is measurable and considers the continual improvement concept. You don't have to include the quality objectives in the quality policy, but it must provide a framework for establishing and reviewing them. Some examples of quality objective areas include customer satisfaction, warranties, shipping/delivery time and meeting regulatory commitments.

Once your team has established the policy, it must be communicated in an understandable way to the entire organization, and if relevant, to other interested parties as well. This means that everyone from the people in the front office to the nighttime cleaning crew understands what the policy means to them and their daily activities. They don't have to memorize it or be able to recite the policy verbatim to an auditor, but they need to understand their role in ensuring all elements of the policy are achieved.

For this to be done effectively, the organization usually needs some kind of awareness training after the policy has been established. Awareness training could be as simple as making sure all personnel read the company's Intranet site on the policy or as complex as sending key people to professional training courses on ISO 9001:2000—that's up to you and top management. But make no mistake—this is one area that auditors will test *constantly*. Without an effective quality policy and without an effective way to communicate that policy, the system will not conform to the standard's requirements and, ultimately, will not meet the customer's requirements (i.e., potential lost business resulting in stagnant or zero growth for the organization).

TRANSITION TIPS: When developing your quality policy in the War Room, be sure to have your organization's vision and mission statements in mind, as well

MANAGEMENT RESPONSIBILITY

as the organization's long-term business plan. Knowing the organization's purpose will help you set a framework as to how the quality policy and the quality objectives can ensure continual improvement for the business. In fact, be thinking in those terms at all times—*improvement, improvement, improvement!*

The 1994 version did not require any specific policy content. Now, policies must include commitments to comply with requirements and continually improve the effectiveness of the system. With that in mind, existing policy statements might be inadequate, so organizations should review them to ensure they meet the new requirements.

Also, remember that the quality policy is an evolving document and should be reviewed and updated when necessary. As your customers' needs change, so will your business and, thus, your policy. But the quality policy is listed under 4.2.1 as a required "documented" statement and, therefore, subject to document control.

And just another friendly reminder: It's a good idea to consider the eight quality management principles when developing your policy. It's not a requirement and won't be audited against explicitly, but it will help you set a solid foundation for your system. For more information on the quality policy, see p. 145.

5.4 Planning

MANAGEMENT RESPONSIBILITY

5.4.1 Quality Objectives (1994 clauses, 4.1.1)

Top management shall ensure that quality objectives, including those needed to meet requirements for product [see 7.1a.], are established at relevant functions and levels within the organization. The quality objectives shall be measurable and consistent with the quality policy.

Source: BS EN ISO 9001:2000

Objectives have been discussed previously on p. 75. As you may have figured out already, this is a new section in the standard and is the cornerstone to connect business operations with the planning stage of ISO 9001:2000 implementation. The setting of objectives was implied in the 1994 version concerning customer needs, but it wasn't specific. Now, all objectives must be measurable and they must come from top management.

Top management is responsible for this important step, because if an organization delegates the setting of objectives too far down the organizational chart, there is a risk that the objectives may not align with the overall objectives of the business. To avoid that risk, top management's fingerprints should be all over every objective.

A quality objective is defined in ISO 9000:2000 as "something sought, or aimed for, related to quality." There is no prescribed number of objectives that must be set for the organization, and the standard doesn't say that each part of the business must have them. But the objectives should be able to demonstrate product quality and they should be cross-functional across the organization. And if your quality policy states you will produce defect-free products, you'd better have an objective that measures defect levels. If the policy states on-time delivery, you should have a shipping objective. (**Note:** Organizations should understand that process objectives also are required in this clause and that reporting on process performance is a required management review agenda item.)

This easy-to-understand language was developed to be more compatible with ISO 14001 and environmental management systems, where the objectives for continual improvement and environmental performance are required to be measured. And, as with ISO 14001, your policy and objectives should go hand in hand.

☞ **TRANSITION TIPS:** To set objectives, organizations need to know where they currently are. In other words, you need to measure first to determine the appropriate target to set.

Chances are, even if you're registered under the ISO 9001:1994 standard, you'll need to revise your quality policy and objectives for the new requirements. But don't make the mistake of establishing too many objectives for the organization. This can become cumbersome and difficult to manage. Strive to set the correct number of objectives. To do that, make sure top management is involved or, at the very least, make sure top management gives its approval.

For more information and examples of quality objectives, turn to p. 147.

MANAGEMENT RESPONSIBILITY

5.4.2 Quality Management Systems Planning
(1994 clause, 4.2.3)

Top management shall ensure that

a) the planning of the quality management system is carried out in to meet the requirements given in 4.1, as well as the quality objectives, and
b) the integrity of the quality management system is maintained when changes to the quality management system are planned and implemented.

Source: BS EN ISO 9001:2000

Now it's time to really get down to business with planning the best quality system for your organization. You've learned about the requirements in 4.1, documentation in 4.2 and, of course, the quality policy and objectives. Now it's time to decide what your intentions are with the level of quality you desire for the organization and out-line a plan as to how you're going to achieve those intentions.

The plan doesn't have to be complex—many organizations choose to create a couple of pages, similar to an executive summary of what and how things happen in the organization related to quality. Issues you should consider include continual improvement, resource needs, the identification of processes and their interactions and change in the organization.

The last element is something new in ISO 9001:2000 (5.4.2.b). Because businesses of all types and sizes are in a constant state of change, TC 176 felt that managing change to maintain the integrity of the system and the organization was an impor-tant concept to consider and understand. In other words, if your organization enters into a new line of business, requiring you to hire more people to spur growth, or if the economy plunges into a recession, forcing you to halt production and lay off employees, significant change will occur at every level. But no matter what happens, you still need to meet your customers' requirements. Your customers must not suffer because your organization is experiencing change—if they do, you won't have them as customers very long.

So the new standard simply requires that you consider change during the planning stage. You should have a process that addresses any type of change in the organiza-tion, which could include a restructuring of the organization, personnel turnover, new products or services (or the downsizing of products or services) and any process improvement. Also, any change should be addressed during a management review.

TRANSITION TIPS: Be sure to understand the terminology in this section when dealing with the "quality plan" and "quality planning." They are related, but the plan is the result of the planning process. Clause 5.4.2 relates to "sys-tem" level planning to satisfy the requirements of clause 4.1 (which address the system and its processes). Later, clause 7.1 will cover "product" level plan-ning for the product realization processes.

5.5 Responsibility, Authority and Communication

5.5.1 Responsibility and Authority (1994 clause, 4.1.2.1)

Top management shall ensure that responsibilities and authorities are defined and communicated within the organization.

Source: *BS EN ISO 9001:2000*

This clause is a great example of how the new standard has been simplified from the 1994 version. The old language was cumbersome and long, resulting in 93 words and five sub-clauses. The new language is clearer, resulting in one sentence and 15 words.

As easy as that may seem, however, most companies have a problem linking the concepts of responsibility and authority. In fact, you have probably experienced this in your own job. For example, let's say your boss just reviewed the first-quarter revenues for a certain product line in your company and he is extremely disappointed in the results. To fix the problem, he has given you the ultimate responsibility to increase the profitability for it in the next quarter—in fact, it's now your No. 1 priority.

How are you supposed to go about achieving this monumental task? Chances are, your boss doesn't care about the details. He just wants results—and fast. But nine times out of 10, your boss won't give you the authority to head over to the marketing department and start spouting off orders for new advertising slogans, followed by a visit to the operations area to lay off 12 workers to cut costs.

This is why top management needs to have ownership in defining and linking these concepts in an organization, and it is often done simply with an organizational chart and detailed job descriptions of personnel. Nothing says you need a chart and job descriptions to accomplish this, but documenting these items clarifies exactly what everyone is—or should be—doing.

5.5.2 Management Representative (1994 clause, 4.1.2.3)

Top management shall appoint a member of management who, irrespective of other responsibility, shall have responsibility and authority that includes

   a) ensuring that processes needed for the quality management system are established, implemented and maintained,
   b) reporting to top management on the performance of the quality management system and any need for improvement, and
   c) ensuring the promotion of awareness of customer requirements throughout the organization.

NOTE The responsibility of a management representative can include liaison with external parties on matters relating to the quality management system.

Source: BS EN ISO 9001:2000

MANAGEMENT RESPONSIBILITY

This clause is very similar to the 1994 language but with a few improvements. In short, the intent of this clause is that top management must appoint a manager (preferably within your own company) as a representative who will be the single point of contact within the company for establishing, implementing and maintaining the quality management system. This representative also needs to report to top management on the performance and effectiveness of the quality system. Note that this person doesn't have to be a member of top management to be the management representative. But in case top management is absent and a decision must be made for the business, the management representative must have the power to act when necessary.

This was one of the shortcomings of the 1994 standard. An organization would have a management representative or "deputy" identified, but the person rarely had the authority to get things done. That's where this clause has been strengthened—it ensures that the management representative is high enough on the chain of command to make decisions.

Another change in this clause is the new awareness that the management representative must bring concerning customer requirements. This person needs to ensure that the business and the quality management system have the fundamentals in place when it comes to communicating the needs of customers. In other words, there needs to be open channels between sales and operations—always.

 TRANSITION TIPS: This clause is important to BSI auditors, and they will likely review the management representative clause to ensure conformance. As a rule of thumb, make sure the management representative knows the business both internally and externally. Some good examples of management representatives could include functional managers, the head of operations or an upper-level customer service manager. Of course, the quality manager is often a good choice as well.

5.5.3 Internal Communication

Top management shall ensure that appropriate communication processes are established within the organization and that communication takes place regarding the effectiveness of the quality management system.

Source: BS EN ISO 9001:2000

This clause is really an extension of Clause 5.5.2 regarding communication, but it is a new concept in ISO 9001:2000. The key here is quite simple: Use whatever means necessary—especially modern technology—to communicate the processes and the effectiveness of the quality management system. This could include your organization's Intranet, monthly progress reports, periodic communication meetings with staff or even e-mail. The possibilities are limitless, but just make sure the channels are always open to promote continual improvement. You should consider what media are used, who uses them, why they use them and how frequently they are used.

TRANSITION TIPS: This clause doesn't require a documented procedure, but it's a good idea to have one or at least a protocol to follow. Communication is vital to any organization's success. Therefore, a formal way to ensure communication happens is the right thing to do. Also, for it to be effective, the receivers must hear and understand the message. It is not enough just to broadcast the message.

5.6 Management Review (1994 clause, 4.1.3)

5.6.1 General

Top management shall review the organization's quality management system, at planned intervals, to ensure its continuing suitability, adequacy and effectiveness. This review shall include assessing opportunities for improvement and the need for changes to the quality management system, including the quality policy and quality objectives.

Records from management reviews shall be maintained (see 4.2.4).

5.6.2 Review input

The input to management review shall include information on

a) results of audits,
b) customer feedback,
c) process performance and product conformity,
d) status of preventive and corrective actions,
e) follow-up actions from previous management reviews,
f) changes that could affect the quality management system, and
g) recommendations for improvement.

5.6.3 Review output

The output from the management review shall include any decisions and actions related to

a) improvement of the effectiveness of the quality management system and its processes,
b) improvement of product related to customer requirements, and
c) resource needs.

Source: BS EN ISO 9001:2000

MANAGEMENT RESPONSIBILITY

Although management reviews were a requirement in the 1994 standard, there are fundamental changes in this clause with the release of ISO 9001:2000. In the old standard, top management was required to review the quality management system's effectiveness at defined intervals, based on the management representative's report. This always was important, and the reports were classified as some of the most important records in the quality system.

However, even though the foundation was there for improvement, it didn't happen effectively in many organizations. Management review meetings would occur, but there was often a lack of action after the sessions.

Now the new standard is broken into three specific sections regarding management review. These sections call for action and improvement, as well as ensuring top management is responsible for getting the job done. The language is much more prescriptive and calibrated for top management to follow, designed to include more input on improvement criteria such as corrective and preventive actions, customer feedback, performance data, internal audit results and actions from previous management reviews. This is a significant change from the 1994 standard, and it is something auditors will check thoroughly.

TRANSITION TIPS: Management reviews should be conducted when it's appropriate for the business to do so, which could range from every week to every quarter. Of course, the big clue here is when there is change in the business, it's probably a good time to conduct a management review—and, of course, act on the findings.

Management reviews should be conducted early and often in the implementation or transition stages and are generally more effective if they are completed before internal audits begin.

The big changes to note in this section are 5.6.2.e and 5.6.2.f, which state that the input to top management reviews shall include information on "changes that could affect the quality management system and recommendations for improvement." These two elements are huge signals for top management to want to be at these reviews because they can be translated as "changes to the business." Examples include new technology, new products, mergers and acquisitions, new office locations, new delivery mechanisms and/or e-business.

And, of course, the real gist of management review is an explicit requirement to improve the business. Companies that don't understand this or don't fully commit to the concept will fail.

One last thing… The standard doesn't say that you must have a documented procedure for management reviews, but again, it's a good idea. Also, it is required that you document the results of the meeting in some form (minutes or a report) so that you have a good record of your progress to improve the business.

MANAGEMENT RESPONSIBILITY

6-Resource Management

If you're like most professionals in the business world, then you've been caught between the proverbial rock and a hard place on more than one occasion. For example, have you ever had sales targets that you knew you couldn't meet without additional staff? Have you ever needed training to get the job done correctly but didn't have the time or the budget to do it? And, of course, everyone has had those classic computer problems that plague information systems and your entire workday because of a needed upgrade in some hardware or software package.

You get the point. Businesses need resources so that the organization can perform effectively and meet or exceed customer requirements. Those resources must come from a strong management commitment, which is what this clause is all about.

Indeed, resource management has become increasingly important for businesses because of growing pressure for new product development, enhanced services and, of course, profitability. Unfortunately, the first items to be cut from the operational budget when sales take a downturn are often resources—people, training, equipment, etc. What most organizations don't see, however, is the long-term effect of those actions: Cutting resources, although sometimes necessary, often translates into *cutting quality*—and everyone knows the effect that can have on customer satisfaction.

Experts from TC 176 recognized a greater need for resource management when revising ISO 9001:2000—in fact, they deemed it to be a strategic imperative for any organization. The concept, however, isn't anything new to quality management systems; resource management was scattered throughout the 1994 version. (Clauses 4.1.2.2 and 4.18 were good examples.) But the concept is greatly enhanced in the new standard. Experts realized that having a vision from management concerning resources is a critical factor for an organization's quality and, ultimately, its success.

That said, there are some changes that implementing organizations should be aware of. In fact, the biggest difference that ISO 9001:2000 has over the 1994 version is a strong focus on improving all aspects of the system. Again, continual improvement is a key ingredient to any organization's success. Try to think about success and profitability of an organization without improving the quality of products, services or even the workplace. A long shot indeed...

RESOURCE MANAGEMENT

> ## 6.1 Provision of resources (1994 clause, 4.1.2.2)
>
> The organization shall determine and provide the resources needed
>
> a) to implement and maintain the quality management system and continually improve its effectiveness, and
> b) to enhance customer satisfaction by meeting customer requirements.

Source: BS EN ISO 9001:2000

The requirements in this clause are straightforward. Clauses 4 and 5 addressed quality planning and management's responsibility to implement the system—now Clause 6 outlines the requirements to provide resources to carry out the plan.

In a nutshell, organizations must dedicate resources (staff, equipment, tools, materials, information and money) in a reasonable timeframe to establish and improve the quality management system and enhance customer satisfaction by meeting customer requirements. While this may seem like an easy concept to follow, it often proves to be one of the most difficult for an organization seeking registration. Resource management is an ongoing issue in every organization and something that needs to be continuously planned for in the quality management system.

From an auditing perspective, this is an area that will be checked in many places. First, just as in the 1994 standard, an auditor will look for a statement that commits management to providing adequate resources in areas such as training, technology, personnel and other relevant spheres of the business.

Second, and perhaps more important, an auditor will be examining the shop floor of the organization to see the "pressure points" of areas that lack adequate resources. This is a fundamental change of ISO 9001:2000 because the standard now aims to improve the effectiveness of the system.

Further, the actions of management are best seen by visiting the production floor to determine if these resources have been planned and allocated.

TRANSITION TIPS: Although this is an important area and one that auditors will likely gauge, the standard does not require a procedure for resource management. The important thing is that the organization is actually providing the resources needed for an effective quality management system and that customer requirements are being met.

6.2 Human resources

6.2.1 General (1994 clause, 4.18)

Personnel performing work affecting product quality shall be competent on the basis of appropriate education, training, skills and experience.

Source: BS EN ISO 9001:2000

This clause is about proper planning and is generally the same as the old standard (4.18) with one major difference. The 1994 standard required that an organization needed qualified people to perform their various jobs. The new standard takes that concept to another level, now requiring "competence" on the basis of appropriate education, training, skills and experience. In fact, "competence" is now given a formal definition in ISO 9000:2000, meaning "demonstrated ability to apply knowledge and skills."

TC 176 included this language in this clause because oftentimes in an organization, a person can be well educated and well trained but have zero competence at doing the job. ISO 9001:2000 now requires that an organization evaluate the qualification criteria of personnel before hiring or promoting them. The competence concept is a direct attempt for the organization to take preventive action before a problem arises.

TRANSITION TIPS: Most companies already have documentation in this area with appropriate training records and procedures, so creating more isn't a necessity. But during the planning stage of the quality management system, organizations should determine the amount of documentation needed for conformance to this clause and follow it accordingly. (**Special note:** Organizations should pay particular attention to Clause 6.2.2.e, which states that the organization shall "maintain appropriate records of education, training, skills and experience." Most organizations likely will have training records only.)

Additionally, this is an area that auditors likely will check to ensure proper resources are available so that the organization achieves appropriate levels of competence. In other words, if you're not already doing so, keeping good records is a must.

RESOURCE MANAGEMENT

6.2.2 Competence, awareness and training
(1994 clause, 4.18)

The organization shall

a) determine the necessary competence for personnel
    performing work affecting product quality,
b) provide training or take other actions to satisfy these needs,
c) evaluate the effectiveness of the actions taken,
d) ensure that its personnel are aware of the relevance and
    importance of their activities and how they contribute to
    the achievement of the quality objectives, and
e) maintain appropriated records of education, training, skills
    and experience (see 4.2.4).

Source: BS EN ISO 9001:2000

Since Clause 6.2.1 addresses proper planning, Clause 6.2.2 follows up with the appropriate action, stating that the organization must "determine competence for personnel performing work affecting product quality." In other words, you and/or your team should complete a "training needs analysis" of personnel to ensure they're qualified to do their jobs, evaluate those training needs with their job descriptions and then provide the appropriate training to make sure customer requirements are met. The analysis doesn't have to be difficult or arduous. It could be as simple as chatting with personnel to make sure they're comfortable with what is expected of them.

However, to meet the requirements of this clause, you should (although not required) have documented procedures for identifying and providing whatever training is required to enable people to carry out work that affects the quality of the product(s) or service(s). The training can be formal or on-the-job experience. For example, if you have decided that the best way for someone to learn a task is to work alongside a skilled person for two weeks, then that is classified as training and must be recorded. A quality record demonstrates such training took place and provides evidence of its effectiveness, and it should be maintained.

RESOURCE MANAGEMENT

TRANSITION TIPS: When you bring a new product or project into the business, make sure that training and competence is a part of the plan. For example, if you're a software manufacturer and you're about to launch a new product, make sure that the customer service and technical support departments have full knowledge of the product before it hits the streets.

Also, it's critical to remember that competence, awareness and training move across the whole organization—from top management to the shop floor. Indeed, it is a common occurrence in many organizations that good workers get promoted past their level of competence. That's not to say that they couldn't do the job if they received the appropriate training, but to be proactive, a competence analysis can be an excellent preventive action to head off any problems before they begin. (**Note:** Competence is the *combination* of education, experience, training and skills. It's up to a responsible management team to determine the right combination for each job classification.)

One more thing… Auditors will be evaluating competence throughout the organization during the audit by talking to people at different levels of the organization to make sure they have a good comfort level of what is expected of them—from their daily tasks to their awareness of how their jobs contribute to the achievement of the organization's quality objectives. Auditors will be looking for communication breakdowns or where communication can be enhanced, and they'll also be looking at management reviews to see where the audit trail will lead them concerning training.

However, the new standard is written to be flexible in this area. For example, if you've done a training needs analysis and are following an appropriate plan, it's an auditor's job to determine if plans were effective (based on results). It is not an auditor's job to decide if the plan will be effective (consulting). The auditor may offer an observation on the system, but that is all. The goal of the auditor is to evaluate the system—in other words, make sure that what is being done is what was targeted to be done.

6.3 Infrastructure (1994 clause, 4.9)

The organization shall determine, provide and maintain the infrastructure needed to achieve conformity to product requirements. Infrastructure includes, as applicable

   a)   buildings, workspace and associated utilities,
   b)   process equipment (both hardware and software), and
   c)   supporting services (such as transport and communication)

Source: BS EN ISO 9001:2000

RESOURCE MANAGEMENT

Although infrastructure issues were partially addressed in the 1994 standard (Clause 4.9), ISO 9001:2000 takes infrastructure needs to a new level.

Believe it or not, a good way to look at this clause is to take the first sentence and reverse it. It states: "The organization shall determine, provide and maintain the infrastructure needed to achieve conformity to product requirements." Break down this sentence and start with "achieve conformity to product requirements." In other words, think about the daily business of your organization (i.e., what it does) and then think about what resources are needed to make the product or service happen.

ISO 9001:2000 is specific when it addresses infrastructure, outlining these issues (but only if they are applicable to your organization):
- Buildings, workspace and associated utilities;
- Process equipment (both hardware and software); and
- Supporting services (such as transport or communication).

For example, if you work at a manufacturing plant that might have a power interruption or water main burst, it is obviously a good idea to have a contingency plan for any utility disruption. Or if you're part of a service organization that receives a large portion of its business through the Internet, having a reliable backup in the event of a server crash is imperative.

These resources, or lack thereof, can have a significant impact on quality. Addressing resources issues early on during implementation is an absolute must.

TRANSITION TIPS: Although resources are an extremely important part of the quality system, it is important that implementers don't get too carried away when dealing with this clause. An important note to manufacturing facilities: If you don't know where this clause applies, discuss it with the facilities manager. They usually address these issues properly and may have already done most of the legwork.

6.4 Work environment

The organization shall determine and manage the work environment needed to achieve conformity to product requirements.

Source: BS EN ISO 9001:2000

This is a new clause of ISO 9001:2000, but it is based somewhat from Clause 4.9 in the 1994 version. It is a very short but precise requirement: "The organization shall determine and manage the work environment needed to achieve conformity to product."

In short, the primary focus of this clause is the workplace environment needed for product conformity. For example, a process step may have to be performed within certain temperature and humidity ranges. However, it also deals with health and safety issues, because they can have a serious impact on the quality of products and services. Indeed, it is the only clause in the standard that explicitly addresses employees—something new that organizations transitioning to the new standard should be aware of.

The concept is fairly straightforward, and again, achieving "conformity to product" should be considered first. For example, medical device manufacturers, microchip makers or food companies have strict requirements for clean facilities—something that is often measured to achieve product conformity in their sectors. That's one way that those facilities must manage the work environment, i.e., human and physical factors that could affect product quality.

TRANSITION TIPS: Examples of issues to consider with this clause include: safety standards for the industry, OSHA requirements, protective equipment, ergonomics, cleanliness of the facility, pollution, adequate lighting, heating and/or cooling systems, humidity or moisture that could damage products and other similar factors.

Additionally, this clause can be addressed if your organization already has implemented a health and safety management system, such as OHSAS 18001. For more information on this standard, turn to p. 189.

Other Issues: Although not requirements of ISO 9001:2000, there are other resources that organizations should consider during planning and implementation. Issues such as information, suppliers, partnerships and natural and financial resources can be essential considerations for making sound decisions affecting quality. Guidance on all of these items is provided in ISO 9004:2000.

RESOURCE MANAGEMENT

7-Product Realization

Although much of this clause was taken from various sections of ISO 9001:1994, the new standard has many new features. The primary new feature is the area of "permissible exclusions," or where this clause—or certain sections of it—might not apply to your organization.

How do you know what applies and what doesn't? That's where it can become difficult, because it's up to you and top management to decide if something might not be applicable. Permissible exclusions are related to Clause 1.2 of ISO 9001:2000, which states:

> **"Where exclusions are made, claims of conformity to this international standard are not acceptable unless these exclusions are limited to requirements within Clause 7, and such exclusions do not affect the organization's ability, or responsibility, to provide product that meets customer and applicable regulatory requirements."**

TC 176 included the clause for permissible exclusions because of the elimination of two standards in the 1994 series—ISO 9002 and ISO 9003. Those standards were developed to achieve the minimum levels of quality or where design and development were not a function of the organization. (Some service organizations or small businesses are examples of organizations that used those standards to achieve product conformity while excluding design elements.)

With ISO 9001:2000, however, the ability to exclude design elements becomes difficult—but not impossible. Organizations must use the quality manual (Clause 4.2.2) to explain any exclusions in their system. But be sure of your decision to exclude anything. If you decide a certain clause is *not* applicable to your organization, auditors will check it *thoroughly* to ensure system conformance and, more importantly, that customer requirements are being met.

Organizations should review the Clause 1.2 *Application* guidance document available on the ISO Web site (www.iso.ch). It explains the issue well and gives numerous examples for different industries. If you have specific questions or concerns about this section, consult your registrar directly.

PRODUCT REALIZATION

7.1 Planning of product realization
(1994 clauses, 4.2.3, 4.10.1)

The organization shall plan and develop the processes needed for product realization. Planning of product realization shall be consistent with the requirements of the other processes of the quality management system (see 4.1).

In planning product realization, the organization shall determine the following, as appropriate:

a) quality objectives and requirements for the product;
b) the need to establish processes, documents, and provide resources specific to the product;
c) required verification, validation, monitoring, inspection and test activities specific to the product and the criteria for product acceptance;
d) records needed to provide evidence that the realization processes and resulting product meet requirements (see 4.2.4).

The output of this planning shall be in a form suitable for the organization's method of operations.

NOTE A document specifying the processes of the quality management system (including product realization processes) and the resources to be applied to a specific product, project or contract, can be referred to as a quality plan.

NOTE 2 The organization may also apply the requirements given in 7.3 to the development of product realization processes.

Source: BS EN ISO 9001:2000

Again, much of Clause 7 was taken from various sections of the 1994 version, including 7.1. However, there is a greater focus on the process approach within the three paragraphs of 7.1, especially the planning aspects of product realization, which makes it one of the most critical clauses in the new standard.

Perhaps the first thing organizations should do regarding Clause 7.1 is define what it is they produce, which is what "product realization" means. (**Note:** Service organizations "produce" a service, so they might not necessarily be excluded in this section.) In other words, this is the point at which your organization uses raw materials and converts it into something that can be sold or used in some way. You also should be aware of the definition of "product" as it relates to ISO 9001:2000:

PRODUCT REALIZATION

"...results of a set of interrelated or interacting
activities which transforms inputs into outputs."

Product realization is typically defined in the quality manual, usually in a section on definitions. The quality manual is discussed further in Module 4.

As in the 1994 standard, organizations must plan the control and production of all processes/activities that affect the quality of products or services. These process controls are particularly important where their absence adversely affect quality. Control should include:

- documented procedures—The detail of these procedures is dependent upon the training/experience of people carrying out the tasks.
- a suitable working environment—Can the product be affected by an adverse environment? i.e., special clean rooms are needed in some industries.
- following appropriate industry codes of practice/standards, quality plans (if applicable) and/or documented procedures.
- monitoring processes using suitable parameters and characteristics, i.e., using statistical techniques.
- an authorized person who can approve all processes and equipment used.
- workmanship criteria—Do the people carrying out the tasks know what is expected of them, how the product should look when they've finished?
- suitably maintained equipment—All equipment used must be suitably maintained to ensure the processes will not be interrupted (also covered in Clause 6.3).

Some processes cannot be tested fully until in final use, (new technology being used might not yet have established any test precedents, i.e., a new paint being developed to withstand 10 years of extreme weather conditions).

In such cases, qualified personnel should carry out all stages of the production process and/or continual monitoring should take place to ensure compliance to procedures. The qualification requirement shall be specified and records will be kept of the processes, equipment used for them and personnel carrying them out—these should be classified as records.

Additionally, as with the 1994 standard, final inspections will need to be carried out according to planned arrangements (this could be a defined process or documented procedure). No products should be dispatched until all the test stages in your procedures have been satisfactorily completed and all documentation completed and authorized.

TRANSITION TIPS: This clause shouldn't be too much trouble for most organizations transitioning to the new standard, but it is a good idea to examine the clause carefully—there may be opportunities to streamline what might already be done. Again, this clause, like many others, is now more flexible than before.

You may discover that fewer procedures are needed in the system to accomplish better results.

Also, this clause has two notes that are important for organizations implementing for the first time and those transitioning to the new standard—but they are not requirements. The first note explains the quality plan concept, which can be used as an easier way to document product realization processes. It is also something that already might be being done.

The second note is also a good piece of advice from TC 176. It states that an organization should consider utilizing similar approaches to planning as those outlined in Clause 7.3 *Design and Development*. Doing so can strengthen and streamline operational planning on a number of levels.

One more thing... This is an important section, so be sure to really think things through on all levels, especially the measurement of objectives and how they relate to customer satisfaction. This will be something that auditors check to make sure your organization is providing evidence that customer and product requirements are being met. Also, you'll notice that there are no requirements for a procedure in this clause, but you should consider creating one to describe how the planning of product realization is done, or at least explain the process in the quality manual.

7.2 Customer-related process

7.2.1 Determination of requirements related to the product (1994 clause, 4.3)

The organization shall determine

a) requirements specified by the customer, including the requirements for delivery and post-delivery activities,
b) requirements not stated by the customer but necessary for specified or intended use, where known,
c) statutory and regulatory requirements related to the product, and
d) any additional requirements determined by the organization.

Source: BS EN ISO 9001:2000

PRODUCT REALIZATION

This section should stand out as one of the most important clauses relating to customer satisfaction because it sets the framework for establishing customer requirements. It also is related to the *Contract Review* section of ISO 9001:1994.

Organizations should understand from the beginning of this revised clause that it is now much more prescriptive than the 1994 version. In the past, many people in the sales department of an organization weren't talking the same language as those who had to deliver the product in operations. In other words, sales would talk to the customer and make the sale but wouldn't always establish the customer's needs effectively.

Establishing customer requirements is no longer an option with ISO 9001:2000. Now the organization must document what the customer wants and prescribe a process for delivery of that product. For example, if you're a ball bearings manufacturer and your customer needs 8-inch bearings delivered by July 1, then there should be a process established to make it happen, as well as a contingency plan if the product malfunctions. (For example, a toll-free number the customer can call to make a complaint and a cost-free way to ship the nonconforming product back to the manufacturer.)

TRANSITION TIPS: Portions of this clause are new concepts within the quality management system framework, particularly subclauses B and C that address requirements not specified by the customer. An easy way to implement this section is to use a checklist approach with these issues.

Additionally, there is no requirement to have a documented procedure or records for determining customer requirements, but because it is such a critical function of the quality management system and the business, it is highly recommended. Depending on the business, establishing customer requirements can be a very complicated process, and if you have a lot of people taking sales calls and speaking with customers, having a documented procedure and records can ensure everyone is on the same page and complying with the process.

One more thing… Subclause 7.2.1.c is new and can be complicated, but it is very important to the business and to your stakeholders. For example, imagine your organization has a large contract to supply a company in Brazil with your product, but it never arrives with the customer because it's stuck on the dock in Santos. After performing a root-cause analysis, it turns out that there is a strange law with the port authority that no one knew about, and it could take weeks to get the situation straightened out. With this in mind, it's a good idea to have the legal department play a role in establishing statutory and regulatory requirements related to the product. This can help you manage risk significantly.

PRODUCT REALIZATION

7.2.2 Review of requirements related to product

The organization shall review the requirements related to the product. This review shall be conducted prior to the organization's commitment to supply a product to the customer (e.g. submission of tenders, acceptance of contracts or orders, acceptance of changes to contracts or orders) and shall ensure that

a) product requirements are defined,
b) contract or order requirements differing from those previously expressed are resolved, and
c) the organization has the ability to meet the defined requirements.

Records of the results of the review and actions arising from the review shall be maintained (see 4.2.4).

Where the customer provides no documented statement of requirement, the customer requirements shall be confirmed by the organization before acceptance.

Where product requirements are changed, the organization shall ensure that relevant documents are amended and that relevant personnel are made aware of the changed requirements.

NOTE In some situations, such as Internet sales, a formal review is impractical for each order. Instead the review can cover relevant product information such as catalogues or advertising material.

Source: BS EN ISO 9001:2000

This clause gets at the heart of customer satisfaction and can be thought of in general terms as preventive action. The key to this clause is the second sentence, which states that the requirements review "shall be conducted prior to the organization's commitment to supply product to the customer." In other words, before that eager sales manager commits to manufacturing a new product for your organization that will supply him with a great year-end bonus, he needs to make sure that top management is aware of the commitment to the customer and that a plan is in place (resources, distribution, etc.) to ensure the product can be delivered.

This can be a difficult requirement for many organizations because, obviously, everyone wants to bring in new business and increase the bottom line. Indeed, it's hard to imagine a salesperson saying to a new customer, "No, I'm sorry, we can't possibly do that." The intent of this clause is not to deny new business but to ensure that the business can fulfill customer expectations. In reality, sometimes expecta-

PRODUCT REALIZATION

tions can't always be met. But proper planning and communication can minimize that from happening in the long term. Research shows that the company that figures out how to plan for these issues and manage risk will grow its business in a sustainable manner.

TRANSITION TIPS: The rest of this clause is similar to the 1994 version. To meet its requirements, you must have documented procedures to ensure that:
- They are clear—everyone understands what is expected.
- Any differences between what the customer is asking for and what can be delivered are resolved between the two parties before acceptance.
- The company can actually deliver what is being asked for.

Additionally, a system for any changes to a contract must be established as well as how the change information is to be passed to the affected departments within the company's organization. Records of these requirements must be kept and classified as quality records. It also is recommended that organizations have a documented procedure for this to avoid trouble.

This clause also has a note regarding Internet sales, and it's important in today's global marketplace. The Internet offers a good way for customers to order a product or service without much contact with the organization—but that doesn't mean a contract review shouldn't be performed. However, it can become cumbersome to do a formal review for every Internet order. Organizations are allowed flexibility here, but customer requirements still must be reviewed and met.

7.2.3 Customer communication

The organization shall determine and implement effective arrangements for communicating with customers in relation to

a) product information,
b) enquiries, contracts or order handling, including amendments, and
c) customer feedback, including customer complaints.

Source: BS EN ISO 9001:2000

This clause is a relatively new concept within the quality management system framework. In the 1994 version, there was a reactive subclause within 4.14.2 *Corrective Action*. It stated that the organization must have a procedure that included a system for recording and handling customer complaints, including actions to resolve them.

The new standard, however, goes much further with the customer communication concept. Organizations are now required to establish an open communication channel with customers in relation to product information, contracts, customer feedback and other important data that can ensure and improve product quality. But organizations should understand that customer communication doesn't have to be difficult or burdensome—it should be appropriate to the organization. Communication can be as simple as beginning with customer satisfaction surveys on the Internet or follow-up calls. Additionally, communication can be an excellent opportunity to convert new sales.

See Clause 8.2.1 on *Customer Satisfaction* for more information and guidance.

☞ **TRANSITION TIPS:** The level of documentation in this clause will depend on the size and scope of an organization. But it is a good idea to track customer communication whenever appropriate. Doing so can be a great incentive for your customers to keep coming back, and it may keep the company out of trouble in the long term.

7.3 Design and development

7.3.1 Design and development planning
(1994 clauses, 4.4.2, 4.4.3)

The organization shall plan and control the design and development of product.

During the design and development planning, the organization shall determine

  a) the design and development stages,
  b) the review, verification and validation that are appropriate to each design and development stage, and
  c) the responsibility and authorities for design and development.

The organization shall manage the interfaces between different groups involved in design and development to ensure effective communication and clear assignment of responsibility.

Planning output shall be updated, as appropriate, as the design and development progresses.

Source: BS EN ISO 9001:2000

PRODUCT REALIZATION

As is evident from the title of this clause, planning is key to the successful design of any project and an important element of ISO 9001:2000. This clause states that an organization must have a specified route to achieve the end goal of each project and, of course, an end goal that is clear to everyone as well.

This isn't anything new to business, or life in general. For example, let's say that you want to build a table for your home. You'll need to do some planning before you begin purchasing wood and other materials, and you'll also need to answer some questions, such as:

- What is the purpose of the table?
- What will be the development phases of building the table?
- Should you build a prototype of the table or just begin the project?
- How will you test the table's functionality before using it in your home?

You get the point. Planning is necessary for a successful project. However, this clause is not intended to be a big paperwork exercise. The level of detail is up to each organization. In fact, the clause does not require a procedure or that records be kept for 7.3.1, although having both is a good idea. (**Note:** "Planning output" must be updated, as appropriate, as design progresses. To some auditors, that implies some type of evidence that the planning was performed and updated as appropriate. Organizations should keep that in mind when addressing this clause.)

One good way to address project planning is through the use of flowcharts, as discussed earlier in this Module. Using diagrams and flowcharts to show the entire project plan and its process also creates documentation, which helps an organization manage risk. Additionally, flowcharts are easy to update or change as the project progresses, which is also a requirement of this clause. Items that you should consider when creating a project flowchart are: project description, affected personnel, delivery dates of the plan's elements, resources and other relevant information concerning how the plan will proceed through completion.

This clause also requires that organizations consider the review, verification and validation of each stage of the project plan. In other words, tests should be conducted periodically and as appropriate to measure the functionality of the product to ensure it performs to the proper specification.

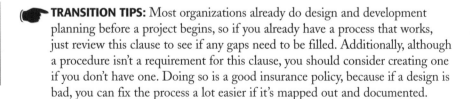 **TRANSITION TIPS:** Most organizations already do design and development planning before a project begins, so if you already have a process that works, just review this clause to see if any gaps need to be filled. Additionally, although a procedure isn't a requirement for this clause, you should consider creating one if you don't have one. Doing so is a good insurance policy, because if a design is bad, you can fix the process a lot easier if it's mapped out and documented.

Also, it is critical to ensure that responsibilities are defined and that communication occurs concerning those responsibilities during the project's stages. Again, this doesn't have to be difficult. Communication can happen through periodic meetings, memos or even e-mail.

7.3.2 Design and development inputs
(1994 Clause, 4.4.4)

Input relating to product requirements shall be determined and records maintained (see 4.2.4). These inputs shall include

a) functional and performance requirements,
b) applicable statutory and regulatory requirements,
c) where applicable, information derived from similar designs, and
d) other requirements essential for design and development.

These inputs shall be reviewed for adequacy. Requirements shall be complete, unambiguous and not in conflict with each other.

Source: BS EN ISO 9001:2000

This clause is similar to the *Design Input* section in the 1994 standard. In a nutshell, whatever is going to be designed must be documented. For example, the requirement could be details from a contract or some other document that shows the communication with the customer. Documents must be clear, leaving no room for misunderstanding.

For example, let's take another look at that table you want to build for your home. After planning its development, you'll need to realize some specific inputs before you begin purchasing wood and other materials. You'll also need to answer some questions, such as:

• What kind of table do you want?
• How many legs should it have?
• What kind of wood should you use?
• What kind of top should it have—transparent or opaque?

Here's another example: A client wants a vehicle designed that must cover 15,000 miles without servicing. You must determine what kind of terrain it will be using, off-road or paved roads, how many people it is expected to carry, how much luggage, what kind of climate it will be operating in, etc. It might be decided that it must have off-road capability, carry four adults and their specialist luggage, with a fuel tank range of 1,000 miles. If legal or regulatory requirements apply, these must be included at this stage. In other words, similar design inputs would apply like the example of the table.

If your organization provides a service, rather than manufactures a product, it may be a case of ensuring that you are fully briefed by the client before offering advice.

TRANSITION TIPS: It's important to think holistically with this clause, and procedures are strongly encouraged. This clause's purpose is to ensure that the development and documentation of customer requirements occur for products and services, which should include the suitability of the product or service for

PRODUCT REALIZATION

the general marketplace. This means examining requirements from the 50,000-foot level often beyond customer requirements, such as:

- regulatory issues—certain sectors have specific requirements, such as the Food and Drug Administration, the Federal Aviation Administration, the Occupational Health and Safety Administration, the Environmental Protection Agency, etc.
- internal requirements—many organizations have their own requirements that must be followed, including labeling, handling and packaging of products. These issues should be considered as well.

After all inputs are considered, be sure to review them so that the organization has an unambiguous statement regarding product requirements. In fact, it's a good idea to hold off on any new project until relevant parties accept these inputs. Some companies go a step further, requiring those parties (usually sales and those developing the product or service) to sign off on the inputs for consideration. This document also can be used as a record as well (a requirement of this clause).

7.3.3 Design and development outputs
(1994 clause, 4.4.5)

The output of design and development shall be provided in a form that enables verification against the design and development input and shall be approved prior to release.

Design and development outputs shall

a) meet the input requirement for design and development,
b) provide appropriate information for purchasing, production and for service provision,
c) contain or reference product acceptance criteria, and
d) specify the characteristics of the product that are essential for its safe and proper use.

Source: BS EN ISO 9001:2000

As with much of ISO 9001:2000, this clause is a logical next step following 7.3.2, and its language hasn't changed that much from the 1994 version. In short, design outputs should be capable of being verified and validated against the design input requirements. For example, if you were designing that oak table for your home as described earlier and your end product was a pine bookcase instead, something went obviously awry during the development phase. There was no verification or validation of the necessary design input requirements, a necessary step toward registration.

This clause requires that verification occurs and that objective evidence is generated to show that customer and other requirements have been met. That evidence can be in the form of test results, checklists, blueprints, technical drawings and other forms of documentation that occur during product development. Evidence also could be reports detailing advice/proposals from the customer or other interested parties, including internal stakeholders.

☛ TRANSITION TIPS: As discussed previously in this book, having the appropriate people involved in the management system is essential. The same is true for this clause—in fact, it's *required*. Make sure the appropriate person or team approves the output before it is released. This ensures a level of accountability (and records) so that a product isn't shipped to a customer without proper authorization.

The design output must be approved, and Clause 4.2.4 states records are maintained to show compliance to requirements. Although a record isn't specifically mentioned in 7.3.3, evidence of the approval is required.

7.3.4 Design and development review (1994 clause, 4.4.6)

At suitable stages, systematic reviews of design and development shall be performed in accordance with planned arrangements (see 7.3.1)

    a) to evaluate the ability of the results of design and development to meet requirements, and

    b) to identify any problems and propose necessary actions.

Participants in such reviews shall include representatives of functions concerned with the design and development stage(s) being reviewed. Records of the results of the reviews and any necessary actions shall be maintained (see 4.2.4).

Source: BS EN ISO 9001:2000

This clause is similar to the 1994 version. In short, at different stages of the design, you must review it. Think of it as a form of progress review. Are you on target? Are there problems, etc.? This review should be a part of planning as described in 7.3.1 and is crucial on a number of levels, including ensuring customer requirements are achieved and making sure the development process is on schedule and on budget.

Perhaps more important, however, is the data that is produced during a proper review. From the beginning stages of manufacturing the product to its delivery, a good review will uncover issues before they become a problem to the customer.

A good example of where a proper review can be crucial is with software design. Reviews can ensure that the product is working properly and won't interfere with

PRODUCT REALIZATION

other software programs and systems. The same is true for any organization—at the end of the day, make sure that the design and the end product will do what you and the customer want it to do.

☞ **TRANSITION TIPS:** Chances are, the elements of this clause already are being performed in most organizations, so be careful not to over-document or stifle the design team's creativity with a lot of paperwork. One of the changes from the 1994 version, however, is that the records are no longer just the results of reviews but also include any necessary actions. Also, it is important that all departments are involved in the reviews and good records are kept of their findings and actions, but do them as appropriate to the organization and the product or service.

> ### 7.3.5 Design and development verification
> (1994 clause, 4.4.7)
>
> Verification shall be performed in accordance with planned arrangements (see 7.3.1) to ensure that the design and development outputs have met the design and development input requirements. Records of the results of the verification and any necessary actions shall be maintained (see 4.2.4).
>
> *Source: BS EN ISO 9001:2000*

This clause is similar to the 1994 version and is a step in the development process that should occur periodically to make sure design outputs meet the requirement inputs.

Examples would be alternative calculations, computer simulations and comparisons to past proven designs. Tests could be involved as part of a prototyping activity. If those tests or verifications reveal product flaws or areas for enhancement, they should be well documented, as should any actions to remedy the problems.

> ### 7.3.6 Design and development validation
> (1994 clause, 4.4.8)
>
> Design and development validation shall be performed in accordance with planned arrangements (see 7.3.1) to ensure that the resulting product is capable of meeting the requirements for the specified application or intended use, where known. Wherever practicable, validation shall be completed prior to the delivery or implementation of the product. Records of the results of validation and any necessary actions shall be maintained (see 4.2.4).
>
> *Source: BS EN ISO 9001:2000*

PRODUCT REALIZATION

Following up on the verifications done on various parts of the product, this clause intends to look at the whole picture of the product and its processes—this is an important distinction to understand, because it differs from Subclause 7.3.5 and *verification*.

Design validation ensures the design (as evidenced by the product) meets requirements for the specified application or intended use. This can sometimes be completed during final test, or it may require validation in the customer-operating environment, e.g., field test, beta test, acceptance test.

For example, if an organization is a manufacturer of all-terrain vehicles and the military ordered a new fleet, they may have specific requirements that need to be tested in the field. Specifications such as bomb-blast resistance, suspension and storage space for military equipment would be much different than if the vehicle is intended for the suburbs of Los Angeles. These issues should be validated before delivery, and the only way to do that is by testing the product in the field.

This step in the process also is critical to other sectors as well, including software, aerospace and even service organizations. Once the product or service passes the validation stage, only then should it go into production for the customer.

TRANSITION TIPS: The results of the validation process and follow-up actions must be recorded, and the records must be maintained—this hasn't changed much from the 1994 standard. However, a record of the design validation and the necessary actions were not mentioned in the old 4.4.8—nor was recording the necessary actions part of the old 4.4.7. But don't be confused about the differences between verification and validation. See Figure 3-6 for elaboration. If you need further assistance, contact CEEM. Information to do so can be found on the inside cover of this book.

PRODUCT REALIZATION

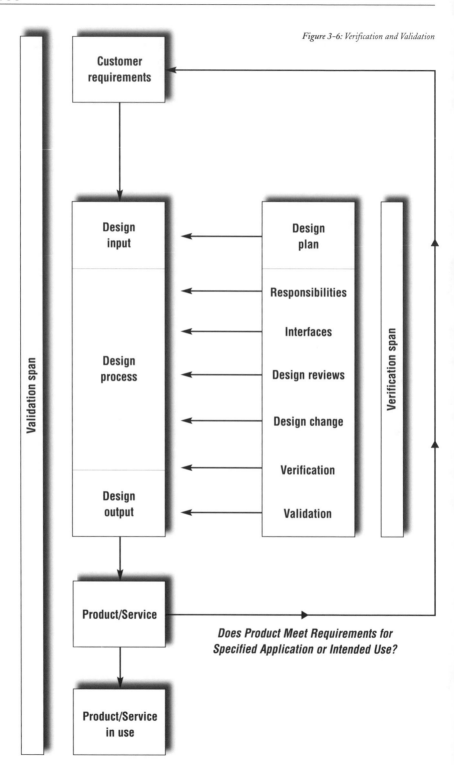

Figure 3-6: Verification and Validation

7.3.7 Control of Design and development changes
(1994 clause, 4.4.9)

Design and development changes shall be identified and records maintained. The changes shall be reviewed, verified and validated, as appropriate, and approved before implementation. The review of design and development changes shall include evaluation of the effect of the changes on constituent parts and product already delivered.

Records of the results of the review of changes and any necessary actions shall be maintained (see 4.2.4).

Source: BS EN ISO 9001:2000

Again, this clause is similar to the 1994 standard in that it requires all changes during the development stage to be identified and documented, then approved by someone with the proper authorization. It is also a clause that requires holistic thinking of the entire process (i.e., the importance of the system as a whole and the interdependence of its parts and/or processes).

Maintaining good records regarding this clause is an important part of the process in terms of the product's development history and future. Using the car as an example again, if you're designing the alternator and discover during its development that it needs to be interchangeable with an old one, that change should be documented immediately. That way, if you ever need to go back and find out why the design was changed, you have a record that points you in the right direction.

This clause also requires that an organization evaluate the effect of any design change on constituent parts and product already delivered. For example, if you change the size of the alternator and it now bumps against the oil pan and the fan belt, a chain reaction of design problems could occur without considering the design changes and their effects.

☛ TRANSITION TIPS: It's important to have control over this process, because you don't want just anyone changing your design—that can become costly or even a liability. Proper communication of all changes to relevant parties involved in design is strongly encouraged and should be considered necessary preventive action. Having a procedure to manage this action is definitely a good idea.

PRODUCT REALIZATION

7.4 Purchasing

7.4.1 Purchasing process
(1994 clause, 4.6.2)

The organization shall ensure that purchased product conforms to specified purchase requirements. The type and extent of control applied to the supplier and the purchased product shall be dependent upon the effect of the purchased product on subsequent product realization or the final product.

The organization shall evaluate and select suppliers based on their ability to supply product in accordance with the organization's requirements. Criteria for selection, evaluation and re-evaluation shall be established. Records of the results of evaluations and any necessary actions arising from the evaluation shall be maintained (see 4.2.4).

Source: BS EN ISO 9001:2000

This clause is also similar to the 1994 standard and is one area where an organization doesn't need a documented procedure—but it's always a good idea to have one. In a nutshell, this clause requires an organization to control purchasing and its processes to ensure that the product or service that was purchased conforms to specified requirements.

Typically in an organization, everyone is authorized to buy certain items to maintain a productive working environment. However, there are often spending limits depending on the level of the employee. A purchasing procedure can define these levels easily in an organization to maintain proper spending controls.

One of the most important features of this clause is its relationship to effective communication with suppliers, which is one of the eight quality management principles highlighted earlier in this Module. (See p. 42.) By communicating with your suppliers, you can ensure that in the process of satisfying your needs, they also gain benefits in terms of decreased cost and improved performance.

Indeed, managing the supply chain effectively is becoming one of the most important elements of modern business. One sector that has made a virtual science of this concept is the automotive industry, which has had a formal process to address supplier relationships for years. By managing suppliers effectively, the automotive sector has enhanced its own systems and performance dramatically.

The same approach is encouraged for any organization, although it doesn't have to be as intense or formal as the automotive industry.

PRODUCT
REALIZATION

One way to address this clause is to have a process (or a procedure) to approve suppliers with your requirements in mind. You can do this by having an "approved vendor or supplier list." This isn't a requirement, but it is one of the easier ways to address the requirements of this clause. Criteria to consider for supplier requirements may include quality, price or even just an organization that you trust. The requirements are up to you, but it's a good idea to document them and communicate them to your supplier continuously.

TRANSITION TIPS: Supplier evaluation is an important step in this clause, requiring organizations to define the criteria to select, evaluate and re-evaluate all critical suppliers. It is also a good idea to communicate the evaluation of your suppliers to enhance performance at every opportunity.

But remember that this clause is designed to be flexible. Also, records must be maintained and, again, having a documented procedure to describe this process is encouraged.

7.4.2 Purchasing information (1994 clause, 4.6.3)

Purchasing information shall describe the product to be purchased, including where appropriate

a) requirements for approval of product, procedures, processes and equipment,

b) requirements for qualification of personnel, and

c) quality management system requirements.

The organization shall ensure the adequacy of specified purchase requirements prior to their communication to the supplier.

Source: BS EN ISO 9001:2000

This clause hasn't changed much from the 1994 standard. Essentially, this clause is talking about "Request for Proposals" (RFPs) or similar documents (requisitions and purchase orders) within an organization. Typically, an organization will send out specific requirements of exactly what they want concerning a product or service, when they want it and their expectation of the vendor's qualifications.

In short, the standard requires that when you are purchasing something, your order must be clear and contain all the relevant information—including personnel qualifications and quality management system requirements—to enable the supplier to supply you with exactly what you want. Additionally, someone must review and approve these purchasing documents for adequacy of specified requirements before release.

PRODUCT REALIZATION

TRANSITION TIPS: It's a good idea to have a documented procedure to outline exactly what should be included in purchasing documents.

7.4.3 Verification of purchased product
(1994 clauses, 4.6.5, 4.10.2)

The organization shall establish and implement the inspection or other activities necessary for ensuring that purchased product meets specified purchase requirements.

Where the organization or its customer intends to perform verification at the supplier's premises, the organization shall state the intended verification arrangements and method of product release in the purchasing information.

Source: BS EN ISO 9001:2000

Suppliers represent an essential link to the quality delivery line. If suppliers ship you the wrong item and you accept it into your stock, you may have just created nonconforming product for your customer, which is obviously undesirable.

This clause has streamlined others into two concise paragraphs. In short, you must ensure that all material coming into your company meets your requirements. This may be by inspection, certificates of conformity, etc. You decide what you require for verification of conformance, and this must be planned and implemented effectively.

Additionally, if you are carrying out an inspection, consider how much control is in place at the supplier's premises, so, in the example of a certificate of conformity, you know whether an incoming inspection could be streamlined or intensified as needed.

 TRANSITION TIPS: Although not required, it is encouraged to have a procedure and documentation for this process and the product's release. For example, if someone is responsible for final receiving and inspection of the product before it is accepted and that person is required to sign for it, there is a feeling of accountability with that authorization to make sure it is right.

PRODUCT REALIZATION

7.5 Production and service provision

7.5.1 Control of production and service provision
(1994 clauses, 4.9, 4.15.6, 4.19)

The organization shall plan and carry out production and service under controlled conditions. Controlled conditions shall include, as applicable

  a) the availability of information that describes the characteristics of the product,
  b) the availability of work instructions, as necessary,
  c) the use of suitable equipment,
  d) the availability and use of monitoring and measuring devices,
  e) the implementation of monitoring and measurement, and
  f) the implementation of release, delivery and post-delivery activities.

Source: BS EN ISO 9001:2000

Again, this clause has been streamlined significantly from the 1994 standard, now requiring organizations to control production and service processes under six conditions. These controls are particularly important where their absence adversely affect quality.

Additionally, although not required, documented procedures and work instructions are encouraged to address these controls and conditions.

PRODUCT REALIZATION

> ## 7.5.2 Validation of processes for production and service provision (1994 clause, 4.9)
>
> The organization shall validate any processes for production and service provision where the resulting output cannot be verified by subsequent monitoring or measurement. This includes any processes where deficiencies become apparent only after the product is in use or the service has been delivered.
>
> Validation shall demonstrate the ability of these processes to achieve planned results.
>
> The organization shall establish arrangements for these processes including, as applicable
>
> a)   defined criteria for review and approval of the processes,
> b)   approval of equipment and qualification of personnel,
> c)   use of specific methods and procedures,
> d)   requirements for records (see 4.2.4), and
> e)   revalidation.
>
> *Source: BS EN ISO 9001:2000*

This clause remains relatively the same as the 1994 standard. In a nutshell, some processes cannot be tested fully until in final use (new technology being used might not yet have established any test precedents, i.e., a new paint being developed to withstand 10 years of extreme weather conditions, heat treating of materials, soldering, welding, glass tempering, etc.).

In such cases, qualified personnel must carry out all stages of the production process and/or continual monitoring must take place to ensure strict compliance to the organization's process. The qualification requirements should be specified, and records must be kept of the processes, equipment used for them and personnel carrying them out—these should be classified as quality records and should be defined according to 7.1 of this standard.

☞ **TRANSITION TIPS:** Written procedures are encouraged for the validation of these processes to ensure that personnel are qualified to perform the validation and the organization has established arrangements to achieve planned results.

PRODUCT REALIZATION

> ### 7.5.3 Identification and traceability
> (1994 clauses, 4.8, 4.10.5, 4.12)
>
> Where appropriate, the organization shall identify the product by suitable means throughout product realization.
>
> The organization shall identify the product status with respect to monitoring and measurement requirements.
>
> Where traceability is a requirement, the organization shall control and record the unique identification of the product (see 4.2.4).
>
> NOTE In some industry sectors, configuration management is a means by which identification and traceability are maintained.

Source: BS EN ISO 9001:2000

This clause combines two related elements of the 1994 standard—product identification and traceability and inspection and test status.

As we know from the old standard, not all products or services necessarily need to have specific identification or traceability. But if this clause applies to your organization (this might be a contractual requirement or a statutory requirement in some industries), you must examine these three issues carefully to ensure conformance. This should include all stages of product realization—from customer-related processes to receipt of all material to be used in your product(s), all the way through production to final delivery to your customer. Additionally, this identification must be recorded and maintained. Often, traceability is included in your scope of registration wording, so customers can see the levels of control in place.

☛ **TRANSITION TIPS:** Traceability is more important in some sectors than others. For instance, a company that manufactures drinking straws might not require specific traceability processes, but the canned beverage industry (which might use straws), lot numbers, the time, date and shift of manufacture are critical so in the event of a problem, the product can be easily or readily recalled. If this is a requirement in your industry, be sure you can trace the history, application or location of that which is under consideration.

PRODUCT REALIZATION

> ### 7.5.4 Customer property (1994 clause, 4.7)
>
> The organization shall exercise care with customer property while it is under the organization's control or being used by the organization. The organization shall identify, verify, protect and safeguard customer property provided for use or incorporation into the product. If any customer property is lost, damaged or otherwise found to be unsuitable for use, this shall be reported to the customer and records maintained (see 4.2.4).
>
> NOTE Customer property can include intellectual property.
>
> *Source: BS EN ISO 9001:2000*

This clause isn't new, but its language becomes somewhat more important in the new standard. Customer property is a product (which also can include intellectual property such as data, specifications, manuals, software, survey sheets for market research, etc.) that the customer owns but provides to an organization to achieve the requirements or necessary outputs. For example, it could be material provided by the customer for injection molding, labels or reusable containers.

Another good example would be a moving company—its whole business involves this clause, which states that the organization "shall exercise care with customer while it is under the organization's control or being used by the organization." Can you imagine a moving company (or an auto repair shop) not adhering to this clause? They wouldn't be in business long.

Standards writers wanted this to be important to all organizations that use customer property for their product or service, and if customer property is lost, damaged or otherwise found to be unsuitable for use, this must be reported to the customer and records must be maintained. These records are important for not only legal reasons, but also for management review so that the process can be improved.

TRANSITION TIPS: This is an area that may not require a documented procedure. It simply depends on the size and scope of the organization and whether the organization deems a procedure as appropriate. Organizations should note, however, that if the customer sells the items to you, then Clause 7.4 applies, not 7.5.4.

PRODUCT REALIZATION

7.5.5 Preservation of product
(1994 clauses, 4.15.2, 4.15.3, 4.15.4, 4.15.5)

The organization shall preserve the conformity of product during internal processing and delivery to the intended destination. This preservation shall include identification, handling, packaging, storage and protection. Preservation shall also apply to constituent parts of a product.

Source: BS EN ISO 9001:2000

There is only one new thing in this clause from the 1994 standard—the last sentence, which reads: "Preservation shall also apply to the constituent parts of the product."

To meet the requirements of this clause, you must have a process for handling, storing, packaging, preservation and the delivery of your materials and products. Consider any specific contractual requirements and always make sure that the materials or products cannot be damaged or suffer deterioration in any way.

☞ **TRANSITION TIPS:** If your system already conforms to the 1994 requirements, this is nothing new.

PRODUCT REALIZATION

7.6 Control of monitoring and measuring devices
(1994 clauses, 4.11.1, 4.11.2)

The organization shall determine the monitoring and measurements to be undertaken and the monitoring and measuring devices needed to provide evidence of conformity of product to determined requirements (see 7.2.1).

The organization shall establish processes to ensure that monitoring and measurement can be carried out and are carried out in a manner that is consistent with the monitoring and measurement requirements.

Where necessary to ensure valid results, measuring equipment shall

a) be calibrated or verified at specified intervals, or prior to use, against measurement standards traceable to international or national measurement standards; where no such standards exist, the basis used for calibration or verification shall be recorded;
b) be adjusted or re-adjusted as necessary;
c) be identified to enable the calibration status to be determined;
d) be safeguarded from adjustments that would invalidate the measurement result;
e) be protected from damage and deterioration during handling, maintenance and storage.

In addition, the organization shall assess and record the validity of the previous measuring results when the equipment is found not to conform to requirements. The organization shall take appropriate action on the equipment and any product affected. Records of the results of calibration and verification shall be maintained (see 4.2.4).

When used in the monitoring and measurement of specified requirements, the ability of computer software to satisfy the intended application shall be confirmed. This shall be undertaken prior to initial use and reconfirmed as necessary.

NOTE See ISO 10012-1 and ISO 10012-2 for guidance.

Source: BS EN ISO 9001:2000

PRODUCT
REALIZATION

This clause also has been streamlined from the 1994 standard (calibration) to make it easier to understand. In short, measurements must be made with product realization processes to ensure the product or service meets the specified requirements. To do that, monitoring and measuring equipment should be compatible with the measurements being performed and should be carried out in a manner that is consistent with monitoring and measuring requirements (i.e., make sure the process is performed in the same manner each time). Additionally, where necessary to ensure valid results, measurement equipment must be calibrated or verified at specified intervals, or prior to use, against measurement standards traceable to international or national standards. Where no standard exists, the basis for calibration or verification shall be recorded.

This type of precise measurement is critical in the modern marketplace as international standards and measurements become more and more critical for product and business success. Indeed, making sure that all units of measure, such as pounds, feet, inches, volts, amps, etc., are equivalent anywhere in the world is absolutely crucial. Imagine if your product was using measurements for feet and inches when the requirement was for meters and centimeters! Not only would your customer be displeased, there also could be a significant danger to users of the product.

We've all heard those horror stories: The Mars landing mission that didn't convert metric and standard measurements, believed to be the cause of the mission's failure; or the bungee-jumper who didn't consider the stretch of the cord and plummeted to disaster.

Accurate measurements and calibrations are key, and so is the equipment that performs these tasks.

When trying to understand this very important clause, let's examine a standard measurement that still causes trouble for everyone—*time*.

In the early 19th century, towns and villages in Great Britain had a local time that varied significantly from place to place, which often caused confusion between the communities when holding events. Then, in 1825, the Stockton-Darlington Railway was established, connecting most of these towns and villages with just a few whistle-stops in between. This forced everyone to standardize time in the region, so the townspeople built station clocks that were synchronized with stationmasters to keep the train on schedule—and everyone else as well. This eventually became the basis for Greenwich Mean Time, which of course has become the time standard for the world.

Clause 7.6 can be explained by using this example of time, the clock towers and the Stockton-Darlington Railway. Examine the clauses and the examples together— 7.6.a already has been explained above.

- 7.6.b—This requires that equipment be adjusted or re-adjusted as necessary. In the case of the clock tower on the railway, this would involve regular time checks between different towns on a daily basis to ensure accuracy. Adjustments would be carried out as appropriate.
- 7.6.c—This requires that monitoring and measuring devices be identified to enable calibration status to be determined. This is easy—the clock towers are our devices—no need to identify them. In business today, this would be done typically by the use of a serial number that can be referenced on its associated calibration certificate.
- 7.6.d—The measuring equipment must be safeguarded. In the day of the railway, this would involved clocks being kept under secure condition to stop people from altering the time.
- 7.6.e—This clause outlines the need to protect equipment from damage and deterioration during handling, maintenance and storage. For instance, the clock on the railway would be enclosed in a robust case that was watertight and resistant to the elements. Maintenance of such clocks and the storage during maintenance and use also ensured that these valuable pieces of equipment remained accurate and reliable.

In addition, the organization "shall assess and record the validity of the previous measuring results when the equipment is found not to conform to requirements...." Again, in the case of the clock, a log would be maintained if adjustments were made to synchronize the clock to GMT. If a clock was found to be varying from GMT excessively, plus or minus one minute, then train officials would have to alert other stations down the line on the possible impact to the schedule, or if necessary, the clock would be decommissioned and a new clock purchased. In any event, records of the results of these calibrations and verifications would be maintained so the history of the timepieces could be used for reference in the event of problems being encountered.

The next section of Clause 7.6 deals with modern-day issues, specifically computer software and its need for all applications to be confirmed. Of course in 1825, the townspeople relied on mechanical or clockwork clocks—they had to be wound each and every day. Today, technology takes society way beyond mechanical clocks for many applications including railways and trucking. Global Positioning Systems, radar, sonar and satellites are used with navigation.

Still, for all their wonders, these technological systems must be reconfirmed periodically to ensure that the computer software continues to be a reliable source of information. The information also should be recorded.

TRANSITION TIPS: Accurate records are essential with this clause, and documented procedures and work instructions for the control and calibration of monitoring and measurement devices are encouraged.

PRODUCT REALIZATION

8-Measurement, analysis and improvement

Clause 8 is the last of the five requirements in ISO 9001:2000. Up to now, the standard has followed the elements of the Plan-Do-Check-Act cycle that was explained earlier in this Module:

- Clause 4, *Quality management system*—sets the framework of the quality management system (planning and doing);
- Clause 5, *Management responsibility*—builds the management commitment you'll need for a successful quality program (planning and doing)
- Clause 6, *Resource management*—ensures the proper resources will be available for the program (planning and doing); and
- Clause 7, *Product realization*—ensures the processes work together (planning, doing and checking).

Clause 8 is primarily about checking and acting. In other words, making sure that organizations have the appropriate tools in place to measure and analyze all processes. Of course, the ultimate goals of this clause are to measure and analyze the business to ensure customer requirements are achieved, and making sure the organization has the tools in place to *improve* the system and processes as well.

For organizations that have implemented and registered to the 1994 standard, you'll find that many of the requirements of this section—such as *Corrective and Preventive Action, Internal Auditing and Statistical Analysis*—haven't changed much from the old requirements. But in the new standard, there is a deliberate emphasis on performance improvement—and actions to make it a continual process. Keep that in mind as you read this clause. Additionally, this section is closely aligned with its companion document—ISO 9004:2000. Be sure to read that standard as well to fully understand the performance improvement concept.

☞ **TRANSITION TIPS:** Organizations familiar with the 1994 standard will find this section to be much more flexible concerning its requirements. Just remember that this clause has a lot of action to it, dealing with four verbs that you should keep in mind: *monitoring, measuring, analyzing and improving*.

MEASUREMENT, ANALYSIS AND IMPROVEMENT

> **8.1 General** (1994 clauses, 4.10.1, 4.20.1, 4.20.2)
>
> The organization shall plan and implement the monitoring, measurement, analysis and improvement processes needed
>
> a) to demonstrate conformity of the product,
> b) to ensure conformity of the quality management system, and
> c) to continually improve the effectiveness of the quality management system.
>
> This shall include determination of applicable methods, including statistical techniques, and the extent of their use.
>
> *Source: BS EN ISO 9001:2000*

As mentioned previously, Clause 8 encompasses actions to check, measure and prove the quality system and the business as a whole. To get there, however, planning is necessary and a significant part of 8.1. Organizations need to think about all the necessary processes that are used to achieve product conformance, i.e., customer requirements. Consider these issues when addressing this clause:

- The other planning elements of this standard, such as *4.1 General Requirements, 5.4.2 Quality Management System Planning and 7.1 Planning of Product Realization* should be included in the planning stage.
- The development of a continual improvement program (if one doesn't already exist) is encouraged.
- The entire clause is applicable to everyone—regardless of size or scope.

In terms of documentation, the 1994 standard required organizations to have documented procedures for all inspection and testing activities—or if your organization provided a service rather than a manufactured product, it required the checks and inspections you had in the process of delivering that service. The new standard is not as prescriptive in this regard, requiring organizations to measure and document what they think is appropriate.

TRANSITION TIPS: The last section of this clause—"determination of applicable methods, including statistical techniques"—is similar to the 4.20 section of the 1994 standard but written in clearer language. Something has changed here, however, and it's very important for organizations to understand. The new standard requires that if organizations plan to use statistical techniques, they must identify how they're going to use them. Manufacturing facilities are familiar with this process, with some having used statistical process control (SPC) methodologies for years. But statistical techniques weren't required for service organizations in the 1994 standard (i.e., it was a permissible exclusion in Clause 4.20). Although not a requirement now, the new standard strongly encourages that all organizations benchmark best practices in some way. This is a great example of the improvement of the ISO 9000:2000 series. Again, organizations should reference 8.1.2 of ISO 9004:2000 to fully understand this clause.

Also, auditors might have a difficult time auditing this section, because it will require them to think "outside the box" and be more flexible than ever before. They'll be looking to see if your organization has objective evidence that shows proper planning and implementation of the monitoring, measurement, analysis and improvement of processes. But because there are no specific documentation requirements, the section is somewhat subjective. Organizations should be aware of this as internal audits and registration assessments begin.

8.2 Monitoring and measurement

8.2.1 Customer satisfaction

As one of the measurements of the performance of the quality management system, the organization shall monitor information relating to customer perception as to whether the organization has met customer requirements. The methods for obtaining and using this information shall be determined.

Source: BS EN ISO 9001:2000

This may be one of the most important and fundamental changes of your quality management system.

The 1994 standard had elements of this clause in sections 1 and 4.14 (complaints handling system), but for the most part, the requirements are new and emphasize that organizations shall monitor information relating to customer perception as to whether the organization has fulfilled customer requirements.

In other words, the new standard goes much further with the customer satisfaction concept. It is no longer acceptable for organizations to merely ask customers if they're satisfied. The new standard requires that customer perception be measured to see the *degree* of satisfaction, which provides data for the organization to improve its performance. Companies may discover that some customers continue to purchase their products or services, but they may not be "satisfied." This requirement gives the customer an opportunity to communicate their "discomfort" and, again, provide an opportunity for improvement.

TRANSITION TIPS: Readers should note that using customer complaints alone does not provide an adequate perception of customer satisfaction. Complaints are only an early warning signal. On the other hand, the standard doesn't require expensive market research surveys. The customer perceptions could be

MEASUREMENT, ANALYSIS AND IMPROVEMENT

obtained through a combination of customer scorecards, product survey cards, sales trip reports, returns and complaints.

Indeed, this wasn't an easy clause for standards writers to develop, and the new ISO 9001:2000 endured a number of drafts before this was approved. In a nutshell, organizations should consider this clause to be the most important thing they do as a business. If customers aren't satisfied, the business won't be around long—and that's guaranteed. Perception is reality for business, and this needs to be measured and improved continuously.

However, standards writers intentionally left out a requirement for a procedure here—but it is encouraged. At the very least, organizations need to develop a process to determine the methods for obtaining and using information relating to customer satisfaction so that the business can improve. It is also important for training purposes so that the organization has a consistent policy on customer satisfaction for all new employees.

8.2.2 Internal audit (1994 clause, 4.17)

The organization shall conduct internal audits at planned intervals to determine whether the quality management system

a) conforms to the planned arrangements (see 7.1), to the requirements of this International Standard and to the quality management system requirements established by the organization, and

b) is effectively implemented and maintained.

An audit programme shall be planned, taking into consideration the status and importance of the processes and areas to be audited, as well as the results of previous audits. The audit criteria, scope, frequency and methods shall be defined. Selection of auditors and conduct of audits shall ensure objectivity and impartiality of the audit process. Auditors shall not audit their own work.

The responsibilities and requirements for planning and conducting audits, and for reporting results and maintaining records (see 4.2.4) shall be defined in a documented procedure.

The management responsible for the area being audited shall ensure that actions are taken without undue delay to eliminate detected nonconformities and their causes. Follow-up activities shall include the verification of the actions taken and the reporting of verification results (see 8.5.2).

NOTE: See ISO 10011-1, ISO 10011-2 and ISO10011-3 for guidance.

Source: BS EN ISO 9001:2000

An organization's internal auditing program is the heartbeat of the entire system—if you have a robust internal auditing program, you have the foundation for a great system. Indeed, the purpose of auditing, which must be conducted periodically as appropriate to the organization, is to evaluate the adequacy and the effectiveness of the quality management system in areas such as documentation, conformance to requirements, improvement, etc. (**Note:** Effectiveness is evaluated by looking at results. Efficiency is evaluated by looking at the use of resources. But efficiency is not an ISO 9001:2000 requirement, only effectiveness is.) You should see the direct connection with customer satisfaction and continual improvement, and you should also note that a documented procedure is required in this clause.

There haven't been a lot of word changes from the 1994 standard with this clause

MEASUREMENT, ANALYSIS AND IMPROVEMENT

that organizations need to be concerned about. But one difference that is new in ISO 9001:2000 is the deployment of a process model. That means if you're conducting a process management approach as required by ISO 9001:2000, you'll also need to conduct process audits. This adds a new dynamic to the auditing process, which organizations need to understand.

The best way to think about this new dynamic is to review the diagram of the process model.

Model of a process-based quality management system. (Note: This graphic is sometimes called the PDCA cycle.)

Auditors will need to understand the organization's processes first, and then, by assessing those processes, they can provide feedback on whether the processes are working and how they might be improved. Auditors should be looking at all aspects of the system, including elements relating to the workplace, health & safety and the environment.

With that in mind, this is also a good place to introduce another standard that will be used very soon in the ISO 9000:2000 series. It is titled, *ISO 19011*. This standard, also known as the "common auditing standard," will soon replace ISO 10011 for quality management systems auditing and ISO 14010, 14011 and 14012 for environmental management systems auditing. At the time of this printing (July 2001), ISO 19011 had been approved as a Draft International Standard, with a tentative publication date set for autumn 2002. Once the standard is published, the aforementioned standards will become obsolete.

The concept behind ISO 19011 is *integrated* auditing, which can lead to tremendous benefits for an organization if done properly. Experts believe this type of auditing is the most cost-effective way to audit an organization now and in the future. For more information on ISO 19011 and integrated auditing, see Module 8.

☛ **TRANSITION TIPS:** Several things have changed that may affect audit procedures. Clause 8.2.2 requires the criteria, scope, frequency and methods be defined. They should have been before, but it is now required. Also, the procedure must define the responsibilities and requirements for planning, conducting, reporting and recording audits. This was not a specific requirement in the past, although it was a good practice based on ISO 10011.

Organizations should examine the new standard carefully in this regard and see where energy can be infused into the internal audit program and the company's audit culture. This is a great time to take things up a notch and really add value to the organization.

To meet the requirements of this clause, you must have a documented procedure for the planning and execution of internal audits. The plan also must reflect the results of prior audits.

Example: If an area had problems during previous audits, it would be a good idea to step up the frequency of visits until the problems are resolved. However, if you have scheduled three visits per year to an area and it has demonstrated that its procedures are being followed and that the procedures are effective, you might want to reduce the number of visits to one per year. Finally, if an area is working to newly introduced procedures, it might be wise to step up the frequency of visits until it is demonstrated that the procedures are effective.

Additionally, a person who is independent (impartial and objective) of the activity he or she is auditing must carry out internal audits. This is a slight clarification from the 1994 standard. However, auditors may audit their own departments, as long as someone audits their work. This approach might be more flexible for some companies.

Audit results must be recorded and should be classified as records. These results must be presented to the person responsible for the audited area. If any nonconformities were found, the next visit must record that they have been addressed and the corrective action is effective. This, too, is classified as a quality record. Quality audit results must be considered during management reviews (5.6.2.a).

Also, when creating an audit plan, organizations should consider not only the frequency of audits as appropriate to the business, but also the cycles of the business. This is a fatal mistake that many organizations make. For example, many companies wouldn't dare conduct an internal audit during their busiest times of the year—but that's the error. The busiest time of the year can be the precise time to conduct an internal audit because that's the time when you'll see firsthand if the system is working as planned. It's not easy, but during the planning stage, organizations should consider doing so.

MEASUREMENT, ANALYSIS AND IMPROVEMENT

8.2.3 Monitoring and measurement of processes
(1994 clauses, 4.17, 4.20.1, 4.20.2)

The organization shall apply suitable methods for monitoring and, where applicable, measurement of the quality management system processes. These methods shall demonstrate the ability of the processes to achieve planned results. When planned results are not achieved, correction and corrective action shall be taken, as appropriate, to ensure conformity of the product.

Source: BS EN ISO 9001:2000

Although this clause takes concepts from three sections of the 1994 standard, organizations should consider the requirements as new. Like many parts of the ISO 9001:2000 standard, this clause takes a holistic approach—applying suitable methods for monitoring and, where applicable, measurement of the quality management system processes. In other words, monitoring and measuring applies to the entire system/business. In the 1994 standard, this requirement dealt only with the processes related to product realization.

While this may seem overwhelming, don't let it be. The important thing to remember is the word "suitable" as it applies to monitoring and measuring, meeting customer requirements and the organization in general. Most organizations already have good control of their most important processes, and for those that don't, this clause can provide valuable data on the processes that need help.

TRANSITION TIPS: This clause is closely related to 8.5.2, *Corrective Action*—something that most organizations already do. Make sure that if your planned results are not achieved, corrective and/or preventive action is taken to ensure product conformity for the long term. Also, organizations should not overlook the tie to Clause 5.4.1 and quality objectives. This is where the process is measured against specified targets.

MEASUREMENT, ANALYSIS AND IMPROVEMENT

Many organizations address the requirements of this clause with a Material Review Board (MRB), whose members are qualified and authorized to inspect products that have been quarantined for not meeting specified requirements. These people could be a team of experts from operations or a just one person, such as a quality manager. Whomever it is, that person will want to inspect the nonconforming product and evaluate the risk of releasing such product in the marketplace. Organizations should note that the authorized person(s) could be the customer as well. **Note:** There will be other perfectly acceptable solutions to satisfying this requirement other than an MRB.

TRANSITION TIPS: There are some subtle changes in this section from what organizations had to do in the 1994 standard. One big change to note is that when nonconforming product is discovered and corrected, it shall be subjected to re-verification to demonstrate conformity to the requirements. In other words, action is required at all times, and auditors will be looking for evidence of it. That wasn't necessarily the case in the 1994 version.

Organizations should review this clause thoroughly to make sure all requirements are met—and remember to examine the PDCA cycle (process model). It is absolutely relevant.

8.4 Analysis of data (1994 clause, 4.14, 4.20)

The organization shall determine, collect and analysis appropriate data to demonstrate the suitability and effectiveness of the quality management system and to evaluate where continual improvement of the effectiveness of the quality management system can be made. This shall include data generated as a result of monitoring and measurement and from other relevant sources.

The analysis of data shall provide information relating to
   a) customer satisfaction (see 8.2.1),
   b) conformity to product requirements (see 7.2.1),
   c) characteristics and trends of processes and products including opportunities for preventive action, and
   d) suppliers.

Source: BS EN ISO 9001:2000

In addition to the traditional statistical technique requirement of the 1994 standard, this clause focuses on the analysis of applicable data as a means of determining where continual improvement of the quality management system can occur. In other words, once the organization has completed the requirements of 8.1 and 8.2 (Checking), it should be ready to analyze the data generated to improve performance. This is tied directly to preventive action, which will be discussed later in this Module.

MEASUREMENT, ANALYSIS AND IMPROVEMENT

The first thing an organization should do is determine what needs to be measured, and hence, analyzed. Of course, customer satisfaction should be one criterion—in fact, it's where all energies need to be focused at all times!

But again, standards writers created this clause with flexibility in mind—the key phrase in this clause relating to analyzing data is "*where* continual improvement of the effectiveness of the quality management system *can* be made." The standard doesn't require action all at once where analysis shows improvements can be made, as is described in Clause 8.5 *Improvement.* It's up to the organization on how aggressively it wants to improve—just be sure that all data gathered and analyzed demonstrate the suitability and effectiveness of a particular process and the overall quality management system.

One area that many organizations are becoming more aggressive in analyzing is the supply chain, which is why "suppliers" are listed in this section. This is an increasingly important part of a management system and exactly why standards writers included this concept in the quality management principles (mutually beneficial supplier relationships). In fact, organizations should reference Pages 4-5 in ISO 9004:2000 while addressing this clause.

☛ TRANSITION TIPS: Be careful with this clause and its requirements. Some organizations tend to overdo data analysis while others do virtually nothing—don't fall into this trap. The fact is, an organization can measure too much, which can hurt the organization's focus by concentrating on things that might not be that important to the business. You're not going to impress an auditor by having a million things measured, because unless you're going to do something about the data in terms of improvement, you're wasting the auditor's and your own time.

You don't necessarily need a procedure for this clause—just make sure the analysis parameters are appropriate to the customer, the product and your business.

And speaking of auditors, this section will be new for them during the assessment in terms of its requirements. Again, this clause is much more flexible than the 1994 standard. Auditors are used to strict control of records with these requirements, and that is no longer the case. No longer will they be in the mode of looking at a piece of paper all the time, and their questioning and assessment process will be different because organizations will be analyzing data differently from place to place.

But documenting the output of the analysis somewhere to show the actions you've taken can be valuable information to the business and one area that auditors may ask to evaluate.

8.5 Improvement

8.5.1 Continual improvement

The organization shall continually improve the effectiveness of the quality management system through the use of the quality policy, quality objectives, audit results, analysis of data, corrective and preventive actions and management review.

Source: BS EN ISO 9001:2000

Without question, this section is one of the top two most important elements of ISO 9001:2000. The most important is measurement of customer satisfaction. Continual improvement is No. 2.

Although only one sentence, this clause is an amazing statement. It simply means, the organization must improve—*period*. This is a big change from the old standard, which only implied the continual improvement concept. ISO 9001:2000 is quite clear in this regard and also provides the recipe and ingredients to make it happen:

- **Quality policy**—states clearly and concisely the vision of the organization in terms of quality and continual improvement.
- **Quality objectives**—sets the targets in place so that the business can improve on them.
- **Audit results**—again, this is the heartbeat of the quality management system, providing data for improvement.
- **Analysis of data**—looking at appropriate information about the business and establishing meaningful measures allows scores of opportunities for improving the system.
- **Corrective and preventive action**—the strategies that take place to make improvements happen throughout the business.
- **Management review**—ensures that all data is analyzed and the appropriate personnel act on the decisions taken by management to improve the processes, quality and other management systems and the business.

In a nutshell, this is what the quality system is all about, and if your organization is wavering on whether to register to ISO 9001:2000, its managers need only to ask this question: *Is improvement necessary for this business?* If the answer is no, then don't bother reading the rest of this book and take an early lunch. Systems either get better or worse. No active system is static over time. You must choose to improve or regress (due to changing requirements, operating environments and competitive pressures).

TRANSITION TIPS: Although this clause is critical, improvement will differ at each company. A documented procedure is not required in 8.5.1, but estab-

MEASUREMENT, ANALYSIS AND IMPROVEMENT

lishing a continual improvement program across the organization is encouraged. Doing so allows everyone to read from the same book, and it is a great way to get input from dozens of valuable sources to improve the business.

8.5.2 Corrective action (1994 clause, 4.14)

The organization shall take action to eliminate the cause of nonconformities in order to prevent recurrence. Corrective action shall be appropriate to the effects of the nonconformities encountered.

A documented procedure shall be established to define requirements for

  a) reviewing nonconformities (including customer complaints),
  b) determining the causes of nonconformities,
  c) evaluating the need for action to ensure that nonconformities do not recur,
  d) determining and implementing action needed,
  e) records of the results of action taken (see 4.2.4), and
  f) reviewing corrective action taken.

Source: BS EN ISO 9001:2000

As mentioned previously in this book, ISO 9001:2000 requires six documented procedures. We've covered four so far. They are:
- 4.2.3 Control of documents
- 4.2.4 Control of records
- 8.2.2 Internal audit
- 8.3 Control of nonconforming product

The last two clauses requiring documented procedures are also the last two clauses of the ISO 9001:2000 standard. They are 8.5.2 *Corrective Action* and 8.5.3 *Preventive Action*. The way the two clauses are written implies that an organization should have two separate procedures. However, they can go together in one procedure, as long as all requirements are established. (Readers should note that standards writers made these two processes deliberately separate so that organizations would not dilute the importance of both corrective and preventive actions. What can happen if the two concepts are combined into a CPAR is a slow closure rate of the corrective action because of the need to have a thorough thought process and implementation of the preventive action. This can become cumbersome for an organization in the long term and cause the quality management system to become reactive. However, there is nothing in ISO 9001:2000 that requires the two concepts to be separate or combined—that's up to you and top management to decide.)

For corrective action, the procedure must include:
- a system for reviewing nonconformities, including customer complaints;
- investigation of the cause of nonconformity and recording the conclusions and results of the investigation;
- evaluating the need for action that must be done to prevent that problem/nonconformity from occurring again;
- a process of determining and implementing appropriate action needed to correct the problem;
- a monitoring and record-keeping system to ensure that the corrective action taken has been effective.

☛**TRANSITION TIPS:** The standard is fairly explicit concerning what organizations need to do in both of these clauses, and many companies already perform these actions quite well. However, one difference that organizations should note is the new emphasis on getting to the root of the problem that needs corrected. In the 1994 standard, this was vague. In fact, if an organization received a complaint from a customer, it usually just asked the customer to return the product and then shipped them a new one.

That's not the intent of the new standard at all. If there is a nonconforming product, organizations now must find out what happened and fix the process so that it doesn't happen again. There is no substitute for implementing a thorough and effective root-cause analysis process or methodology.

8.5.3 Preventive action (1994 clause, 4.14)

The organization shall determine action to eliminate the cause of potential nonconformities in order to prevent their occurrence. Preventive actions shall be appropriate to the effects of the potential problems.

A documented procedure shall be established to define requirements for

- a) determining potential nonconformities and their causes,
- b) evaluating the need for action to prevent occurrence of nonconformities,
- c) determining and implementing action needed,
- d) records of results of action taken (see 4.2.4), and
- e) review preventive action taken.

Source: BS EN ISO 9001:2000

MEASUREMENT, ANALYSIS AND IMPROVEMENT

Again, this clause requires a documented procedure. The new emphasis should be on planning to avoid problems, not just analyzing past problems to avoid them in the future. The strong planning content of the standard (5.4.2, 4.1, 7.1 and 8.1) supports preventive actions to stop potential problems from occurring.

Indeed, this clause is really about the big-picture approach and, as the title clearly describes, preventing nonconformities *before* they occur. But organizations should be reasonable with this clause as well. If a problem occurs, don't go and fire everyone on the shop floor—analyze it and develop a practical solution to prevent it from happening again. However, preventing a problem from "happening again" is still part of corrective action and is not considered true preventive action. True preventive action is accomplished via proactive measures, such as analyzing data (8.4) and identifying trends and opportunities for improvement before problems occur.

TRANSITION TIPS: Some people confuse corrective and preventive actions. Organizations take corrective actions to prevent recurrence of the detected problem. However, preventing the recurrence is just part of a complete corrective action; it is not considered "preventive action." Preventive action avoids a potential problem by preventing its occurrence.

This is not a new requirement from the 1994 standard—organizations should simply review the language of ISO 9001:2000 and determine if any gaps exist. Just make sure that the procedure calls out all of these requirements listed, and you should be fine. Also, consider how prevention can be linked with other requirements and processes and try and change the mind-set to change to a culture of prevention rather than just correction. This approach can pay enormous dividends in saved time, money and resources, and can help to significantly reduce customer complaints.

Congratulations! You now have worked through all the clauses of the standard, and hopefully, you have identified the gaps in your activities and your documentation. The next stage is to write your Quality Manual. But before doing so, if you have any questions relating to the standard, contact CEEM. Information to do so can be found on the inside cover of this book.

MEASUREMENT, ANALYSIS AND IMPROVEMENT

Notes:

Notes:

Notes:

Notes:

module 4

Developing the Quality Manual

  What is a Quality Manual and why do I need one?

A Quality Manual is a high-level document that outlines your intention to follow operational procedures and achieve consistency throughout the organization while also meeting customer requirements. The manual can be used in many ways, including:

- a marketing tool—There is no reason why the manual cannot be sent to potential customers to prove that you take quality seriously and have systems in place that ensure quality (but be careful not to send confidential or proprietary information);
- a communication and training tool that allows everyone in the business to see exactly how it fits together and operates;
- a document that allows third parties, such as BSI, to understand your business and assess your activities as they relate to ISO 9001:2000.

There are many different ways to create a Quality Manual and its supporting documentation. One such method is described below:

The Quality Manual sits at the top of this documentation and outlines why you are in business, what your quality intentions are, i.e., how you are applying the standard's requirements and how your business operates.

A Procedures Manual outlines what you do to meet your intentions detailed in your Quality Manual (i.e., how you operate as an organization). Therefore, it is very important that the documentation you produce all links together. Module 5 will show you how to produce the Procedures Manual you need (if you need one); this Module will concentrate on producing the Quality Manual.

 ## How do I write the Quality Manual?

Although the Quality Manual can be written solely by one person, to get the level of involvement required, it is best to gain the views of others in the business, especially the management team (see Modules 1 and 2).

There are many ways to write a Quality Manual and BSI is flexible in this regard, but organizations should make sure that their approach is appropriate to their operations and includes all of the requirements of ISO 9001:2000 that are applicable to their scope of activities.

However, two methods stand out the most. The first is one of the most common, with organizations following the sequence of the standard and its requirements.

The second most common method is to construct a typical Quality Manual, which can range in length from 10 to 25 pages, and includes the following sections:

Cover page—This should carry the name of the company and identify the document as a Quality Manual.

Contents page—This should be a list of subject headings followed by the page numbers where the details can be found in the document.

Quality Policy statement—A Quality Policy is a statement of intent of about two or three paragraphs that is tailored to your business and covers the answers to the following questions. The answers should be relevant to your business and therefore describe your policy on quality (some possible answers are given after each question):
    1. What does "quality" mean for your business and your customers?
       • on-time deliveries;
       • products and services that meet customers' specified requirements;
       • products that meet design specifications;
       • continually improving standards/methods of working.
    2. How do you achieve "quality"?
       • listening to customers;
       • using technology;
       • working together;
       • training employees.
    3. What do you expect from employees?
       • use the quality system to produce products and services consistently;

- commit to serving the customer in a professional manner;
- contribute to continual improvement.
4. How do we achieve quality?
   - quality objectives

Having completed the questions, the answers can be brought together to form the Quality Policy. An example is shown below:

> *"It is the policy of (your organization) and its staff to provide products and services that conform to the requirements of our customers, to deliver them on time and without defects. This will be achieved through the involvement of a well-trained team striving to continually improve what they do."*

Although not a requirement of the standard, the business owner should sign and date the Quality Policy to demonstrate commitment both to employees and customers. (Remember that quality policies are not set in tablets of stone. They should be regularly reviewed to confirm they still meet the needs of the business. Organizations work in a dynamic environment and hence are faced with continuous change; quality policies, quality objectives and quality systems should change as the business changes.)

Organizational chart—Traditionally, this is a tree diagram showing how the functional departments in the business are organized. An example is shown on the next page.

Remember that you don't want to keep changing your Quality Manual every time somebody joins or leaves the business, so you might want to use job titles only and not the actual names of the individuals concerned. Also, be sure to identify the Management Representative here as well.

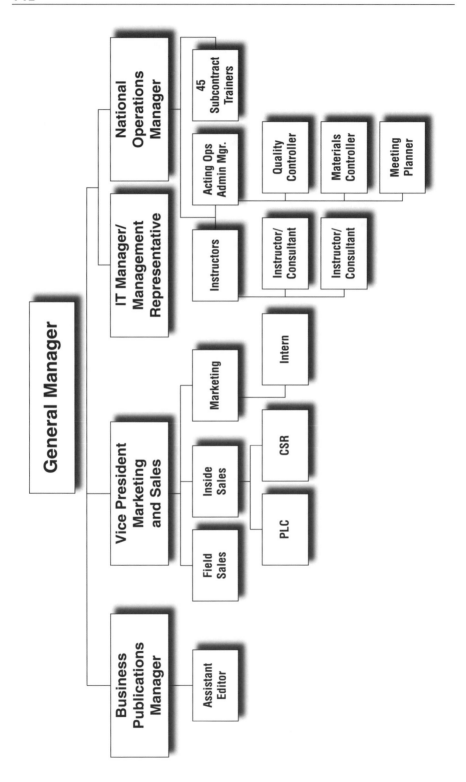

Responsibilities and authorities of key personnel including the management representative—In this section, write down the responsibilities of key personnel with regard to the quality of the product or service delivered to your customers. Who is or is not "key" is dependent on your business. At a minimum, you should identify document controllers, internal auditors, top management, inspectors, the management review team, anyone measuring quality objectives, anyone conducting calibration and, of course, the management representatives, whose responsibilities are shown in the standard. Any additional responsibilities that you feel need to be added can be.

Quality System procedures—Under this heading, simply list the procedures that you have identified. It is suggested that they be listed in numerical order together with their title. If you have decided to group these, for whatever reason, then use the same groupings here. Write a short description of what each procedure does under the appropriate title. This only needs to be one or two sentences.

Permissible Exclusions—Clause 7 allows permissible exclusions, as described in Module 3 (p. 56). If your organization has permissible exclusions, then add a statement explaining the need to NOT apply the clause's requirements.

Appendices—Appendices are not necessary but can be added if they give greater detail to the statements made in the main body of the Quality Manual.

With this approach, organizations should start by developing the first five sections as outlined above (through "responsibilities and authorities"). That will give you a good framework to use for the rest of the manual and the quality management system as well.

Having started the Quality Manual with the first five sections, the next stage is to identify the procedures that describe how you operate.

To complete your Quality Manual, you will need to identify your procedures. You will have reviewed your existing activities and documentation as part of completing Module 3. Organizations that are transitioning to the new standard should note that it is perfectly acceptable to use existing documentation in this vein, but many businesses find that creating new documentation often saves time in the long run.

Just remember that ISO 9001:2000 is really applying common sense. You already know from Module 3 that some documentation is required, specifically, six documented procedures. Once again, those six required procedures are:

- 4.2.3 Control of documents
- 4.2.4 Control of records
- 8.2.2 Internal audit
- 8.3 Control of nonconforming product
- 8.5.2 Corrective Action
- 8.5.3 Preventive Action

Of course, most organizations will (and probably should) have additional procedures for their operations, depending on their complexity, and there are a number of ways to go about identifying those procedures and processes. One widely used approach to identifying procedures is to:
- conduct a process-mapping exercise;
- call a meeting of the cross-functional management team. If the management team is small, then also invite other employees who have an understanding of how the business operates as a whole;
- brainstorm all business activities and record each item on a "Post It" note. Don't forget that you will need to include activities that you do not carry out at present, as identified in Module 3;
- put the "Post Its" into logical groups, i.e., items that relate to each other;
- name the groups—these will become the procedure titles;
- number each group—these are the procedure numbers.

You may find that it takes quite some time to think of all the activities your business undertakes and to agree on the groups and, therefore, the processes and required procedures. It is important that this step is completed correctly as the results will describe what you do to meet the needs of your business and your customers, conform with the standard and give direction to the rest of the documentation design.

After the meeting, save the "Post Its" in their groups as these will be needed later.

Complete the procedures section of the Quality Manual, recording their titles and numbers. Then identify any omissions.

Once the Quality Manual has been produced, make sure, using your *Control of Documents* procedure, that it is controlled. Typically, the Quality Manual will then show:
- an issue number;
- a date of issue;
- a record of who has a copy.

An example of a completed Quality Manual is shown at the end of this Module.

Note: Keep in regular contact with your Lead Auditor to inform when your Quality Manual is ready for review.

If my organization registered to ISO 9001:1994, do I need to re-write my existing Quality Manual?

Most companies will already have documentation in place that addresses the requirements of the new standard. Certainly, those organizations that have implemented the 1994 standard or QS 9000 are currently practicing some of the elements defined within ISO 9001:2000.

The documentation for a conforming quality management system must include the quality policy, quality objectives, quality manual, required procedures and other documents deemed necessary for its effective planning, operation and control.

Documentation requirements are defined in section 4.2.1 of the standard. Companies must have a documented Quality Manual that defines their scope of the quality management system, including details of and justification for any exclusion. The manual must either include the documented procedures or make reference to them, in addition to a description of the interaction between the processes of the quality management system.

What the standard does not say is how all this should be documented, and therein lies the golden opportunity to be creative in the preparation of the quality system.

Starting with the Quality Manual, this could vary from being a creative one page to a very large document. Look at what is best for your business. Companies must avoid creating burdensome documentation, as this is not the intent of the standard. This may cause some auditors to fully review their auditing techniques, and some may find difficulty with this approach.

The use of electronic media may be a good way forward, especially for organizations starting this venture for the first time. Business mapping or process mapping will help identify product realization and other processes and will enable the organization to clearly identify what documentation is critical in the application of its quality management system.

Naturally, the extent of documentation and applicability of more creative forms of documentation will vary with organization size, activity type, process complexity and personnel competence. While documents can be in any form or media, they must be maintained and controlled.

How do I write the Quality Policy?

As you've read from Module 3, an organization's Quality Policy is the most important statement that the company can provide to interested parties and its own employees concerning its vision for quality of its products and/or services. It is a single statement of commitment from the highest-ranking members of the organization that articulates their vision of how they will meet their business objectives and satisfy their customers.

Writing the Quality Policy isn't a difficult thing to do, but organizations should take their time and think holistically about their business and their vision for the future. In fact, it's appropriate to consider the organization's mission and vision statements (if they exist) when beginning the process of writing the Quality Policy. Linking those concepts with quality is usually the first step a company takes.

Of course, an organization needs to follow the five requirements of ISO 9001:2000 when creating its Quality Policy. Those requirements ensure that the document:
- is appropriate to the purpose of the organization;
- includes a commitment to comply with requirements and continually improve the effectiveness of the quality management system;
- provides a framework for establishing and reviewing quality objectives;
- is communicated and understood within the organization; and
- is reviewed for continuing suitability.

As you can see, the language of the five requirements is clear: The first three address the requirements of the policy, and the remaining two address how the policy will be communicated throughout the organization and how it will be reviewed for its "suitability" to the business. It's that simple.

There are some additional issues organizations should consider when drafting the Quality Policy as well. Remember that every quality policy out there will be different because every organization in the marketplace is different. Indeed, implementers shouldn't use a "cookie cutter approach" when designing the Quality Policy—it should be relevant to what the organization does. Still, some organizations will take the language right from the standard and put the company's name in the header, while others will simply use the policy that the organization has used for years. Both approaches are OK, but taking the time to draft a meaningful policy while considering all of these requirements is encouraged. Doing so will ensure your business is proactive and starting with the continual improvement concept from the beginning. Remember that organizations are dynamic and change over time. Consequently, the vision and mission statements, quality policy and quality objectives should continually reflect and be aligned with these business changes.

Here are some other tips to consider while drafting the Quality Policy:
- The policy should create "a framework" for the organization's quality objectives, meaning that every goal you establish for the business is measurable and considers the continual improvement concept. Some examples of topics that quality objectives might address include customer satisfaction, warranties, shipping/delivery time and meeting regulatory commitments.
- Consider the eight quality management principles when developing your policy. It's not a requirement and won't be audited, but it will help you set a solid

foundation for your system.
- Once your team has established the policy, make sure that relevant authorities sign it and make it official. Again, management commitment is crucial for success, and it should start with the Quality Policy.
- Once the document is signed, make sure it is communicated in an understandable way to the entire organization and, if relevant, to other interested parties as well. Examples of communication can include bulletin boards, a Web site, Intranet, visible signs throughout the organization, a company newsletter, identification badges and/or marketing materials.

How do I write effective quality objectives for my organization?

Objectives have been discussed previously in Module 3 (p. 78). A quality objective is defined in ISO 9000:2000 as "something sought, or aimed for, related to quality." In a nutshell, quality objectives are measurable goals based on sound market research, data relating to customer satisfaction and business processes relating to customer requirements and the organization's ability to deliver those requirements. Some common quality objectives that organizations measure include:
- Customer satisfaction (and perception);
- On-time delivery of products and services; and
- Product conformity results.

There is no prescribed number of objectives that must be set for an organization, and the standard doesn't say that each part of the business must have them. But the objectives should be able to demonstrate product quality and they should be cross-functional across the organization. Additionally, all objectives must be measurable and must come from top management.

When developing quality objectives, organizations also should consider the organization's business objectives. The two sets of objectives shouldn't be the same, but they certainly can be related. Here is an example of both so you can see the link:

Business objective—To be profitable for the year.
Quality objective—To reduce rework costs by 20 percent.

Both objectives address the bottom line, but the quality objective could be measured for a number of reasons. For example, remaining under budget with expenditures will keep the organization's costs down, thus not affecting the price of the product or service to the customer (which in turn affects customer satisfaction). Or staying under budget could affect the end-of-the-year shareholder report to the public, which demonstrates effective management of the organization's goals and translates to a good investment for shareholders.

Organizations also should evaluate Clause 5.4.1 (Quality objectives) in ISO

9004:2000, which provides excellence guidance on establishing quality objectives.

One note before reading an example of a quality manual. Don't make the mistake of establishing too many objectives for the organization. This can become cumbersome and difficult to manage. Strive to set the correct number of objectives with sound metrics for measurement. To do that, make sure top management is involved or, at the very least, make sure they approve them.

BSI Quality Manual Review Checklist (Example)

Assessor:_____ Date:_____ Report no._____

Document title:
Document number:
Revision level:
Date of release:

Ref: ISO/TC 176/SC 2/N 525 Current Issue

Care must be taken when reviewing quality manuals to the new standard. The information identified below is the minimum that could be expected to be found in the manual.

You may have to request additional information from the company including where necessary a listing or copies of documented procedures.

The areas that will need to be reviewed carefully are:

• The scope of the quality management system, including details of and justification for any exclusions.

• A description of the interaction between the processes of the quality management system.

A=acceptable, element is adequately addressed   N=not present or not acceptable

4: Quality Management Systems		A	N
4.2.2 Quality manual			
The organization shall establish and maintain a quality manual that includes			
a) the scope of the quality management system, including details of and justification for any exclusions (see Standard 1.2 of ISO 9001:2000),			
• Has the scope been fully documented within the quality manual?			
• Are details of any exclusion documented?			
• Has justification be documented and is it valid for the organization (reference to 1.2 Application)? Is it limited to clause 7?			
b) the documented procedures established for the quality management system, or reference to them, and			
• Control of Documents			
• Control of Records			
• Internal Audits			
• Control of Nonconforming Product			
• Corrective Action			
• Preventive Action			
c) a description of the interaction between the processes of the quality management system.			
The following could be ways to satisfy this requirement, but remember the company may have other ways to address this requirement.			
• Process Mapping			
• Business Mapping			
• Flow Charts			
• Quality Plans			
• Organization Charts			

Basic Process Model:

	Management
Customer	Activities	Desired → Customer
Satisfaction Inputs	Enablers	Outputs

Additional documents will be available such as, documented quality objectives, documents identified by the organization to ensure the effective planning, operation and control of its processes.

Most of these will be audited at site as part of the assessment.

It may be normal practice to integrate Corrective and Preventive Action procedures.

Manual reviewed on the:
first (element) level   ☐ yes   ☐ no
second (sub-element) level   ☐ yes   ☐ no
detail level   ☐ yes   ☐ no
Manual broadly meets requirements of the standard   ☐ yes   ☐ no

a member of the BSI group

QUALITY MANUAL
(example)

1 August 2001

(NOTE: Readers should understand that the following document is merely one example of the many possibilities to create and format a quality manual. For more information, contact CEEM.)

Table of Contents

1   Manual Change History

2   Company History

3   Process Map & Quality Policy

4   QMS Requirements

5   Management Responsibility

6   Resource Management

7   Service Realization

8   Measurement, Monitoring & Improvement

Quality Policy Manual Document Change Control History

Section	Issue Date	Summary of Changes
1. Change History	12/16/2000	Font size of complete document increased, full justified and other minor changes.
2. Company History	12/16/2000	No change to Issue 2.
3. Process Map	12/16/2000	No change to Issue 2.
4. The QMS	12/16/2000	No change to Issue 2.
5. Mgmt Responsibility	12/16/2000	No change to Issue 2.
6. Resource Mgmt	12/16/2000	No change to Issue 2.
7. Product Realization	12/16/2000	7.5.2 was removed as a permissible exclusion (as per KEMA desktop), clarified "product can mean service"
8. Metrics	12/16/2000	Numbering of the section made coherent.

Company Overview

Since 1979, CEEM has served its clients with pride, servicing its internal and external customers in the areas of public training and publications for specialty management systems. CEEM's Customer Service is the "front line" and primary contact to its external customers, taking all incoming orders via mail, telephone, fax and e-mail. Additionally, Customer Service addresses the fulfillment of all public courses and publications orders for the Sales and Publications departments.

CEEM was acquired by the British Standards Institution in August 1998 with the mission of serving all of the Americas to deliver training, consulting and information services.

CEEM Quality Policy:

See the next page with Quality Policy, Organizational Chart and overview of processes:

a member of the BSI group

QUALITY POLICY...

To Achieve Business Excellence
In Everything We Do.

The provision of world class management systems consulting, technical training and publications products and services to meet our customers' expectations consistently.

Our policy will be achieved through...

- Delighting the customer through value-added products and services

- Implementing and following a quality management system that meets the requirements of ISO 9001 in order to comply with our customer's requirements

- Applying a culture of continual improvement by setting quality objectives throughout the business to provide the best service to all of our customers, improve the QMS and meet our business objectives

- Developing products to enhance our training services

- Meeting our regulatory and accreditation commitments

- Communication of this policy to our employees

- Providing an environment conducive to staff development

Joseph C. Lissenden
General Manager
Issue: 3 Rev C
December 2000

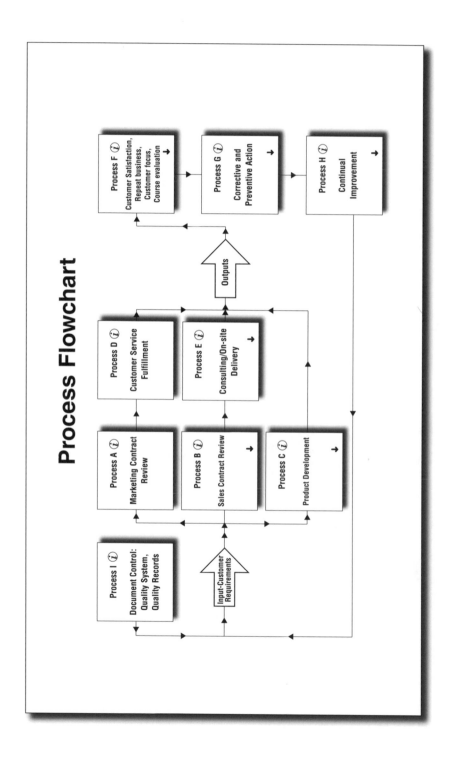

Process Flowchart

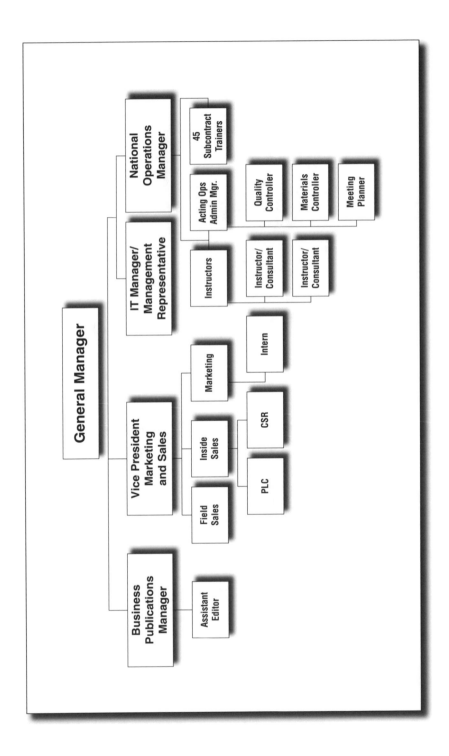

Description of the Interaction of the processes

This relates to the Overview of CEEM processes on the previous pages.

CEEM develops annual business plans in a collaborative fashion. These high level plans set the foundation for running CEEM to the process model. Throughout the business the P-D-C-A cycle is found. CEEM has a Marketing function that primarily creates and markets catalogs for public training courses and publications. Marketing also generates leads for the Sales force.

Process A defines the planning and execution of these activities as well as the contract review with the customer.

A similar but different process occurs with the Sales Team, as they plan their annual activities to win consulting, software and on-site training defined in Process B. Concurrently, newsletters are designed and written, courses are developed and customized from a Plan.

Process C explains how courses are designed (sometimes from subcontractors) and accepted and newsletters are planned, produced and edited.

Process D details the delivery of public courses and the shipment of the newsletter.

Process E details the nuances of delivery of on-site training and consulting engagements.

Process F encapsulates the measurements we have placed on the business and how we evaluate the extent to which we are satisfying our customers.

Process G sets out how CEEM responds to problems in the business. Controlling nonconforming product is essential and we address the root cause as well as preventative measures.

Process H is the continual Improvement Program, which is driven from customer feedback and employees feedback.

Process I represents infrastructure activities such as Purchasing, Document Control and other activities that may take place throughout the system.

Details regarding the activities that comprise these processes including procedures, flow charts, forms, records and other related documents are contained in a controlled format within Process Expert Professional™.

Section 4   Quality Management System

Section 4.1   General requirements

CEEM has established, documented, implemented and maintains a quality management system that is continually improved for effectiveness and meets the requirements of ISO 9001:2000.

While implementing and maintaining the QMS, CEEM:
- identifies processes needed for the QMS and their application throughout the organization (currently nine processes A-I);
- determines the sequence and interaction of these processes by using Process Expert I Professional software;
- determines the criteria and methods required to ensure effective operation and control of these processes;
- ensures the availability of resources and information necessary to support the operation and monitoring of these processes;
- measures, monitors and analyzes these processes and (see Process F);
- implements action necessary to meet planned goals and continual improvement. This is achieved through the weekly company meetings and the results of internal audits.

CEEM manages these processes in accordance with the requirements of ISO 9001:2000 Standard.

CEEM outsources some course design and delivery, some marketing design, printing of marketing material and newsletters and replication of some course material. All suppliers are evaluated formally and regularly as part of our QMS including performance requirements for them. These processes impact product conformity and we control these processes by using approved suppliers, by evaluating their performance, sharing our QMS with them and performing inspection where appropriate. This control of outsourced processes is described in the QMS.

Section 4.2   Documentation requirements

CEEM's documented QMS includes:
- A documented quality policy and quality objectives (under the QMS/Documents folder);
- a Quality Manual;
- documented procedures, including those required by this standard (including the required documented procedures for Control of Documents, Quality Records, Control of Nonconforming Product, Internal Audits, Corrective & Preventive Action and identified on the master list of documents)
- documents CEEM requires to ensure the effective planning, operation and control of our processes.
- quality records required by ISO 9001:2000 (see QR – I4.1).

The extent of our documentation has been determined by:
- the needs of a small, fast-paced organization concerned with the provision of training, consulting and publication services to our customers requirements.
- complexity of our operations;
- the competence of CEEM employees;
- regulatory obligations including our accrediting authority with ANSI/RAB;
- relationships to our parent, BSI and sister operations.

Quality manual

CEEM has established and maintains a quality manual that includes:
- the scope of our QMS, including details and justification of any exclusions;
- the documented procedures established for the QMS, or references them, and;
- a description of the interaction between the processes of the QMS in the way of an overview process flowchart.

Control of documents

There are certain documents that CEEM requires to be under document control. We acknowledge that quality records are a special type of document and are controlled as per control of quality records.

Process I1 is the documented procedure that defines how we apply the control needed to:
- approve documents for adequacy prior to issue,
- review and update as necessary and re-approve documents,
- ensure the changes and current revision status of documents are identified,
- ensure the relevant versions of applicable documents are available at points of use,
- ensure that documents remain legible and readily identifiable,
- ensure that documents of external origin are identified and their distribution controlled, and
- prevent the unintended use of obsolete documents, and to apply suitable identification them when they are retained for any purpose.

Control of quality records

CEEM views quality records as the historical, objective evidence that we have followed our QMS and met customer requirements. We ensure that our quality records are legible, readily identifiable and retrievable. CEEM uses a documented procedure (Process I, Procedure I4) to define the controls needed for identification, storage, protection, retrieval, retention time and disposition of quality records.

Section 5   Management Responsibility

Section 5.1   Management commitment

The General Manager of CEEM must provide evidence of commitment to the development and implementation of the QMS and continually improving its effectiveness by:
- Communicating to the organization the importance of meeting customer as well as regulatory and legal requirements via our weekly meetings, following RAB requirements and BSI corporate policy on risk management and regulatory compliance.
- Establishing the quality policy;
- Ensuring quality objectives are established (posted on the GM's bulletin board),
- Conducting management reviews on a quarterly basis (See Process H, Procedure H1)
- Ensuring the availability of necessary resources.

Section 5.2   Customer focus

The General Manager ensures customer requirements are determined by recruiting and training a competent sales team. These are fulfilled with the aim of enhancing customer satisfaction by setting quality objectives that impact the speed in which our customers get what they have asked for and their general state of satisfaction. Specific details are contained in procedures. (See Processes A, B &H.)

Section 5.3   Quality Policy

The General Manager ensures that our quality policy:
- is appropriate to the purpose of CEEM,
- includes a commitment to meeting requirements and to continually improve the QMS;
- provides a framework for establishing and reviewing quality objectives;
- is communicated and understood at all levels within CEEM,
- is reviewed for continuing suitability at management reviews

The quality policy is controlled showing issue status and date.

Section 5.4   Planning

Quality Objectives

The General Manager ensures that quality objectives are established within CEEM, including those that are needed to meet product and service requirements. The quality objectives are measurable and consistent with the quality policy including our commitment to continual improvement. Quality objectives described within our business plan were selected to improve those services required by our customers. (See Business Plan current issue)

Quality management system planning

The General Manager ensures that:
- the planning processes of the QMS (See Process I, Procedure I7) is capable of meeting the requirements of this standard and the agreed quality objectives.
- the integrity of the QMS is maintained when changes to the QMS are planned and implemented. This enables implementation of effective changes to the QMS.

Section 5.5   Responsibility, authority and communication

Responsibility and authority

The General Manager uses the Integrated Job Model to identify job descriptions, KPI's, and goals and objectives for each employee in CEEM. The development and interrelationship of staff is defined and communicated via Process Expert Professional™, training and weekly company meetings.

The management representative

The General Manager has appointed the Technology Manager as the Management Representative, in addition to other responsibilities. The responsibilities of the management representative include:

- ensuring processes needed for the QMS are established, implemented and maintained,
- reporting to the General Manager on the performance of the QMS and any need for improvement, and
- ensuring the promotion of awareness of customer requirements throughout the organization, as this is a function of our weekly company meetings.

Internal Communication

The General Manager ensures that appropriate communication processes are established (See Process I, Procedure I5) within the organization and that communication takes place during weekly company meetings regarding the effectiveness of the QMS.

Section 5.6   Management review

General

The General Manager plans and conducts management reviews of the QMS at least quarterly to ensure its continuing suitability, adequacy and effectiveness. The review includes a review of opportunities for improvement and the need for changes to the organizations QMS, including quality policy and quality objectives (See Process H, Procedure H1). Records of the management reviews are maintained.

Review input

Inputs to management reviews include information on:
- results of audits,
- customer feedback,
- process performance and product conformity,
- status of preventive and corrective actions,
- follow-up actions from earlier management reviews,
- planned change that could affect the QMS, and
- recommendations for improvement.

Review output

Outputs from management reviews detail actions and decisions related to:
- improvement of the effectiveness of the QMS and its processes,
- improvement of products and services relative to customer requirements,
- resource needs with an emphasis on staff development.

Section 6   Resource Management

Section 6.1   Provision of resources

CEEM determines and provides resources needed to implement / maintain the QMS and continually improve its effectiveness, and to enhance customer satisfaction by meeting customer requirements. Resources are identified and provided during management reviews (See Procedure H1) and weekly meetings.

Section 6.2   Human resources

General

All CEEM personnel affect product and service quality. Assignments are based on competence on the basis of applicable education, training, skills and experience.

Competence, awareness and training

CEEM:
- determines competency needs for all personnel by holding regular management team staff development meetings,
- provides training or takes action to ensure competency needs are met
- evaluates the effectiveness of actions taken,

- ensures that employees are aware of the relevance and importance of their activities and how they contribute to the achievement of quality objectives,
- maintains records of education, training, skills, experience and certification.

This process is documented. (See Process H, Procedure H2)

Section 6.3   Infrastructure

CEEM determines, provides and maintains the infrastructure needed to achieve conformity to product and/or service requirements. Infrastructure includes:

- buildings, workspace and associated utilities;
- process equipment, both hardware and software, and
- supporting services such as transport or communication.

These are discussed as appropriate during weekly meetings. (See Process H)

Section 6.4   Work environment

CEEM maintains and manages a work environment that is conducive to the achievement of conformity to product requirements. Work environment characteristics include cleanliness and orderliness of work spaces, ambient temperatures and positive recognition of improved product characteristics and customer satisfaction.

Section 7 Product realization

Planning of realization processes

Product realization is described in detail in Processes A - I. Planning of these processes at CEEM is consistent with the requirements of our QMS and is documented in formats that fits the way we operate.

Our planning process determines the following, as appropriate:

- quality objectives and requirements for the product or service;
- the need to establish processes, documents, and provide resources specific to the product;
- required verification, validation, monitoring, inspection and test activities specific to the product and the criteria for product acceptance;
- necessary records to provide confidence of conformity of the processes and the resulting product.

As a small business, planning activities are done in weekly company meetings.

Customer-related processes

Determination of requirements related to the product

CEEM determines:

- service requirements specified by our customers, including the requirements for delivery and post-delivery (servicing) activity,
- requirements not stated by our customer but necessary for their known or intended use,
- statutory and regulatory requirements related to the product/service, and
- any additional requirements determined by CEEM.

Review of requirements related to the product

CEEM reviews customer requirements by categorizing them into two separate processes. The process to establish customer requirements for Public Training Courses and Publications Orders is as detailed in Process A1. Processes B1 and B2 outline a different process for consulting and on-site training engagements.

This review is always conducted prior to CEEM's commitment to supply product or service to the customer to ensure that:

- Product requirements are defined,
- Contract or order requirements that are different from those previously expressed are resolved, and
- CEEM has the ability to meet defined requirements.

The results of these reviews are documented. This occurs in the sale for all CEEM products. The contract review of on-site training and consulting (See Process A1) and the marketing contract review of publications and public course registrations (see Process B1 and B2) is documented.

When the customer provides no documented statement of requirement, the customer requirements are confirmed verbally or by fax before acceptance.

When the customer changes their requirement(s), CEEM ensures that appropriate documents are amended and relevant personnel are made aware of the changes. (See Processes A & B)

Customer communication

CEEM determines and implements effective communication with our customers (see Process A, Procedure A1) in relation to:
- product information via the CEEM Web site, catalog and marketing communications,
- inquiries, contracts or order handling, including amendments conducted by the responsible sales team member,
- Customer feedback, including customer complaints which are managed by the Customer Service Representative.

Section 7.3   Design and development

Design and development planning

CEEM plans and controls design planning (See Design Process C and New Product (Course) Development Procedure C1, Newsletter Story Development C4 and C1.2 the Course Development Plan). Design and development planning determines:
- stages of the development process,
- review, verification and validation processes appropriate to each design stage, and
- responsibilities for the design and or development activities.

Interfaces between the different groups involved in design and developments are managed to ensure effective communication and clarity of responsibilities.

Planning is updated as the design and or development progresses.

Design and development inputs

Inputs relating to product requirements are defined and documented. Inputs include:
- functional and performance requirements,
- applicable regulatory requirements,
- applicable information derived from previous similar designs, and
- any other requirements essential for design and or development.

These inputs are reviewed for adequacy. Incomplete, ambiguous or conflicting requirements are resolved.

Design and or development outputs

The outputs of the design and/or development processes are documented in a manner that enables verification against design and development inputs.

Design and or development output shall:
- meets the design and or development input requirements,
- provides appropriate information and service operations,
- contains and or references process acceptance criteria,
- defines characteristics of the product that are essential to its proper use.

Design and development output documents are approved prior to release.

Section 7.3.4 Design and or development review

At suitable stages, systematic reviews of design and development are conducted to:
- evaluate the ability to fulfill requirements,
- identify problems and propose follow up actions

Participants in design reviews include representatives of all functions concerned with the design and development stages being reviewed. The results of these reviews and subsequent follow up actions are recorded. (See Process C, Procedure C1)

Section 7.3.5 Design and development verification

Design and developments are verified to ensure that outputs meet the design and development input requirements. The results of the verification and subsequent follow-up actions are recorded. (See Process C, Procedure C1)

Section 7.3.6 Design and development validation

Design and development validation is performed to confirm that the resulting product is capable of meeting the requirements for the intended use. Wherever applicable, validation is completed prior to the delivery or implementation of the product. Where it is impractical to perform full validation prior to delivery, partial validation is performed to the extent applicable.

The results of the validation and subsequent follow-up actions are recorded. (See Process C, Procedure C1)

Design and or Development changes

Design and or development changes are identified, documented and controlled. The changes are reviewed, verified and validated, as appropriate, and approved before implementation. This includes evaluation of the effect of the changes on the constituent parts and delivered products.

The results of the review of changes and subsequent follow-up actions are documented. (See Process C, Procedure C1)

Section 7.4　Purchasing Information

Purchasing Control

CEEM controls its purchasing process through the use of Process I, Procedure I3 to ensure purchased products and services conform to requirements. The type and extent of these controls are dependent on the impact of the products or services of CEEM's product realization processes and final product.

CEEM evaluates and selects suppliers based on their ability to supply products or services in accordance with requirements. Criteria for selection is identified and recorded and the process for periodic reviews as defined in Process I, Procedure I3.

Suppliers are evaluated based on their ability to meet CEEM requirements and are scored on a 100-point scale. The supply chain is segregated into approved, approved (but under evaluation for new suppliers) and unapproved. Unapproved suppliers consist of previously approved but currently disqualified suppliers. The Approved Supplier List is QR I3.5.

Any follow-up activity required of the supplier is recorded.

Purchasing Information

CEEM purchasing documents contain all the information describing the product to be purchased, including:
- requirements for approval of product, procedures, processes and equipment,
- requirements for qualification of personnel (including training needs) and
- QMS requirements.

Purchase requirements are reviewed for adequacy prior to communication with the supplier. Process I, Procedure I3 identifies the purchasing levels and details purchasing policy including the use of Purchase Orders, the Approved Supplier List and the Expense Report.

Verification of Purchased product

CEEM monitors incoming products and services against purchase specifications. The results of cumulative data is fed back to suppliers. Records of this monitoring are maintained. The purchaser resolves all discrepancies.

CEEM conducts verification at supplier's premises when decided by the General Manager. Those university partners that CEEM has relationships with that print their own course material are audited once per year and a record of the audit is maintained at CEEM.

Section 7.5   Production and service provision

Control of production and service provision

CEEM plans and carries out production and service provision under controlled conditions. We address the following controlled conditions as essential:
- the availability of information that describes the characteristics of the product,
- the availability of work instructions from Process Expert Professional software,
- the use of suitable equipment,
- the implementation of monitoring and measurement, including RAB field visits of CEEM accredited courses, and
- the implementation of release, delivery and post-delivery activities.

Since the use of monitoring and measuring devices is not inherent to the nature of CEEM's industry, the requirement for the availability and use of these devices (ISO 9001:2000) does not apply.

Validation of processes for production and service provision

CEEM is capable of determining deficiencies in publication products prior to delivery. CEEM plans and carries out production and service provision of public courses, on-site courses and consulting under controlled conditions. Controlled conditions include:
- the availability of information that describes the characteristics of the product or service provided (consulting, newsletters/publications or courses),
- the availability of work instructions,
- the use of suitable equipment (projectors, laptops, CD-ROMs, software, etc)
- the implementation of monitoring and measurement (Process E),
- revalidation (as a result of design reviews and customer feedback).

Identification and traceability

CEEM uses a job profitability system that codes each training or consulting engagement. These product codes are initiated at the outset of activities. The system provides the ability to trace and track all courses (public and on-site) and consulting projects from the Project Planning Schedule.

At all times, the status of any product in the storage areas is known. Where additional traceability is required the unique identification of the product is further defined.

Customer Property

CEEM takes care of customer property while under our control or being used by us. We identify, verify, protect and maintain customer property provided to us. On occasion, disks with course material are provided by the customer and then converted into a master print copy.

CEEM identifies, verifies, protects and maintains customer property while under our control.

If any product is lost, damaged or otherwise found to be unsuitable for use, CEEM records and reports this fact and details to the customer.

module

5

Developing Appropriate Documentation

42 How does formal documentation add value?

Documentation adds a desirable value to the quality management system by enabling communication of intent and consistency of action throughout the organization. Indeed, using appropriate documentation can contribute positively in the following ways:

- Achievement of conformity to customer requirements and continual improvement of the business;
- Provision of effective training;
- Repeatability and traceability of processes;
- Individual's understanding and accountability;
- Elimination of ambiguity;
- Provision of objective evidence; and
- Evaluation of the effectiveness and continuing suitability of the QMS.

In the context of ISO 9001:2000, documentation refers to both planning-type documents (procedures, quality plans) as well as records (evidence).

Generation of documentation should not be an end in itself, but rather, a value-added activity leading to the above benefits. The amount of documentation prescribed as mandatory by ISO 9001:2000 is considerably less than called for in the 1994 version. The responsibility to determine just how much and what types of documentation is necessary is left up to you and the organization, within the guidelines of the quality principles and defined objectives. But this Module should help you understand the requirements and how your organization could benefit from going beyond merely what is required.

Although the actual types of documentation vary between different organizations—considering the different processes, degree of product complexity and level of employee skills and competence—generally, the following types of documents are used in a quality management system:

- Documents that provide consistent information, both internally and externally, about the organization's QMS. The Quality Manual is an example of such.
- Documents that describe how the QMS is applied to a specific product, project or contract. Such documents are referred to as plans, or quality plans.
- Documents stating product or service requirements. These are called "specifications."
- Documents giving recommendations or suggestions, referred to as "guidelines."
- Documents that provide information about how to perform activities and processes consistently; such documents could include written procedures, work instructions, drawings, flowcharts, etc.
- Documents that provide objective evidence of activities performed or results achieved; such documents are referred to as "records."

Additionally, although documentation is a function of nearly every organization at some level, top management should define the appropriate documentation for the organization and its quality management system. This ensures that the documentation satisfies the needs of all interested parties, especially customers.

TRANSITION TIPS: The requirements for documentation are presented in a completely different manner than the 1994 standard. In essence, Clause 4 of ISO 9001:2000 describes that documentation will be necessary for the QMS. Again, there is a requirement for six documented procedures in ISO 9001:2000, but organizations will need to determine how many additional procedures might be needed for a truly robust quality management system. The amount and depth of documentation content should be balanced against and be reflected in the investment an organization makes in the recruitment of people with the required skills and competence, education and training.

43 What is a procedure?

Simply stated, a procedure outlines what you do to complete a task, a flow of activity that describes who does what, in what order and to what standard. Its purpose is to document consistent processes in an organization to reduce variation and achieve specified targets.

Collectively, the procedures make up a significant portion of your quality management system. Your procedures will describe how you operate and control your business and how you meet the requirements of the standard (which must include the continual improvement concept).

Again, you already know from Modules 3 and 4 that six documented procedures are required in ISO 9001:2000. They are:

- 4.2.3 Control of documents
- 4.2.4 Control of records
- 8.2.2 Internal audit
- 8.3 Control of nonconforming product
- 8.5.2 Corrective action
- 8.5.3 Preventive action

However, organizations will find that throughout their business processes, additional procedures will likely be required.

How do you know when to create an additional procedure?

That's a good question, and one that can only be answered by you and top management. Procedures exist in an organization to ensure that all activities in the process are done consistently day in and day out. But as this book has stressed numerous times, there is no need to over-document and create a procedure for everything.

Just remember that as a rule of thumb, procedures are a good idea whenever and wherever not having one would affect the quality of a product or service in a negative way (i.e., resulting in nonconforming product and/or failing to meet customer requirements).

Also, be sure to consider that the whole point of having processes and procedures is *operational control*. Review Clause 7.5.2 (Identification and traceability) to ensure "validation of processes."

 How do I write a procedure?

First, you must choose a format. There are many different formats you can use, and the choice is up to you. Two examples are shown at the end of this Module. The Module describes how to complete the first, but the principles outlined are equally valid for both formats.

To complete a procedure using the first example, the first step is to establish the need for a procedure. After the business goes through a process–mapping exercise, these decisions should be relatively easy. Once you've established the necessary procedures, assign a procedure owner to each of the procedures that you identified in the Quality Manual. The procedure owner is the person responsible for approving the initial procedure and its subsequent changes.

Although one person can write procedures, it is suggested that you seek involvement of the personnel responsible for carrying out the procedures. It is best to start with the *Control of documents* procedure (Clause 4.2.3), as this will determine the format of all procedures, how they are created, approved and issued.

The attendees should consist of the personnel who are or will be involved in carrying out the work. Involving personnel at this stage will:

- enable the correct procedure to be written; and
- assist in easing implementation, i.e., the change process helps to carry personnel along, and they are more likely to adopt something they, themselves, have written.

At the meeting, carry out the following actions:

- identify the need for the procedure, and if not required, clearly understand the reasoning why it is not required;
- create an objective for the procedure, i.e., what is its purpose?;
- create a scope—a short statement outlining how the procedure operates;
- list the activities in the order they occur to meet the overall objective. Keep the statements concise, introducing any documents/forms and approvals/authorizations/checks as required. Record job titles in the left-hand column; (**Note:** Initially, it may be a good idea to include forms as attachments, although with a mature system where everyone is clear as to what forms must be used, these can be referenced only. This can reduce the updates required to procedures if a form should be updated.)
- add any notes in the "Notes" column that aid in the understanding of how the procedure flows—for example, exceptions, references to other documents/procedures etc.;
- write what happens now, not what you would like to see. At this stage, the only new work you should introduce is work needed to meet the requirements of the standard. For example, if you do not review a contract when it is received to make sure you are capable of handling it, then you will need to include this in your procedures;
- replace the job title with "All Staff" or "All Staff in Production," etc., if you identify a responsibility that everyone has to follow;
- include references to other procedures, so the procedures link together to form the system;
- use the "post-its" that you generated when completing the Quality Manual as a source of information; and
- make sure you include any areas highlighted from Module 3—you may have to allocate new responsibilities.

At the end of this meeting, you should have a draft procedure similar to the one located on page 2 of the first example (p. 177). Notice that the document is concise, written in a "do this, do that" style and flows down the page as the responsibilities change. Writing documentation in this manner automatically meets many of the requirements of the standard. As a guide, two, or at most, three pages for each procedure is probably sufficient.

Better still, try to convey the information in a flowchart format, and try and keep it to one page.

NOTE: When running the meeting and discussing what people's responsibilities are and what the flow of work is, you may find that different understandings of "what the procedure is" begins to emerge. Where this occurs, try and reach a consensus regarding what is written; try and aim for a "best practice" approach in these circumstances and then make a decision.

 How detailed should the procedures be?

The answer to this question is up to you and your organization. But keep in mind that there are many quality systems where businesses have documented everything they do to such an extent that the bureaucracy is stifling. Avoid that at all costs!
NOTE: Over-documented systems often contain much duplication and this alone presents a good opportunity for an improvement exercise.

There isn't a special clause that says you must have volumes of documentation. If you want to create this level of documentation, then you may, but it is simply not necessary. (**NOTE:** The use of "smart forms" that are self-explanatory can eliminate the need for lengthy instructions on how to complete a task.)

If your business is small, you are in an ideal position to react quickly to the marketplace. Thus, you need procedures that reflect this flexibility. The skill is to write procedures that meet your needs and reflect the skills and experience you and your staff already has, but that are sufficiently detailed to describe how the business runs and conforms to the standard. (**TIP:** Once again, only six documented procedures are required in ISO 9001:2000, but you should consider other procedures as necessary to ensure the effective operation of the quality system). Always keep that in mind as you continue the documentation process.

 What are work instructions?

Organizations should think of work instructions as specific guidance or step-by-step direction on how to perform a specific job task, procedure and/or job function. Work instructions usually are written when a specific process is too complicated for the language of the procedure.

The complexity of your business also helps to determine whether you need detailed work instructions in addition to your procedures. Many businesses include work instructions to:
- aid in training;
- make it clear how a job is done;
- reduce mistakes;
- provide a memory aid for staff;
- provide a point of reference for jobs that are not often carried out;
- exhibit a basis for reviewing activity if something goes wrong. The work

instructions can be changed and a new method of working introduced in a controlled manner to prevent the problem from recurring; and
- ensure both procedures and work instructions are clear and concise.

But organizations should use caution when considering the use of work instructions. Often times, work instructions aren't necessary because their content can be covered sufficiently in the appropriate procedure. This is a common mistake in dozens of organizations, but one that can be avoided by aggressively looking to reduce documentation whenever possible. Indeed, the use of flowcharts, pictures, video clips or other visual tools are excellent examples of utilizing work instructions when necessary.

Ask the staff responsible for doing the work what the best method is and, where required, to write the work instructions, as they are likely to know how the job is best completed. This can be done on an individual basis or as a team effort if more than one person carries out the job. As before, there may be more than one way of completing a job. If there is, try and reach a compromise to find the best approach. For work instructions, consider these issues:
- keep the statements short and to the point—a "do this, do that" style; and
- allocate a reference number to the work instruction and record this in the "Notes" column of the procedure, so it is clear what the links are.

Once the work instructions have been written, test them by asking selected staff not involved in their production to work to them and request their feedback. When the comments are received, review them and change the work instructions as required.

 TRANSITION TIPS: When developing documentation for the quality management system, organizations should evaluate the need for work instructions carefully to avoid any duplication. Deciding this factor is really about finding the right balance in the organization between appropriate training, education and competence and the need to explain the process in detail with work instructions.

Whatever your organization decides, be sure to keep work instructions as simple as possible, keeping the user in mind at all times. Make them easy, understandable and appropriate to the process and the organization.

Also, make sure that all work instructions follow the same format and reference the applicable procedures (the procedure should reference the applicable work instruction as well), standard(s), specifications, drawings etc.

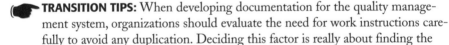 ## If my organization is registered to the 1994 standard, will we need to re-write all of our documentation?

Organizations that already have good documentation in place (records, procedures, flowcharts, work instructions, etc.) won't need to reinvent the wheel when it comes to documentation requirements. But it would behoove every process/procedure owner to re-evaluate applicable documentation and the new requirements of ISO 9001:2000 to streamline operations and paperwork as much as possible.

When reviewing existing documentation, remember that in order for your organization to have a conforming quality management system, you must include the quality policy, quality objectives, Quality Manual, required procedures and other documents deemed necessary for its effective planning, operation and control.

To do that, review section 4.2.1 of the standard where the required documentation steps are defined. Companies must have a documented Quality Manual that defines their scope of the quality management system, including details of and justification for any exclusion. The manual must either include the documented procedures or make reference to them, in addition to description of the interaction between the processes of the quality management system.

Also, keep in mind that the use of electronic media for sound documentation control is an excellent idea. Business mapping or process mapping will help identify product realization processes and will enable the organization to clearly identify what documentation is critical in the application of its quality management system.

 ## What are corrective and preventive actions, and why are they important?

In a nutshell, corrective actions are steps an organization must take to fix problems (processes that result in nonconforming product and/or other nonconformities of the system) when things go wrong so that they don't happen again.

Preventive actions are steps taken to eliminate problems (potential nonconformities) before they happen.

Both steps are important elements of any quality management system, and documented procedures are required for an organization to comply with the requirements of ISO 9001:2000 (clauses 8.5.2 and 8.5.3). Additionally, both requirements have the intent of continual improvement of the system and the business as well. (See Module 3, p. 132.)

For firms that are registered to the 1994 standard, the essence of these requirements remains the same. The two main differences include a requirement for an effective root-cause analysis program at work and the idea that the business should now be focusing on the *potential* nonconformities, not just ones that have already occurred.

Do I need to have copies of ISO 9001:2000 available for everyone?

Having accessible copies of ISO 9001:2000 (and ISO 9004:2000) available to relevant personnel is a good idea, but not a requirement of ISO 9001:2000 or BSI. But the organization should have copies available to those who deal with quality issues in their daily tasks, and at least one copy on file to meet the requirements of Clause 4.2.

Organizations should note, however, that having the standard available for all personnel creates an excellent opportunity to build awareness and understanding of the system's requirements.

Copies of the standard or any British Standard can be purchased from CEEM Inc. For more information, call CEEM's Standards Line at 800-378-8619; or visit the CEEM Web site for complete details: www.ceem.com.

 Do I need to create a procedures manual?

This is an area where organizations should be careful not to over-document. The new standard doesn't require a procedures manual, but some organizations choose to have one in order to have a specific place for all procedures and other documentation.

If you do create a procedures manual, consider the following:
- Prepare a registered holder's list—these will be the individual(s) responsible for updating the manual. You must make sure that there are sufficient manuals available for staff to use when required.
- Include a contents page so it easier to find the procedures.
- Approve all the documentation by following your Control of documents procedure—see clause 4.2.3 in Module 3.
- Issue the procedures manual to the registered holders.

Once you have issued your procedures manual, the next stage is to implement the system.

When you issue your procedures manual and complete your documentation requirements, contact BSI. At this point, you will need to discuss and agree (if you have not already done so before) the time scales for your assessment and registration.

 What other documentation do I need?

While the documentation requirements of ISO 9001:2000 are more flexible when compared to the requirements of the 1994 standard, organizations need to understand exactly what is expected of them from a registrar, and perhaps more important, what they should expect from themselves.

As you've read from previous Modules, the documentation requirements are clear in ISO 9001:2000. At a minimum, the requirements are:
- Six documented procedures (as specified in Module 3)
- A Quality Manual
- A Quality Policy
- Quality objectives
- Documents needed by the organization to ensure the effective planning operation and control of its processes
- Records as required in Clause 4.2.4 (Control of records)

But organizations should be careful to limit their documentation to only these requirements—these are *minimum* requirements. You may need to detail additional information in procedures and other documentation areas as well.

As a general guide, review Clauses 1.2 and 4.2 to fully understand all documentation expectations. Be sure you understand the language here completely, paying particular attention to not only the requirements outlined in 4.2, but also the intention of ISO 9001:2000 as described in 1.2. This is very important, and something auditors will review thoroughly.

Documentation tips

Experts have advised tens of thousands of companies on how to document their management systems to achieve quality, and nearly all of them will recommend the KISS principle—*Keep It Short and Simple.*

Even with all of the new improvements of ISO 9001:2000, this advice is more valid today than ever before. Consider these 10 tips while developing your documentation throughout your organization:
- Use simple words and phrases.
- Keep sentences short.
- Stay focused on the specifics of the process.
- Avoid using the language of the standard's requirements verbatim. Interpret their meanings as applicable to your organization and generate your own language that is easy for all to understand.
- Avoid using language that could be interpreted as condescending or insulting.
- Keep the user in mind at all times while drafting documentation.
- Use illustrations or pictures whenever possible to show processes and examples of best practices.
- Maintain a consistent language style and format for all documentation.
- Have the language reviewed by users and top management before releasing it.
- Communicate all documents effectively upon release, especially if there is a change.

☞ **TRANSITION TIPS:** Readers should note that TC 176 developed excellent guidance on ISO 9001:2000 documentation requirements, which can be downloaded from the Internet: http://isotc176sc2.elysium-ltd.net.

PROCEDURE EXAMPLE #1

Internal Quality Audits

Issue: 1   Procedure Owner: Managing Director
Procedure No: QS05
Date: 31 July 2001

Objective:

The objective of this procedure is to outline how internal quality audits are scheduled, planned and reported to ensure that the quality system is effective in meeting the needs of the business.

Scope:

The procedure describes how various activities carried out by the business are assessed against stated requirements and objectives. Based on this assessment, the audits are scheduled with independent resource being added to the schedule. The schedule is agreed and then communicated to managers in the business.

Individual audit plans outlining who will be audited are generated for each audit. Trained staff, who report findings to the manager concerned, carry out the audit. Corrective and preventive action is carried out to resolve any nonconformities raised in the audit.

A Follow-up Audit is carried out to review the effectiveness of the corrective and preventive action. Assuming that all actions have been effective, the audit is closed down. The trend of nonconformities is analyzed and the schedule revised to reflect the risk to the business.

Activities and Responsibilities

Management Representative: Prepare an annual Audit Schedule (form QS/05/1) ensuring that all areas of the business and procedures in the quality system are covered. The scheduling must take into account the risk to the business of the activity under consideration. Each audit is given a sequential number.

Management Representative: Allocate independent and trained auditors to the Audit Schedule. Communicate the schedule to the auditors.

Auditor: At least three weeks before the audit, contact the manager of

the area(s) being audited and create and agree an Audit Plan (form QS/05/2). The audit plan must show:
- audit number;
- date and times of the audit;
- who will be interviewed and when;
- what part of the quality system is being audited;
- the signatures of the auditor and the manager; and
- times of opening and closing meetings.

Auditor(s): Review past audits and documentation relevant to the audit and prepare an Audit checklist.

Auditor(s): Carry out the audit in accordance with the agreed Audit Plan using the Audit Checklist as a guide. Any nonconformities identified must be agreed with the auditee.

Auditor(s): Prepare and present the Audit Report (form QS05/3) to the manager showing:
- date of the audit;
- area and procedures audited;
- name of the auditor(s); and
- details of nonconformities.

Gain agreement to the report and ask the manager to sign the report.

Auditor(s): File all completed documents in the Audit File held by the Management Representative and retain for 5 years.

Manager of area being audited: Identifies and implements corrective and preventive action to resolve the nonconformities raised. Agree with the Auditor when a Follow-up Audit should be carried out to review the effectiveness of the action.

Auditor(s): Carry out a Follow-up Audit to review the effectiveness of the corrective action to prevent the nonconformity from recurring. Report accordingly. File Audit Plan and Audit Report in the Audit File. Advice the Management Representative that the audit has been closed down.

Management Representative: Amend the Audit Schedule to show that the audit has been completed. Assess findings and their risk to the business. Schedule/reschedule the next audit accordingly.

PROCEDURE EXAMPLE #2

Internal Quality Audits

Issue: 1   Procedure Owner: Managing Director
Procedure No: QS05
Date: 31 July 2001

Purpose: The purpose of this procedure is to outline how internal quality audits are scheduled, planned and reported to ensure that the quality system is effective in meeting the needs of the business.

Scope: All of the Quality Management System.

QS/05/1: The Management Representative shall appoint staff to act as internal auditors. The Management Representative is responsible for ensuring that auditors receive adequate training and that this training is recorded.

QS/05/2: The whole quality system is to be audited at least once in each financial year, with one audit being carried out each quarter.

In April each year the Management Representative is to prepare an Audit Schedule (QS/05/1) covering the whole year. The Managing Director must approve this activity.

QS/05/3: Before each audit, the Management Representative shall call a meeting with the auditors appointed to carry out the audit to:
- assign audits to the audit team or individual auditors by reference to specific procedures of the quality system;
- number the audits sequentially with the details being recorded in the Register of Audits (QS/05/2);
- review progress of audits during the current year to-date; and
- assess auditor performance and review training records (see QS/08).

QS/05/4: Prior to carrying out the audit, the auditor should review the records of relevant previous audits carried out within the previous three years and identify any areas for consideration for the planned audit.

An Audit Checklist should be prepared covering the scope of the audit.

The Auditor should arrange convenient time with the staff involved in the work areas being covered by the audit.

The audit then should be carried out as planned with the results being discussed with the Management Representative. The Management Representative will communicate the results to the staff involved.

A report will be issued by the Auditor and sent to the Management Representative.

The Audit Report is form QS/05/2.

Corrective Action will be carried to resolve any nonconformities raised by implementing QS/04.

The Management Representative will record the results of the audit in the Register of Audits and file the Audit Report.

QS/05/5: If the Audit Report shows that nonconformities have been raised as a result of an audit, the management representative will request that the Auditor carries out a Follow–up Audit within 40 days of the original audit.

The purpose of the Follow–up Audit is to review the effectiveness of the corrective and preventive action implemented to correct the non-conformity raised.

Once the Follow–up Audit has been completed, the auditor should complete the Follow up Audit Report (QS/05/3) and send this to the Management Representative who will make the appropriate entries in the Register of Audits.

Notes:

module 6

Implementing the System

 How do I implement the system?

Now that you have written your documentation according to the standard's requirements, the next step is to implement the system.

The key to implementation is communication and training. During the implementation phase, everyone must operate to the procedures and collect records that demonstrate the organization is doing what it says it's doing. Consequently, if personnel are to implement the system correctly, they need to be aware of what they're supposed to do.

The first thing to remember is that many on the staff will have been involved in writing the documentation; therefore, acceptance of the procedures should be easier—there are no surprises. You could just inform the staff that the procedures have been written, issued and everyone is now expected to comply with them.

Alternatively, if you have a procedure to address clause 6.2.2 (competence, awareness and training), you could initiate it and brief the staff accordingly on the necessary process. The training can then be entered in the training records as evidence that proper instruction has been provided (as is required in 6.2.2.e). Adopting this approach also demonstrates to staff that you are serious and committed to the system.

Once the training process has been completed and staff are implementing the procedures, periodically walk around the business informally asking if the procedures are working or being implemented.

Additionally, if you need assistance to train staff, CEEM has a full suite of accredited courses that can train personnel effectively in the following areas:
- Understanding ISO 9001:2000
- Implementing ISO 9001:2000
- Quality Systems Documentation

- ISO 9001:2000 Lead Auditor
- ISO 9001:2000 Internal Quality Systems Auditor
- ISO 9001:2000 Auditor Transition

CEEM also can customize courses to an organization's specific needs. For more information, contact CEEM. Information to do so can be found on the inside cover of this book.

What is a gap analysis?

In a nutshell, a gap analysis is a process an organization goes through to determine the difference between what the process or quality management system is like now and what it should be when it conforms to the requirements of ISO 9001:2000 (or any management system standard). It's much like a full audit of the entire system, but it's an activity that is done at the beginning of the implementation process rather than after.

When organizations perform a gap analysis and effectively examine each process against established requirements, they usually discover a world of data as well as several opportunities to improve business performance. Some issues that are often probed during a gap analysis include:
- The organization's quality culture;
- Knowledge of the quality management system and ISO 9001:2000;
- Whether procedures have been established when necessary and/or required;
- Compliance to established procedures and processes;
- Proper resource allocation;
- Effective communication of objectives and responsibilities;
- Awareness of the quality policy and quality objectives;
- Competency of personnel and training programs;
- The organization's ability to make changes when necessary; and
- The suitability and effectiveness of the quality system.

Once these areas are evaluated, the organization can make strategic decisions on how best to fill those gaps that were discovered so that established requirements can be met and customer satisfaction enhanced.

TRANSITION TIPS: If you need assistance, BSI can help you develop an assessment plan to meet the desired timing for your registration to the ISO 9001:2000 standard. However, it is important that you maintain conformance with the ISO 9001:1994 standard during the transition period to keep your current certificate in place. A key consideration is to maintain the currently required procedures (you can't drop these procedures, even if ISO 9001:2000 doesn't require them) during the transition period.

Clause 5.4.2 of ISO 9001:2000 (Quality planning) requires planning any system changes and maintaining the integrity of the system during the changes.

Switching to the ISO 9001:2000 standard is a significant change for your system and "planning" the transition may be the subject of an audit. Have your planning evidence ready.

Also, registrars want to see usually three months of system operation before conducting an audit. Your will need to collect records as evidence your system is complying with planned arrangements, meeting requirements and effectively achieving the planned results.

What new requirements do I need to consider with the new standard?

When you are planning a trip, you must know your starting point and ultimate destination to decide on the most efficient and effective route. Similarly, you need to understand the new and changed ISO 9001:2000 requirements before plotting your transition path.

Start by ordering the ISO 9000:2000, ISO 9001:2000 and ISO 9004:2000 family of standards. Copies can be purchased through CEEM at discounted rates. Visit www.ceem.com for more details.

Before opening the ISO 9001:2000 *Requirements* standard, review the quality concepts described in the ISO 9000:2000 *Fundamentals and Vocabulary* standard. If you are unsure of any of the terms, look up their definitions in section 3 of ISO 9000:2000.

When you examine ISO 9001:2000, pay particular attention to the process approach described in its Introduction section. The process model illustrates the clause linkage based on the Plan-Do-Check-Act approach.

Refer to Annex B in the new ISO 9001 standard to see the clause correspondence between ISO 9001:2000 and ISO 9001:1994. Now you are ready to begin reading through the requirements to understand the differences.

The ISO 9004:2000 standard provides guidance on performance improvements beyond the basic requirements of ISO 9001:2000. For ease of reference, these requirements are shown in ISO 9004:2000 as boxed text.

Since ISO 9004:2000 uses the same clause structure as ISO 9001:2000, it can be used to gain a better understanding of the requirements by seeing possible practices. Remember, however, that your system will be evaluated against ISO 9001:2000, not ISO 9004:2000.

Also, you can view the Transition Planning Guidance that ISO TC 176 developed to assist organizations during the transition phase. It highlights the key requirement differences and can be downloaded from the Internet on ISO's Web site: www.iso.ch.

55 ## How should I communicate the relevant elements of our quality system to personnel and our suppliers?

The first activity is to identify specifically who your interested parties are. Then, it is important to keep everyone within the scope of your quality management system informed of your plans and progress. Clause 5.5.3 of ISO 9001:2000 requires internal communication channels be established to share information about the effectiveness of your quality management system. (See the next page for an example of an Internal Communications procedure.)

Top management will rely on internal communications to convey the importance of meeting customer requirements. The organization also must make employees aware of the relevance and importance of their activities and how they contribute to achieving the quality objectives.

Providing this information will involve everyone in helping to improve performance and meet the established objectives for their areas. Management should actively encourage feedback and communications from people within the organization for process improvements.

In terms of suppliers, communication is also a key ingredient for success. If your suppliers don't understand your requirements for quality, breakdowns will surely occur and customer satisfaction will not be achieved. Purchase orders are often the place to identify any unique requirements.

ISO 9001:2000 requires strict control of outsourced processes that can affect product conformity with established requirements, so the same process that you use to communicate with personnel can be used for suppliers as well. Just make sure that the information that is shared with suppliers is relevant to product conformity and not proprietary in nature. (**Note:** It is your responsibility to manage all outsourced activities and processes, e.g., design).

EXAMPLE OF AN INTERNAL COMMUNICATIONS PROCEDURE

Purpose

This procedure describes the tools and mechanisms for effective communication within ABC Corp. and provides guidance on how each may be utilized.

Scope

This procedure applies to all of ABC Corp. and those whom we interface to meet customer requirements.

Related Documents

ISO 9001:2000

Responsibilities

Process Owner—CEO, Communications Director
Process Users—All ABC Corp. employees

1.0 Procedure

1.1 The Communications Director shall be responsible for ensuring that effective communication of the organizations goals, objectives and customers needs and expectations are communicated within the organization. The CEO will ensure these are enabled with resources to meet organizational objectives and customer requirements.

1.2 The following mechanisms are available to communication tools:
- Face-to-face discussions
- E-mail
- Weekly staff meetings
- Intranet
- Monthly team meetings
- ABC Corp. managers meetings
- Monthly Reports
- Communication Day
- Cork boards
- Memos
- ABC Corp. all-hands meetings
- Business Plan

1.3 Continual improvement shall be fundamental to the ongoing development of the quality system. The Continual Improvement Team Leader will organize, enable and report to the CEO on these initiatives. Improvement items are addressed at each staff meeting and management reviews.

What happens if we need to change our procedures?

As everybody works to the quality system, there are bound to be changes that need to be identified and addressed. At BSI, we expect this; indeed, changes and improvements are a good sign that you are operating to the system and that it is maturing. So don't be afraid to change your procedures or work instructions.

To do this effectively, however, make sure that your documented procedure to address change (which is a requirement of Clause 4.2.3 Control of documents) is established and followed. For more information on this clause, go back to Module 3, p. 68.

 If I'm starting from scratch, how long will it take to implement ISO 9001:2000?

The time scale to implement a quality management system that conforms to the requirements of ISO 9001:2000 depends on a number of factors such as resources, a sound plan, commitment from top management and personnel and the complexity of the system. It is very important that you consider all of these issues during the planning phase.

But of course, the main purpose of the implementation phase is to introduce the quality system to the business and get staff working to the system as soon as possible.

Ideally, the phase should last about six months to allow you sufficient time to collect enough records to verify that the system is working, but you should be getting data back for analysis within two to three months. There may be parts of the quality system that you operate infrequently, such as on an annual basis, e.g., preparing a business plan in the fall of the year. If you then implement your system in February, it will be 11 months before that process will be exercised again. Most registrars will accept this situation and will review this procedure at a later date during a continuing assessment (surveillance) visit.

However, most registrars will expect action in areas that affect your business on a regular basis, e.g., audits, corrective action, management reviews as well as your normal operating procedures; hence, the two to three months time period.

The BSI ISO 9001:2000 Transition Process

Define Processes

The process flow to the left is the arrangement that BSI auditors will follow throughout the transition. It is not in the same sequence as ISO 9001:2000.

1st Assessment Visit: Review Quality Management System and Product Realization

Following discussions with clients, we decided to start the transition process from the 1994 standard with the Quality Management System and Product Realization sections. These sections address the majority of the clauses in ISO 9001/2:1994.

2nd Assessment Visit: Review Measurement, Analysis and Improvement

This process provides the opportunity to transfer gradually from the old standard to the new over two years, at no extra cost through your scheduled continual assessments.

3rd Assessment Visit: Review Management Responsibility

After the first Continual Assessment Visit, the focus will move onto Measurement, Analysis and Improvement. This will provide the Management Representative with information to report to their Top Management, which will cover Management Responsibility.

4th Assessment Visit: Review Resource Management

The final visit will cover Resource Management. It is at this final visit that registration to ISO 9001:2000 will be reviewed, and if appropriate, recommended.

If my organization already is registered to the 1994 standard, how long will it take to transition to the new standard?

ISO—and in turn, BSI and CEEM—are keen to manage the transition process to minimize the disruption and make it as seamless as possible. The transition period set by ISO within which registrars such as BSI are required to move clients into ISO 9001:2000 is three years. (This is, incidentally, far longer than on the two previous occasions when revisions were introduced to ISO 9000).

However, BSI believes that the vast majority of organizations that already have management systems in place to ISO 9001-2:1994 will have many of the requirements already accomplished. Therefore, it is BSI's strategy to encourage clients to transfer to the revised standard within two years—and to offer a maximum support to ensure that the transition is as comfortable as possible. Consequently, BSI assessment staff will be building transition plans with clients and moving incrementally through the revisions until December 2002. This will then allow an additional 12 months for those who need more time.

Examine the transition flow chart on p. 187 for a tentative plan. Contact BSI for more information.

How do I determine the needs of my customers?

There's an easy answer to this question: *Just ask them!*

But of course, in order to do that, you should have a good process to not only establish customer requirements, but also make sure they're being achieved. This is a requirement that has been woven into several clauses of ISO 9001:2000, particularly 7.2 Customer related processes and 8.2.1 Customer satisfaction, which states that the "organization shall monitor information relating to customer perception as to whether the organization has met customer requirements." Further, the clause requires that methods for obtaining and using this kind of information must be determined.

There are scores of issues to consider concerning customer needs, but perhaps the first thing you should do is make sure that customer requirements are established thoroughly. There is no requirement to have a documented procedure or records for determining customer requirements, but because it is such a critical function of the quality management system and the business, it is highly recommended. Customer needs can be identified by asking specific questions when your organization interacts with the customer or you can use approved forms to document those requirements. Forms can be used for records as well—just in case you ever need them!

ISO 9001:2000 also requires that you determine requirements *not specified* by the customer, but are needed for the product's intended use. These are issues that are usually implied, but not necessarily specified. For example, if you purchase a new car, you expect it to start, right? You may not specify that, but you certainly expect it.

Organizations also need to consider regulatory and other requirements as well, including those related to the environment or health and safety. For example, if your processes produce a byproduct that could be harmful to personnel or the community's drinking water, you may need to control your processes to comply with those requirements.

So as you can see, there are a number of things to consider with customer needs and expectations, and they can be overwhelming if you don't manage them and document them in some fashion. Once you do that, you'll have a much easier time prioritizing those needs. And if you haven't addressed customer requirements all at once, don't panic. You can always address the remaining issues through continual improvement processes and procedures—just make sure you do it!

Here are some issues to consider when dealing with customer requirements:
- Quantity of product;
- Product price;
- Correct color, size, shape, style, etc.
- Expected delivery date of product;
- Defect ratio;
- Service received when taking order was satisfactory; and
- Packaging.

 TRANSITION TIPS: When you establish customer requirements, be sure to also establish methods to communicate information back to your customers as well. This can help your business improve in many ways, especially customer satisfaction.

 ## How can I ensure my quality management system is compatible with other systems, such as ISO 14001 or OHSAS 18001?

The revised ISO 9001 was developed to have enhanced compatibility with ISO 14001, particularly with regard to terminology and content. There was and continues to be close collaboration between the technical experts of ISO TC 176 and ISO TC 207 (the Technical Committee responsible for the ISO 14000 series of standards).

A recent review of ISO 14001 and ISO 14004 by TC 207 has led to the initiation of a revision of those standards as well. This will provide the opportunity for further enhancement of the compatibility between the ISO 9000 and ISO 14000 standards.

As mentioned previously in this book, auditing will be affected specifically for quality and environmental management systems, to be called ISO 19011. This new standard will replace the existing ISO 10011 and ISO 14010/14011/14012 documents. The planned publication date for this new standard is the third quarter of 2002.

As for OHSAS 18001 (occupational health and safety assessment series), it, too, was developed to be consistent with both ISO 9000 and ISO 14001 in order to facilitate the integration of these business systems. So there shouldn't be any problems with compatibility now or in the future.

If your organization needs assistance in these areas, CEEM has qualified professionals that can help you integrate these systems to improve overall business performance.

Additionally, BSI has trained its auditing professionals to assess integrated systems that include ISO 9001:2000, ISO 14001 and OHSAS 18001. For more information, contact BSI or CEEM. Information to do so can be found on the inside cover of this book.

Notes:

Notes:

Measurement

61 How do I determine what needs to be measured and analyzed in the business?

Measurements and data analysis will differ between organizations, depending on the size, scope and complexity of the management system and the business. Generally, small- and medium-sized enterprises (SMEs) will need to establish and define these processes a little more than larger organizations, simply because traditionally, they often do not have the resources allocated to measure and analyze all processes for improvement, whereas larger organizations do.

But in basic terms, and at a minimum, every organization should measure and analyze data that affects product conformity, customer satisfaction or the effectiveness of the quality management system. Refer to Module 3 for more information on measurement and metrics.

TRANSITION TIPS: While ISO 9001:2000 requires organizations to measure and analyze "appropriate data," it's also important for every organization to understand how to measure effectively. Here are some tips to consider when prioritizing what needs to be measured and analyzed in your organization:
• Make sure your measurements address your organization's quality objectives, as outlined in Clauses 4.2.1 and 5.4.1 (Documentation requirements and Quality objectives).
• Make sure that your measurements and methodology for measurements are appropriate to the business, and that personnel can understand what is being collected and analyzed and why.
• All measurements should be qualitative and quantitative.

- Make sure you measure and analyze processes outlined and described in your procedures—not personnel performing the processes (this is the job of internal audits and annual performance reviews). The processes should be efficient and effective.

 ## 62 Should I measure my suppliers' performance, and if so, how?

Without question, yes, but make sure your evaluation is appropriate to your organization and the supplier's. This type of relationship development with your supply chain can make a world of difference for the quality of your products and services as well as the bottom line.

The premise here is that no organization can survive or completely satisfy their customers without the help of critical suppliers providing raw materials, information or human resources. The marketplace consists of many organizations interdependent on each other. Most organizations quickly find out how providing nonconforming product, product or information beyond the due date or in some other way hurts an organization's ability to deliver the product/service to the end user. Under this premise, organizations should be careful not to react and dismiss suppliers for one-off errors but instead, quantify their performance and endeavor to communicate expectations.

There are a number of ways to accomplish effective measurement of a supplier's performance and its relationship to quality. One way that some sectors (such as automotive) have increased the level of quality and profitability in their own organizations is by requiring third-party registration of ISO 9001 throughout their supply chains (or in some cases, ISO 9000's automotive counterparts—QS-9000 and TS 16949). These mandates have been a significant driver for registration since the early 1990s, because registration can represent a clear signal to the world that a sound quality management system is in place now and for the long-term.

Such a mandate can also reduce liability concerns within an organization. Trends show that in many parts of the world, manufacturers are increasingly held liable for nonconforming product, regardless of fault or negligence. A quality management system registered by an independent third party can demonstrate that an organization is capable of meeting customer requirements and has business processes in place to realize the desired outcome.

But registration mandates aren't the only way to measure a supplier's performance. In fact, ISO 9001:2000 provides clear guidance through its requirements concerning supplier selection, supplier use and management of suppliers (Clauses 7.4 *Purchasing*, 8.4 *Analysis of data* and the eighth quality management principle are examples). Again, as discussed in Module 3, it is advised to have a sound process in place for purchasing, and developing at least one procedure to cover clauses 7.4.1 through 7.4.3 is strongly encouraged (although not required). Most organizations should recognize that the service deliver line is certainly impacted by the ability of a supply chain to delivery of critical products and services at agreed date, correct to order and at a reasonable price.

When developing measures for supplier performance, consider the following steps:
1. Establish strict vendor selection criteria. Criteria can include whether the supplier has a documented quality system, evaluation of on-site audits of the supplier, supplier questionnaires regarding quality or inspection of product(s) at the supplier's site.
2. Develop sound metrics to measure criteria performance.
3. Analyze the data the metrics provide.
4. Review data during management review for action if necessary.
5. Communicate relevant feedback to suppliers.

The last point is an important step. Greater relationships and increased communication with suppliers strengthen the bond with the supplier for a win-win situation. This starts with feedback from you.

NOTE: Process owners might be Supplier Quality Assurance or Purchasing divisions. Also, quality records of supplier evaluations and any purchase order process are required.

 How do I know what "appropriate" data is as described in Clause 8.4?

Analyzing data is largely a cognitive skill, and "appropriate data" will vary greatly among organizations. Companies often make the mistake when they measure too much and become inundated with information. Strategic decisions should be made early on as to what exactly is useful to measure. These decisions are by no means random. Determining what needs to be measured can only be completed after identifying your processes and describing their interaction and sequence. The answer to what should be measured begins with what the objectives of the business are, what the quality objectives are and what critical aspects of certain processes need to be measured to ensure customer satisfaction.

The quality management principles should be evaluated at this stage concerning supplier development, as the measurement of supplier performance should be based on partnerships and improving the relationship.

TRANSITION TIPS: The requirement in Clause 8.4 is new and is quite specific in what must be analyzed, which at a minimum, must include:
- customer satisfaction;
- conformity to product requirements;
- characteristics and trends of processes and products, including opportunities for preventive action; and
- suppliers.

Keep in mind that different managers and employees in the organization will be analyzing this information. Care should be taken as measurements around Clause 7 are required, but are not the only measurements required in the quality management system.

 ## What is nonconforming product?

A nonconforming product is a product (service, software, hardware or processed material) developed through specified processes that does not meet customer requirements. ISO 9001:2000 Clause 8.3 (Control of nonconforming product) requires a documented procedure to ensure that if nonconforming product does occur, there is a process to handle it effectively so that it isn't released to the customer.

Most organizations have a specific quarantine area (usually near the inspection area) to hold nonconforming or suspect product when it occurs so that proper action can take place to handle it. Remember that it's perfectly fine to take the nonconforming product and fix it, authorize its use for the customer under concession or relevant authority or if it can be used for another customer in some way, it can be authorized for another application. Just make sure that a relevant authority addresses any use of a nonconforming product and that proper procedures and records are followed and kept.

 ## How do I measure customer satisfaction?

"Customer satisfaction" is recognized as one of the driving criteria for any organization. In order to evaluate if the product meets customer needs and expectations, it is necessary to monitor the extent of customer satisfaction and/or dissatisfaction. Improvements can be made by taking action to address any identified issues and concerns.

The revised standards improve customer satisfaction significantly because the management system described in the ISO 9001:2000 is based on management principles that include the process approach and customer focus. The adoption of these principles should provide customers with a higher level of confidence that the product meets their needs and increases their satisfaction.

In terms of specific measurements, organizations can use a slew of metrics to measure customer satisfaction, customer dissatisfaction and customer perception, and more important, improve on those issues. Indeed, many organizations that used the 1994 standard already have the some of the required infrastructure in place to measure customer satisfaction in an appropriate manner. Here are some examples of methods used to track this type of data:

- Warranties
- Customer/user group studies
- Questionnaires
- Surveys
- Customer complaints
- Product returns
- Information from trade associations
- Direct information/feedback from customer

(Turn to the next few pages for examples of surveys and evaluation forms.)

The important thing to remember concerning this requirement is to think holistically about not only *how* your organization will measure customer satisfaction, but more important, *what* your organization will do with the information to improve performance. As this book has stated numerous times, the intent of the standard is *improvement, improvement, improvement!*

CEEM
a member of the BSI group

12110 Sunset Hills Road
Suite 100
Reston, VA 20190-3231

ORDER INFORMATION

PLACE PRODUCT INFORMATION
LABEL HERE

PLEASE FEEL FREE TO MAKE ADDITIONAL COMMENTS:

THANK YOU FOR HELPING US TO SERVE YOU BETTER!

Customer Satisfaction Card

Quality and customer satisfaction go hand in hand at CEEM. Please take a moment to evaluate the product(s) and service(s) you received from CEEM, so that we may serve you better in the future. Or just e-mail us your comments: solutions@ceem.com.

DATE CEEM RECEIVED REQUEST | DATE YOU RECEIVED ORDER

DID YOU RECEIVE THE PRODUCT(S) YOU ORDERED? ☐ YES ☐ NO
IF NO, PLEASE EXPLAIN:

WERE YOU SATISFIED WITH YOUR ORDER? ☐ YES ☐ NO
IF NO, PLEASE EXPLAIN:

ON A SCALE OF 1-10, WITH 10 BEING GOOD AND 1 BEING BAD, HOW WOULD YOU RATE OUR SERVICE?

needs improvement   acceptable   excellent
1   2   3   4   5   6   7   8   9   10

WOULD OTHER CEEM PRODUCTS/SERVICES ASSIST YOU?
training   consultancy   software   videos   books

WOULD YOU LIKE E-MAIL UPDATES ON CEEM'S NEW PRODUCTS?
IF YES, PLEASE ENTER YOUR E-MAIL ADDRESS BELOW:

a member of the BSI group

Training Evaluation Form

Course Name _____

Today's Date _____

Project No.   01-0-0713

Dear CEEM Course Attendee,

Thank you for taking part in a CEEM training course. We truly hope your experience was productive, educational and satisfactory in every way.

To ensure your overall satisfaction and our own continual improvement, please take a few moments to evaluate the course by circling the number that corresponds with your experience.

Please feel free to add any comments that you might have, so that we might serve you and others better in the future. And of course, confidentiality is guaranteed.

When finished, please return to the instructor. If you have additional comments or if you would like to speak with a CEEM customer respresentative, please call 800.745.5565, or drop us an e-mail: solutions@ceem.com.

Instructor(s)

The instructor was knowledgeable, well-prepared and fun.

strongly disagree					neutral				strongly agree	
0	1	2	3	4	5	6	7	8	9	10

Comments

Course

The course materials and content are easy to use and are informative.

strongly disagree					neutral				strongly agree	
0	1	2	3	4	5	6	7	8	9	10

Comments

Facilities

The training room provided an atmosphere suitable for learning.

strongly disagree					neutral				strongly agree	
0	1	2	3	4	5	6	7	8	9	10

Comments

Service

CEEM employees are helpful, knowledgeable and responsive.

strongly disagree					neutral				strongly agree	
0	1	2	3	4	5	6	7	8	9	10

Comments

Overall

The following describes what I liked best about this course.

The following describes what I liked least about this course.

The following features are important to me, with 10 being the most important.

Instructor: 0	1	2	3	4	5	6	7	8	9	10
Course: 0	1	2	3	4	5	6	7	8	9	10
Facilities: 0	1	2	3	4	5	6	7	8	9	10
Service: 0	1	2	3	4	5	6	7	8	9	10

How does CEEM measure against the competition? (0 - 10 scale)

Would you choose CEEM again based on this experience?   Yes or No

F1 I—5.21.01
Issue 1 Rev. A
Page 1 of 1

Notes:

Auditing

 Why should my organization conduct internal audits?

In order for your quality management system to be effective, it is absolutely essential to conduct periodic assessments of its processes to ensure that it is achieving its stated objectives. Additionally, internal audits:

- help organizations identify opportunities to correct or prevent problems so that customer requirements are met and/or exceeded.
- act as an input to the management review process.
- provide valuable data for analysis so that improvements to the system can be made.
- help ensure regulatory requirements are met.
- improve customer satisfaction.
- support organizations' attempts to register through a third party.
- are an essential activity to identify opportunities for continual improvement.
- are required of any system conforming to the ISO 9001:2000 standard (Clause 8.2.2).

As stressed in Module 3, an organization's internal auditing program is the heartbeat of the entire system. Just remember that one new requirement in ISO 9001:2000 is the deployment of a process model. That means if you're conducting a process management approach as required by ISO 9001:2000, you'll also need to conduct process audits. This adds a new dynamic to the auditing process, which organizations need to understand when developing their audit plans.

TRANSITION TIPS: Some organizations might already be conducting a form of process audits, they just don't know it. The point to remember is that conducting internal audits where the audit team is determining conformance to established procedures is just a shell of what process audits can do for an organization. They allow for dynamic auditing providing information on risk that has been identified and should be able to determine if processes are robust. As was mentioned earlier, auditors do not audit the individual, but in fact, assess the *system*.

Additionally, the management system is a tool to enable business objectives. One merit of internal auditing is that an organization might focus on a particular business objective as a theme to an internal audit. By way of an example, the company might seek to undertake an aggressive acquisition strategy and integrate these new businesses into the larger company's way of operating. Internal audits can ensure that the processes of these activities are going as per the plan and can correct any issues early in the process.

67 ▸ How often should internal audits be conducted?

Since the purpose of internal auditing is to improve the system, regularly scheduled audits are strongly encouraged. ISO 9001:2000 (Clause 8.2.2) requires an organization to conduct internal audits at planned intervals to determine whether the quality management system:

- conforms to the planned arrangements (see 7.1), to the requirements of ISO 9001:2000 and to the quality management system requirements established by the organization, and
- is effectively implemented and maintained.

Of course, the requirement of Clause 8.2.2 is designed to be flexible as well, especially when determining the frequency and scope of each audit. Just make sure that you define and plan everything accordingly and appropriately, and perhaps more important, stick to your plan.

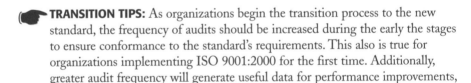

☞ TRANSITION TIPS: As organizations begin the transition process to the new standard, the frequency of audits should be increased during the early the stages to ensure conformance to the standard's requirements. This also is true for organizations implementing ISO 9001:2000 for the first time. Additionally, greater audit frequency will generate useful data for performance improvements, and will allow personnel to become more comfortable with the audit process.

Also, organizations should conduct at least one full assessment of the entire system before attempting a registration audit with a third party. Doing so allows everyone to understand the entire process, the system and its many links.

68 ▸ What is a typical audit process?

Those who have experienced an audit before know the heightened awareness that often occurs within an organization during audit days. Everyone reviews their job descriptions, processes and procedures, managers clock in early to review records and make sure everything is operating smoothly and the quality manager probably hasn't slept well all week anticipating the "Big Day."

Although understandable behavior (everyone wants to look good, right?), no one should be putting on their "best performance" for an auditor. In fact, that's exactly what the auditor *doesn't* want to see!

Remember, proactive organizations conduct audits to improve business performance. It's a service that adds value to the organization and how it operates, delivers and considers customer requirements. A skilled auditor doesn't want the red carpet rolled out for their arrival—they'd rather sit down with the people on the shop floor and really see how the operation ticks on a normal day. That way, they can see the system for what it is—not for what it aspires to be during an audit.

The audit process differs between organizations and their respective audits. The scope, frequency, size and complexity of the audit are all considerations that must be planned before the audit begins.

The audit process differs for third-party audits and between registrars as well. At BSI, auditors make it very clear as to what will transpire during an audit—surprise inspections have no positive effect for an organization in the long-term. All through the process, BSI auditors will tell you exactly what to expect, what they've learned during their audit and provide specific documentation concerning their findings in a formal report and presentation.

For a complete agenda of what you can expect from a BSI auditor during a registration audit, turn to Module 10.

What is the auditor's role?

The primary role of any auditor is to collect objective evidence and determine if the organization:
* has a documented quality management system;
* is meeting the requirements of ISO 9001:2000;
* has a suitable and effective system.
* has interpreted collected data.

Other roles of the auditor are to:
* make a judgment about the overall quality program;
* report all findings back to the organization.

This role is crucial to the system, the business and can help make the determination as to whether the organization meets the criteria of ISO 9001:2000 in order to receive registration status.

Auditors gather objective evidence through staff interviews, observing the business processes in action, evaluating documented procedures, records and other documents. Of course, auditors can't look at everything—most organizations have vast amounts of data to evaluate and no one could get through all of it during the limited time of an assessment. Think if it as a sampling of your system, or a snapshot in time of what your company was doing on a particular day.

Once they gather the appropriate information, auditors will record their findings and provide feedback to the organization in some fashion. This is called an audit report, and is usually presented in a formal way to an organization during a closing meeting.

Often times, many people literally groan when they here that they or their department will be audited. They imagine a dictatorial presence standing over them and evaluating every little thing they do in their daily jobs.

But that's a misperception, or at least one that skilled auditors are trying to overcome. Auditing is not about finding faults with personnel or the business—it's about adding value to the organization, improving business processes, linking customers and suppliers through information sharing and enhancing customer satisfaction.

Indeed, a good auditor is a great person to have on staff. A person who can not only collect valuable data about the organization but interpret it as well is a valuable asset to any business.

How should I choose an internal audit team?

Choosing the right team to implement and audit to the ISO 9001:2000 standard was first introduced in Module 3, and it must be stressed again in this Module. The key to any successful quality management system is an effective auditing program— period.

Again, it is optimal to have people on the team with different skill sets from cross-functional parts of the business, providing valuable input to the entire process. This allows business synergies and communication to occur across the business.

Auditors should be identified early in the implementation process, but make sure you have people who represent relevant departments and have the right personality traits. The following are a few traits that often make up good auditors:
- **Action-oriented**—The team needs to be ready to act and implement change.
- **Experienced**—It's a good idea to have auditors who know the business of the organization. People who have been around a while and know how things operate can be invaluable.
- **Detail-driven**—Auditing is all about the details and finding the right audit trails by asking the right questions.
- **Holistic thinkers**—When auditing to ISO 9001:2000, auditors must be able to see the "Big Picture." In other words, they must think cross-functionally and understand the business as a whole.
- **Good communicators**—Auditors must ask a lot of questions, and they must be articulate, intelligent and cordial at all times. Communication is the most important skill of every auditor.

Of course, these aren't the only traits for a good auditing team. Auditors also should be well-trained, pragmatic, have strong ethics and remain objective at all times. For more information on selecting an audit team, obtain a copy of ISO 19011— *Guidelines for quality and/or environmental management systems auditing*. Contact CEEM for details.

 TRANSITION TIPS: This is a process that you should establish early on, enabling you to begin the audit process and launch the corrective/preventive action program to coincide with the audit. Additionally, there should be some type of qualification of auditors. Even if auditors take an outside class, their interpretations and ability to conduct an internal audit should be measured and approved by the company prior to allowing audits to begin.

 ## 71   What are nonconformities, and what happens if BSI finds them during an audit?

A nonconformity is a situation where there is a likelihood that nonconforming product or service will occur, or where the benefits of ISO 9001:2000 are not being realized because of the absence of, or lack of, adherence to a procedure.

However, there are established levels of nonconformities within BSI. Here's how they break down and how they'll be reported on an audit report:

- **Major nonconformity**—This is a nonconformity of such severity that its existence would indicate that nonconforming product or service could be released to the customer, or where the requirements of an appropriate clause of ISO 9001:2000 has not been adequately addressed or implemented. Of course, BSI recognizes that some clauses in ISO 9001:2000 are new and that some procedures that address those clauses may be newly implemented and operational evidence limited. Still, some objective evidence on implementation must be found, as merely documenting procedures is insufficient. If there is only limited objective evidence, the immaturity of the system will be reported and followed up with checks during continuing audit visits. An example of a major nonconformity could be an organization having no formal process and procedure to conduct internal audits.
- **Nonconformity**—This is single lapse of a process or procedure that has been observed during an audit where the impact is relatively low to the customer. This is sometimes called a "minor nonconformity." It is usually raised against a procedure or a certain clause or requirement of the standard. An example of a minor nonconformity could be an auditor examining 50 purchase orders during an audit and 10 of them were unsigned by a relevant authority.
- **Observation**—This is what many auditors usually consider an "almost" nonconformity, but there may not be enough evidence to categorize it as such. Observations are important to resolve, but it's up to the organization or auditee to fix them as appropriate. During a registration audit, observations are often raised as opportunities to improve the business, but it is not required that the

organization address them immediately. However, addressing observations in a timely manner demonstrates that the organization is interested in continual improvement. An example of an observation could be that an organization has a process and procedure for inspection and receiving, but records might show that there are only a few forms that prove the process is being performed effectively. **NOTE:** Third-party auditors (registrars) must be very careful when it comes to issuing observations. There are strict guidelines from the Registrar Accreditation Board that state registrars cannot be "consultants" when it comes to auditing. Rather, they must be strictly independent and objective. Observations are allowed by RAB, but they are scrutinized—and should be. Additionally, observations can also be "positive" in nature, and often are.

Normally, businesses are concerned that they will not be ready for an audit when BSI arrives. They perceive that things need to be perfect for an audit; however, this is hardly ever the case. BSI does not expect a system to be perfect from day one or during a registration audit. Furthermore, they do not arrive for the audit with any preconceived ideas or expectations on finding nonconformities.

If indeed the auditors find nonconformities in your system, don't panic—remember, these are simply opportunities for improvement!

If your organization does receive nonconformities, they will be recorded within the body of the final assessment report. Only objective evidence of system, service or product nonconformities is recorded, which includes nonconformities issued against the organization's documented procedures. Observations and any opportunity for further improvements are also recorded.

Apparent nonconformities will be discussed at the time of discovery with the client's representative since they may be able to give clarification, or may know where other information can be found. Each auditor will be objective and open-minded when judging conformity and shall never make decisions based on preconceived ideas or familiar practice.

If a major nonconformity is raised, the audit team leader will notify you as soon as possible that the recommendation will be not to certify (if it is a registration audit). The team leader will advise you of this notification and will either terminate or continue the audit, at your discretion. If you request that the audit should be terminated, the audit team will complete the audit report with a recommendation of further assessment and the closing meeting will be held. If you decide to continue the audit, this is recorded within the audit summary and the recommendation of further assessment is made.

But again, don't worry too much about nonconformities. BSI is there to help you improve, and the way to do that is through effective auditing and reporting of all findings. Indeed, that's what we do every day!

What should auditors be looking for during an audit?

First, auditors—whether they are internal auditors or third-party auditors—must be well-trained before they begin auditing anything, so they should already have a good idea of what to look for and how to look for it. Auditors of all types should assume conformance until testing the management system identifies a nonconformance. The inverse should be prevented at all costs.

Second, a successful audit is one that is well-planned, identifying the scope and duration of the audit, what areas are to be audited and which people will need to participate long before the audit begins. And of course, the audit plan should be confirmed with the organization or relevant departments that are going to participate as well.

Once the audit begins, many auditors have a checklist approach in which they have specific questions and objectives of what processes and documentation they want to evaluate. This allows them to stay focused on the process, ensuring that all areas of the standard are covered. Audits can be grueling affairs for auditors, so most registrars and internal auditors use checklists of some kind to help them keep track of what areas they've audited.

BSI auditors, however, do things a little differently. Rather than using a specific checklist, BSI auditors use the actual standard as their checklist to understand your entire business process and how it conforms to the requirements of the standard. To do that effectively, BSI auditors are trained exclusively and intensely to the elements of the ISO 9000:2000 series, making sure that they understand the standards themselves and how your organization uses their requirements and guidance. Doing so enables BSI auditors to ask the right questions from auditees—and know what answers to expect as well.

Of course, all auditors are looking for generally the same information. In a nutshell, they're looking for consistency across the organization with its processes, procedures and documentation. They'll obtain that information by reviewing documentation, observing processes and business activities and interviewing employees with open-ended questions (i.e., *"Can you tell me how this process or procedure works in your area?")*

NOTE: As stressed earlier in this Module, auditors are not looking for fault when they perform an audit. They're only looking to verify the information they've collected and report where the system may not be operating to its full potential—or not operating at all. Remember that audits add value to the business and its overall performance each and every time they're done!

73 What is ISO 19011?

ISO 19011, also known as the "common auditing standard," is a jointly prepared document from experts of TC 176 on quality management and quality assurance and TC 207 on environmental management. It is a new standard that will help organizations streamline their auditing practices for management systems. When it is completed and released by ISO, it will replace ISO 10011 for quality management systems auditing and ISO 14010, 14011 and 14012 for environmental management systems auditing. At the time of this printing (July 2001), ISO 19011 had been approved as a Draft International Standard, with a tentative publication date set for autumn 2002. Once the standard is published, the aforementioned standards will become obsolete.

In a nutshell, ISO 19011 provides effective guidance on the conduct of internal or external quality and/or environmental management system audits, as well as on the management of audit programs as required by both ISO 9001:2000 and ISO 14001:1996. Intended users of ISO 19011 include auditors, organizations implementing quality and/or environmental management systems and organizations involved in auditor certification or training, certification/registration of management systems, accreditation or standardization in the area of conformity assessment.

The group of experts that created ISO 19011 has worked diligently to ensure that the standard is flexible and can apply to a range of potential users. Its clauses and requirements break down into seven clauses:

- **Clauses 1, 2 and 3** deal with scope, normative references and terms and definitions respectively.
- **Clause 4** describes the principles of auditing.
- **Clause 5** provides guidance on establishing and managing audit programs. Issues such as assigning responsibility for managing audit programs, establishing the objectives, coordinating auditing activities and providing sufficient audit team resources are addressed here.
- **Clause 6** contains guidance on conducting quality and/or environmental management system audits, including the selection of audit teams.
- **Clause 7** provides guidance on auditor competence. It outlines the knowledge and skills needed to be competent to conduct an audit and provides guidance on the personal attributes needed to be an auditor, such as education, work experience, auditor training and audit experience that are indicators of whether a person has acquired the appropriate knowledge and skills. It also outlines a process for the evaluation of auditors. Clause 7 has been the most controversial of ISO 19011's development because of it broad applicability.

Of course, the concept behind ISO 19011 is *integrated* auditing, which can lead to tremendous benefits for an organization if done properly. Experts believe this type of auditing is the most cost-effective way to audit an organization now and in the future. Where quality and environmental management systems are implemented together, ISO 19011 can be used to conduct joint audits with enhanced results. However, it is at the discretion of the user audits are conducted separately or together.

How does ISO 19011 address internal audits for ISO 9001:2000 and ISO 14001?

ISO 19011 doesn't have specific guidance for internal audits of ISO 9001:2000 or ISO 14001:1996. It is a generic document that offers guidelines for all types of auditing, including other management system audits such as OHSAS 18001. Its guidance also can be used to monitor conformance to other requirements as well, such as product specifications or laws and regulations.

ISO 19011 content includes generic guidance on the following topics:
- Principles of auditing
- Managing an audit program
- Audit program implementation, monitoring and reviewing
- Initiating the audit
- Appointing the audit team leader and establishing the audit team
- Defining audit objectives, scope and criteria
- Determining the feasibility of the audit
- Establishing initial contact with the auditee
- Conducting document review
- Preparing the audit
- Conducting the opening meeting
- Communication during the audit
- Collecting and verifying information
- Generating audit findings
- Conducting closing meeting
- Preparing, approving and distributing the audit report
- Conducting audit follow-up
- Competence of auditors

As you can see, the document is comprehensive. Organizations should obtain a copy and review its content before beginning assigning auditors and conducting internal audits. To obtain a copy, contact CEEM. Information to do so can be found on the inside cover of this book.

Do auditors need to be retrained to the new ISO 9000:2000 series?

Absolutely. Without question, auditors will need to be re-trained to the new requirements of ISO 9001:2000 and the consistent pair concept with ISO 9004:2000. The level of training, however, is up to you and top management.

For internal purposes, a great start to understanding the new requirements of ISO 9001:2000 is reading this book. It answers some of the most frequently asked questions and interprets each clause of the new standard for implementing and registration endeavors.

However, you and your organization should consider formalized, accredited training to ISO 9001:2000 as well. A number of organizations specializing in the quality management arena provide accredited training courses. Those organizations must follow specific guidelines established by the Registrar Accreditation Board (RAB), the U.S. accreditation body recognized by the American National Standards Institute (ANSI) and ISO. The primary focus of any training to the new standard encompasses the process approach to plan and conduct of audits as described in ISO 9001:2000. Other benefits of formalized training can include:
- Understanding the purpose of a quality management system and its role in helping an organization operate with increased efficiency and consistency and enhanced customer satisfaction;
- Understanding the eight quality management principles described in ISO 9000 and ISO 9004;
- Understanding the requirements of the new ISO 9001:2000 and the objective evidence needed to show conformance and effectiveness of the quality management system;
- Understanding the differences between ISO 9001:1994 and ISO 9001:2000; and
- Understanding the changes to audit methodology in areas such as continual improvement, top management commitment and responsibility and the process approach.

If you have specific questions concerning ISO 9001:2000 training, contact CEEM. Information to do so can be found on the inside cover of this book.

 ## What is corrective and preventive action?

In a nutshell, corrective actions are steps an organization must take to fix problems (processes that result in nonconforming product and/or other nonconformities of the system) when things go wrong so that they don't happen again.

Preventive actions are steps taken to eliminate problems (potential nonconformities) before they happen.

Both steps are important elements of any quality management system, and documented procedures are required for an organization to comply with the requirements of ISO 9001:2000 (clauses 8.5.2 and 8.5.3). Additionally, both requirements have the intent of continual improvement of the system and the business as well. (See Module 3.)

Notes:

Notes:

Management Review

 How can I use the management review process to help identify opportunities for continual improvement?

As you've read from Module 3, standards writers put a strong emphasis on management review in the new ISO 9001:2000 because of its direct link to many parts of the quality management system—especially continual improvement. Thorough reviews are necessary for improvement because they determine the suitability, adequacy and effectiveness of the quality management system, its objectives and the business as a whole. Indeed, a management review is an explicit requirement in ISO 9001:2000 and should occur as appropriate to the organization (or as often as possible).

When planning a management review, organizations should create an agenda (based on the requirements of Clauses 5.6.1 and 5.6.2) to discuss internal audit results and then draw conclusions on how the business addresses:
- customer satisfaction;
- nonconforming product data and trends;
- corrective and preventive actions;
- training;
- resource allocation;
- customer complaints; and
- other critical factors of the system and business.

In terms of the process, organizations should consider (or at least review) the Plan-Do-Check-Act model before conducting management reviews. This will help you understand how the process works—especially the most important aspect of it—ACTING. Whatever process you choose, be sure that all of your activities focus on two things: improvement and customer satisfaction. The two are obviously linked, but having those two items as your major agenda items will help the management team stay focused.

TRANSITION TIPS: Management reviews are really where the rubber meets the road, so having a sound process to achieve results is essential. But one of the most important things to understand and do concerning management reviews is to make sure that the right people are at the table. If the decision-makers who understand the process aren't present, improvements and actions will be difficult.

How often should management reviews be conducted?

Again, the timetable to conduct management reviews should be at "defined intervals" or as appropriate to the organization. Just make sure that your management reviews are well planned and documented, and stick to the schedule religiously.

Most organizations that have registered to the 1994 standard already should have a robust management review process in action. If that's the case, be sure to review the new requirements and make necessary adjustments. However, if you are implementing ISO 9001:2000 for the first time, your organization should begin conducting management reviews before the system is fully implemented—and they should occur often (perhaps once a month or more). This shows strong support to the team, employees and to auditors during the early implementation stage, and it also provides valuable data that can show results and areas for improvement.

How should I track action items to ensure they are being completed after a management review?

There are a multitude of ways to track action items from management reviews, depending on your organization's size, scope and level of available technology. Choose a process that's appropriate and easy to track.

Larger companies often use a spreadsheet approach and log items carefully. Or you can just write them down and assign an alpha-numeric figure, and the management representative can tick them off when completed. The software program Process Expert Professional™ also can be an excellent tool to help you track action items, providing functionality such as e-mail, the Internet and Intranet to aid your tracking efforts. See p. 45 for more information on Process Expert Professional™.

What's the best way to communicate selected output of the management review process to people within my organization?

Again, internal and external communication should be thoroughly considered by top management. The organization's size, scope, complexity and level of available technology also should be considered.

At the management review, make sure that all functional representatives or department heads are present and understand the communication channels and requirements of the management review process. The representatives who attend the management review should incorporate the actions items that are relevant to their department in their own functional meetings. For example, if your operations manager attends the management review, any actions that are assigned to his/her department should be addressed when the operations department holds its next meeting or as appropriate.

Of course, a plant with hundreds of workers may not need to communicate all of the information down to everyone on the shop floor, but the person responsible for the action should confirm that the action needs to be addressed and should also confirm its completion to relevant parties. Here are some examples of ways to communicate actions: Process Expert Professional™, e-mail, the company's Intranet, bulletin boards, Internet, memos or just talking to the responsible party to ensure the action occurs.

NOTE: Organizations should review Clause 5.5 of ISO 9001:2000 before implementing communication channels. The (responsibility, authority and communication) process should be used with management reviews.

Should I communicate management review issues to interested parties?

Communicating management review issues externally is a good idea, but assume that interested parties don't understand your review process and, frankly, don't care.

Interested parties want to see results, actions, improvements and how your customers are going to be satisfied with your products and services, which is exactly what you should communicate. Make sure you exclude any of the "ISO language" of the review process and just put it in plain English (or whatever language you choose).

There are a number of ways to report this kind of data, and companies are being proactive in doing so. Many communicate relevant management review data on their Web sites, in their annual reports and some actually invite interested parties into the management review session to show them how the operation ticks on a normal day.

Whatever method you choose, be sure to communicate—in a general way—the status of the business, its quality objectives and improvement trends. Stay away from sending out proprietary data or anything that might be sensitive to the business.

☛ TRANSITION TIPS: To ensure you don't send out proprietary data, be sure you take the time to identify interested parties thoroughly. Interested parties could include venture capitalists, customers, employees or other people or organizations that have a stake in requisite changes that occur to your business. By communicating effectively, your organization closes the information loop effectively, which is optimal for all parties.

How should my organization plan changes that affect the quality management system?

The key word here is planning. See Section 5.4 of ISO 9001:2000. Make sure the integrity of the quality management system is maintained as you transition to the new standard. Also ensure that planned changes complement the quality policy and quality objectives. This is particularly true for organizations that already are registered.

Start by obtaining copies of the new ISO 9000:2000 series. Next, ensure that you have a clear understanding of the transition plan to the new standard that affects you. This should be readily available from your respective registrar. The transition plan flows down from TC 176, sector-based groups (e.g. AS 9100, QS-9000, TL 9000 etc.), the International Accreditation Forum, accreditation bodies and, finally, the individual certification bodies/registrars.

Also, internally, make sure that you leave the review meeting with a clear action plan. Everyone needs to be clear of exactly what is required; there are various software packages in the marketplace that can help you to keep track of the progress being made.

Additionally, make sure you allow time to follow up on any actions raised. When you finally close out the actions, make sure the changes are in line with ISO 9001:2000, any legal and regulatory requirements and that the changes made have been effective. The detail associated with the changes must be communicated, and management must show an interest in the progress made, making sure that any resources needed are provided in a timely manner.

Once the changes are implemented and any documents re-issued, it is vital that the changes are audited, because what sounds good and looks good on paper is not necessarily good in practice. Test the changes thoroughly.

TRANSITION TIPS: Again, flowcharts are an excellent way to show the stages of change. Use them whenever possible.

 How can I use management reviews to assist the organization with strategic planning?

Think about management review as a process that should incorporate "systems-thinking," which leads to sound decision-making. Management review is a vehicle for management to review overall performance and gather information on which to base decisions and actions that will have both an immediate as well as a strategic impact. Selected output from the management review process can then become an input into the strategic planning process.

You also should look at the results of processes and products, customer feedback, preventive and corrective actions and continual improvement and evaluate these things to see where you are now and where you want to go in the next few years. Don't just think about conformance. You need to look at the big picture. Consider issues such as line efficiency, ergonomics, conversion rates, scrap and rework. What are your competitors doing that you don't?

Think about the structure of your business. Are you doing the right things? Are there other complementary services that you can provide to your customers that you are not currently involved with? Good focused market research can pay off dividends in this area.

Raw materials are another important area to consider. Just because you have used a propriety compound for the last 10 years does not mean that something better does not exist. Communicate with your suppliers to see how they can help your organization to improve. Packaging methods, new printing technology for labeling and traceability may be available.

In some industries, it is possible to compare "like-for-like" data on deliveries. Delivery of plastic resins for injection molding and extrusion is one example. Accumulated data of flow-rates, bulk density and rheology can tell you a great deal about your vendors' manufacturing processes, often before they know what is happening and your plant grinds to a halt.

Material handling is another important area to consider. The world is full of companies either not taking full advantage of the systems they have or working with systems that are in their final death throes. Organizations often take unreliable conveyor systems and/or handling equipment as a running cost of doing business, but the question is: How much material do they contaminate or waste as a result? It may be a better alternative to resolve the cause of the problems rather than work with unreliable equipment.

To summarize, management review is not just about missing signatures. Look at the big picture, because your survival as a business depends on it!

Notes:

recorded. The relevant clause of the standard is also recorded. This data forms an essential part of the final audit report and provides a comprehensive cross-reference. The team leader ensures that the audit takes account of all requirements of the management standard and the scheme. The team leader is responsible for ensuring that each auditor supplies the required information and that the progress is regularly reviewed during the audit. Auditors should particularly note points that require data from, or for, other auditors.

- **Preparing Recommendations**—When each auditor has completed his/her allotted task, the audit team will meet, with the team leader as chairman. The objectives are to:
  1. Check that all aspects of the planned audit have been completed.
  2. Obtain all team members' views on what they have assessed.
  3. Categorize each observed nonconformity.
  4. Consider whether there are any patterns of related nonconformities.
  5. Decide upon the team's recommendation.

  The audit team reaches its recommendation by consensus. If they are unable to reach consensus, the team leader makes the final decision. The team leader is responsible for recording in the report that the decision was not reached by consensus. After this meeting, the team leader prepares the audit report, which contains the team recommendation and a statement of the situation found by the auditors based on the observed nonconformities. The report highlights particular areas that require corrective action but does not advise the client on how to correct nonconformities.

- **Closing Meeting**—Once the audit report is developed, all relevant personnel gather to hear a formal presentation of the findings. The purpose of the closing meeting is to inform the client of the team's recommendations and to present to them any nonconformities raised. A record of the meeting is made and any significant discussion points are recorded. The client's representative (usually a ranking member of the organization, which could range from the quality manager to the management representative to the CEO) is asked to sign the report during the final meeting and a copy of the report is left with that person.

After the report is presented and the BSI auditors thank you for your hospitality, a copy of the report and its corrective actions are sent to the BSI technical and certification manager or deputy for review. It is then forwarded to a BSI client administrator upon approval, and a certificate is issued within a few weeks.

What kind of questions should I expect during an audit?

The first thing a good auditor will do is make everyone feel comfortable, stressing the fact that he or she is not there to audit any particular person—just the processes and the quality system as it conforms to ISO 9001:2000. An atmosphere of trust, transparency and open communication is an absolute must to conduct a successful audit, so auditors will be using every communication tool they have to make this happen.

Good auditors will avoid "yes or no" questions, generally asking open-ended questions so that the auditee has a chance to respond in his or her own words. How the auditor asks the question greatly affects the amount of information he or she receives back from the auditee.

Of course, the type of question will depend on who the auditor is interviewing. He could be asking holistic questions to top management about the organization's quality objectives or resource allocation or specific questions to a plant worker about a detailed process—it simply depends. But again, you can expect a lot of open-ended questions, no matter where you are on the organizational chart. Here are a few examples of open-ended questions that may be asked during an audit:

- How does your organization ensure that the quality policy is reviewed for continuing suitability?
- How does your organization ensure that appropriate communication processes are established?
- What process(es) does your organization have to ensure that customer feedback is reviewed during management review?
- How does your organization ensure the effectiveness of corrective actions?
- How does your organization ensure that nonconforming product doesn't reach the customer?
- How does your organization ensure that continual improvement occurs?
- How does your organization conduct internal audits?

The list can go on and on; however, these examples should give you a good idea of what to expect during any type of audit.

How do we act during an audit?

Organizations often go into a crisis mode on audit day, which isn't necessary at all. Remember, auditors are there to help your organization improve your processes, which in return, should improve the bottom line.

The best thing your organization can do is simply act normally, just like any other day. The only difference is, someone will be asking you and your personnel a lot of questions about what they do and how they do it. And because people typically spend one-third of their lives doing their jobs, they should know the answers without much of a problem.

Just remember these words of advice on audit day:
- Relax and breathe deeply.
- Keep your self-esteem high.
- Answer the auditor's questions as completely as you can.
- Ask for clarification if you don't understand the question.

It's that easy! Again, don't worry about audit day. BSI is there to help, not hurt your organization. In fact, that's our mission and passion as a business!

How long does it take to go through a registration audit?

The time scale of a registration audit depends on a number of factors, including the size and complexity of the organization and its system, as well as the scope of the audit.

In general terms, an average-sized organization will require an audit team (usually two to three auditors) to spend two to six days to conduct a complete assessment at a facility. After the audit, internal personnel will review any nonconformities, and a certificate will be issued about a month after receiving a suitable corrective action plan.

In terms of a surveillance or follow-up audits, BSI will conduct the assessment usually on a semiannual basis, but it is not a full evaluation. Surveillance audits usually are one-to two-day affairs.

However, BSI recognizes that obtaining specific information regarding audit days is needed to plan and implement your quality management system. For complete information or to obtain a quote, contact BSI directly.

When do I find out the results?

The closing meeting will be held on the last day of the audit. At the meeting, the auditor will go through the report, giving you a copy and highlighting any nonconformities. The auditor will categorize the nonconformities as minor and major. Here are their definitions, repeated from Module 8:

Minor nonconformity: A single observed lapse in following a procedure. A number of minor nonconformities do not necessarily indicate a major nonconformity as defined below. Minor nonconformities shall not produce a situation where nonconforming product or services will occur.

Major nonconformity: (definition from the International Accreditation Forum [IAF]). "The absence of, or failure to implement and maintain, one or more required management system elements, or a situation, which would, on the basis of available objective evidence, raise significant doubt as to the quality of what the organization is supplying."

If a major nonconformity is identified, then your business will not be recommended for registration. This is unlikely, particularly if you have had a pre-assessment and have implemented any required corrective and preventive actions. (**NOTE:** A successful pre-assessment is no guarantee that the outcome of the initial assessment will result in a positive recommendation for registration.) Minor nonconformities will not prevent registration. However, if a large number of minor nonconformities are found in one particular area or against one particular part of the standard, then this would highlight a major weakness and prevent registration. These should be regarded as areas where the controls in your organization can be improved. BSI is one of the most experienced registration bodies in the world with a first-class international reputation. We take the task of auditing seriously and do not raise petty issues for the sake of raising a nonconformity; our approach is to help you to improve your business processes and achieve conformance.

Provided you have truly implemented a process-based approach, are doing what you say you are doing and have met the requirements of the standard, then you will be recommended for registration to ISO 9001:2000. A few nonconformities should not detract from the success and the achievement of gaining registration.

After the auditor has presented the report, and assuming you have been recommended for registration, you will be given typically 20 days to submit a plan to correct the nonconformities raised. In this plan, you must clearly specify what corrective action you will undertake as well as when and who will do it.

The plan must be sent to your lead auditor. Once received, the lead auditor will review the plan and, assuming it covers all the points needed to correct the nonconformity, will arrange for your registration to be approved. The lead auditor will let you know of the approval as soon as possible and arrange for your certificate to be issued. An example of a certificate is included at the end of this module.

 ## What is an audit report?

An audit report is BSI's formal document prepared by the ICAD auditor that contains the audit team's recommendation and a statement of the situation found by the auditors based on the observed nonconformities. The report highlights particular areas that require corrective action but does not advise the client on how to correct nonconformities.

Once the audit report is developed, all relevant personnel gather to hear a formal presentation of the findings, usually called a closing meeting. The purpose of the closing meeting is to inform the client of the team's recommendations and to present to them any nonconformities raised and ensure that they are fully understood. The client's representative is asked to sign the report during the closing meeting, and a copy of the report is left with you.

 ## What happens after I get registered?

Indeed, obtaining registration is only the beginning. But now that you have worked so hard to achieve registration and received your certificate, you can begin to advertise your success and promote your business as a BSI-registered firm.

To maintain your registration, all you need do is to continue to use your quality system. During the coming years, we expect your system to change and improve to meet the needs of your business and your customers. BSI Inc. checks periodically, typically every six months, that you are using the quality system and that it continues to meet the requirements of the standard. Your lead auditor will let you know when these surveillance visits, or continuing assessments, will occur.

Of course, at the heart of the ISO 9000:2000 series is improvement, and there are many ways you can improve the quality of your business. The most logical next step is to identify areas where you can improve your existing quality management system. This could include:

- reducing waste;
- lowering costs;
- producing goods quicker and more effectively;
- identifying the costs of non-quality;
- measuring your performance;
- measuring the levels of customer satisfaction;
- identifying new ways of operating or learning from other businesses (benchmarking); and
- assessing the marketplace and the quality of your product in comparison with your competitors.

Looking at any areas in detail will identify areas where you can improve. And of course, use the ISO 9004:2000 document as often as possible. Its guidance can offer a great deal of support as your ISO 9000 quality journey continues.

How can I reward my team for a job well done?

Because your organization has worked hard to achieve registration—you have a great reason to celebrate! If you have been following these modules, it is likely that everybody will have been involved in the success to varying degrees. So why not recognize that effort and hard work as well as the achievement?

Many organizations celebrate this accomplishment by having a formal presentation of the certificate. If your organization is interested in such a presentation or if BSI can assist you in any way, please don't hesitate to contact us. After all, we like to celebrate, too!

BSI Client Ref:
12345678

Certificate No:
N/A

Report Number:
87654321

Prepared by:
BSI Auditor

Date:
7/11/01 – 7/12-01

XYZ CORP.
1234 Any Street
Boston, Mass. 00001
U.S.A

ASSESSMENT SUMMARY

This report relates to the initial assessment for XYZ Corp. held July 11-12, 2001. Details of the assessment are contained within this report.

During the assessment two nonconformities were identified and, if applicable, these are detailed within Appendix 2. Any opportunities for future improvement are detailed within the body of this report.

CONCLUSIONS

Congratulations, we are pleased to recommend Registration.

This is subject to the submission of a satisfactory plan for investigating the identified nonconformities and implementing effective, corrective and preventive actions. Failure to effectively implement the corrective actions identified to BSI could result in a major nonconformity being raised at the next assessment. Please submit a plan to determine action, time scales and responsibilities to Mr. BSI Auditor for review, no later than August 12, 2001.

On receipt of your corrective action plan and verification of the recommendation your certificate will be issued.

We believe in a partnership approach that provides an added value service. It is on this basis we propose a program of continuing assessment that is planned to commence in six months, we will re-assess your activities by carrying out four visit(s) every two years for one day(s) per visit.

On completion of each two-year cycle, or sooner as required, a Strategic Review that focuses on the strengths and weaknesses of your Management System(s) will be undertaken in order to facilitate new company initiative and continuous improvement.

RECOMMENDED SCOPE OF REGISTRATION

XYZ Corp. was established 1970, with the sole purpose of manufacturing widgets for automotive parts and satisfying customers.

OPPORTUNITIES FOR FUTURE IMPROVEMENT

Evaluation forms would be better served when signed by a relevant authority and employee.

EFFECTIVENESS OF INTERNAL AUDITING

Internal audits are up to date to the matrix. Well done and effective.

OBSERVATIONS

Each employee has been more then helpful with the audit. It is a pleasure to work with a staff willing to give of their time and knowledge.

BSI Client Reference: 12345678   Report Number: 87654321
Prepared by: BSI Auditor   Date: 7/11/01—7/12-01

CERTIFICATION DETAILS

CLIENT INFORMATION

Client name to appear on certificate:
XYZ Corp.

Invoice address if different from that on report cover
NA

Location address(es)

Approved site address (if applicable)
N/A

Contact name
John Q. Smith

Telephone number:
1-888-555-1234

Alternative contact:
John Jones

Telephone number:
1-888-555-1234

ACCREDITATION REQUIREMENTS

UKAS [ ]   RAB [X]   RvA [ ]   INMETRO [ ]

The 'T' codes allocated to the client are T69A

VISIT DETAILS

THE ASSESSMENT TEAM

The assessment was conducted by:
BSI Auditor

on behalf of BSI.

The principal staff involved on behalf of the company were:
John Q. Smith
John Jones
Bryan Johnson

THE MANAGEMENT STANDARD
The management standard used as the basis for this assessment was: ISO 9001:2000.

BSI Client Reference: 12345678
Prepared by: BSI Auditor

Report Number: 87654321
Date: 7/11/01—7/12/01

APPLICATION: ISO 9000:2000

Where exclusions are made, claims of conformity to the International Standard are not acceptable unless these exclusions are limited to the requirements of clause 7, and such exclusions do not affect the organization's ability, or responsibility, to provide product that meets customer and applicable regulatory requirements.

Exclusions:

7.3   Design and Development

THE COMPANY'S DOCUMENTATION

The company's management system documentation forming the basis of assessment was: Quality System Manual Dated 7-10-01

SCOPE OF THIS ASSESSMENT VISIT

The activities assessed in depth are listed in Appendix 1.

The assessment was based on random samples, and therefore, nonconformities may exist which have not been identified.

If you wish to distribute copies of this report external to the organization, then all pages must be included.

Signed for on behalf of BSI

BSI Auditor
Client Manager
Date: 7-12-01

Signed for on behalf of the client

John Q. Smith
Management Rep
Date: 7-12-01

BSI Client Reference: 12345678
Report Number: 87654321
Prepared by: BSI Auditor
Date: 7/11/01—7/12-01

APPENDIX 1 – AREAS ASSESSED THIS VISIT

Areas Assessed	4.1	4.2	5.1	5.2	5.3	5.4	5.5	5.6	6.1	6.2	6.3	6.4	7.1	7.2	7.3	7.4	7.5	7.6	8.1	8.2	8.3	8.4	8.5	NCR Ref
Quality Office	✓	✓						✓										✓	✓					
Manager			✓	✓	✓	✓														✓	✓	✓	✓	
Personal									✓	✓	✓	✓												JC-1
Office Staff													✓	✓	N/a		✓							JC-2
Purchasing																✓								

Management Standard Clause Number · Nonconformity Summary

Quality Management System Requirements

4.1	General requirements	6.1	Provision of resources
4.2	Documentation requirements	6.2	Human resources
5.1	Management commitment	6.3	Infrastructure
5.2	Customer Focus	6.4	Work environment
5.3	Quality policy	7.1	Planning of product realization
5.4	Planning	7.2	Customer-related process
5.5	Responsibility. Authority and communications	7.3	Design and development
5.6	Management review	7.4	Purchasing

7.5	Production and service provision
7.6	Control of monitoring and measuring devices
8.1	General
8.2	Monitoring and measurement
8.3	Control of nonconforming product
8.4	Analysis of data
8.5	Improvement

BSI Client Reference: 12345678
Report Number: 87654321
Prepared by: BSI Auditor
Date: 7/11/01—7/12-01

APPENDIX 2 – NONCONFORMITIES IDENTIFIED DURING THIS VISIT

Area	NCR Ref	Description	Ref Standard
Personal	JC-1	Standard requires maintaining appropriate records of education.. Upon review of Ethan Jones file there was no record of education.	6.2.2 e
Office Staff	JC-2	Procedures require each Counsellor check sheet to be signed by the counsellor. On review of account 18866 it was found that the Counsellor check sheet was not signed.	7.1

ATTACHMENT 1 –ASSESSMENT PLANNING

BSI Client Reference: 12345678
Report Number: 87654321
Prepared by: BSI Auditor
Date: 7/11/01—7/12-01

Location(s):	XYZ Corporation
Visit Cycle/Years:	4 Time in 2 Years

Planned assessments:

Report Number:				
Planned Month:	December 2001	June 2002	December 2002	June 2002
Actual Date:	December 18th			
Activity/Department/Operation:				
Review previous NCRs	✓	✓	✓	✓
Management review	✓	✓	✓	✓
Internal audits	✓	✓	✓	✓
Corrective & preventive actions	✓	✓	✓	✓
Customer Service	✓		✓	
Personal	✓		✓	
New enrollment		✓		✓
Purchasing		✓		✓

Certificate of Registration

Certificate No. FM 12345

XYZ CORP.
1234 ANY STREET
BOSTON, MASS. 00001
USA

Operates a quality management system which complies
with the requirements of BS EN ISO 9001:2000

Signed on behalf of BSI

Registered 1 August 2001

This certificate remains the property of the BSI Inc. and shall be returned immediately
upon request. This certificate does not expire. To check its validity telephone (703) 437-9000.
If relevant, additional certified addresses are recorded on an appendix to this certificate.

BSI Inc. • 12110 Sunset Hills • Suite 140 • Reston, VA 20190-3231

A507 (USA)

BSI Inc. Registered Firms Scheme
Appendix

to Certificate No. FM 12345

This appendix declares the scope of registration of the certificate granted to:

XYZ CORP.
1234 ANY STREET
BOSTON, MASS. 00001
USA

License Scope

The manufacture of square and round widgets.

Signed on behalf of BSI Inc.   Date: 1 August 2001

This Appendix is an integral part of the Registered Certificate and should only be read in conjunction with the Certificate.
This appendix is the property of the BSI Inc.

BSI Inc. • 12110 Sunset Hills • Suite 140 • Reston, VA 20190-3231

A508 (USA)

Notes:

Today and Tomorrow

 What's next?

If you choose to take the path of registration, you should know that once you receive your certificate, the journey for greater quality and enhanced customer satisfaction has only just begun.

Indeed, there are many paths you can take from this point, and some of them are explained in this section. But don't forget that the fundamental intent of the ISO 9000:2000 series is continual improvement, and going beyond the requirements of ISO 9001:2000 is strongly encouraged. With that in mind, be sure to read and thoroughly understand the ISO 9004:2000 standard, which offers excellent guidance for performance improvements. Doing so should enhance every aspect of your quality management system, and your business as well.

 Can I get help from anyone else?

Now that you are registered and operating a quality management system, you have joined a club, a *quality* club. You do not have to pay a subscription or actually join, but it is accepted in the quality world that we share experiences and best practices to help us all learn to be more effective and efficient in what we do. Of course, we keep some things confidential if we need to, especially from competitors, but you may find that others will want to discuss how you do things. Reciprocate and you will be surprised what you can learn as you spread the word about *quality*.

 What is the Malcolm Baldrige Quality Award?

According to the American Society for Quality (ASQ), the U.S. Congress established the Malcolm Baldrige National Quality Award in 1987 to raise awareness about quality management and to recognize U.S. companies that have successful quality management systems.[*]

The award program focuses on quality as an integral part of today's business management practices. The award's criteria are widely accepted as the standard for quality excellence in business performance. They are designed to help companies deliver ever-improving value to customers and improve overall company performance and capabilities.

The U.S. Commerce Department's National Institute of Standards and Technology (NIST) manages the award in close cooperation with the private sector. ASQ assists in administering the award program under contract to NIST.

The management principles of the new ISO 9000:2000 series are now better aligned with the philosophy and objectives of most award programs, including the Baldrige criteria. These principles are:

- customer focus
- leadership
- involvement of people
- process approach
- system approach to management
- continual improvement
- factual approach to decision-making
- mutually beneficial supplier relationships

For more information on the management principles and their relation to the Baldrige criteria, visit the BSI Global Web site: www.bsi-global.com.
(Source: ASQ Web site)

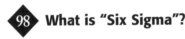 What is "Six Sigma"?

Six Sigma is a philosophy similar to the concepts embedded in the ISO 9000:2000 series—in other words, it focuses on customer goals, continual improvement, sound metrics and a process approach to doing business. It also is a statistical measure of a process, emphasizing a fundamental belief of achieving zero defects in the process. That means a strict measurement of sub-par products in a manufacturing environment or perhaps on-time delivery of products in a service organization.

However, in order for an organization to achieve the distinction of conforming to the Six Sigma principles, performance doesn't have to be perfect. Indeed, Six Sigma improvement rates allow for a limited number of defects—specifically, three parts per million. This is "virtual perfection" within an organization but still allows room for improvement.

Some global companies, such as General Electric and Motorola, have achieved Six Sigma, but the cost associated is often expensive. It can take up to 10 years for an organization to really achieve the Six Sigma rate, which requires high levels of training, education and top management commitment.

Still, the concept is catching on in a number of organization because of the anticipated results. Here are a few examples of the difference Six Sigma can make:

99.74% Good = 3 Sigma	99.9998% Good = 6 Sigma
20,000 lost articles of mail per hour	Seven articles lost per hour
Unsafe drinking water for almost 15 minutes each day	One unsafe minute every seven months
5,000 incorrect surgical operations per week	1.7 incorrect operations per week
Two short or long landings at most major airports each day	One short or long landing every five years
200,000 wrong drug prescriptions each year	68 wrong prescriptions per year
No electricity for almost seven hours each month	One hour without electricity every 34 years

Source: ASQ Web site: www.asq.org

 What is "Just-In-Time"?

Just-In-Time, or JIT, is a concept used by many organizations with purchasing and
distribution functions of a process. The goal of JIT is to maximize efficiency, reduce
or eliminate waste and consider all customer requirements to ensure on-time delivery of the product or service.

In a JIT environment, everything moves fast. Products, materials or resources are
delivered in smaller quantities "just-in-time" to be used for the manufacturing
process. Suppliers of those products usually are located near the organization or
facility so that deliveries can be made faster, cheaper and frequently. This concept
also allows for a higher quality of products being delivered because the requirements
often are precise. (They have to be to operate in a JIT environment or the production line will stop!)

A JIT world operates on a constant cycle, which allows for a lean, smooth operation. It also helps ensure that process variation is at a minimum due to the arrival of
the materials at specified times. For example, if your packaging materials arrive
before the raw materials needed to make the product, the JIT process could col-
lapse. JIT stresses strong customer-supplier relationships (much like ISO
9001:2000) so that the process doesn't break down.

For more information on JIT processes, contact BSI. An associate can assist you.

 Are there any more of these Modules?

This Module is the last in this set. We hope that you found this book to be useful
when designing and implementing your quality management system.

At CEEM, we believe passionately in quality and continual improvement. As part of that belief, we are always looking to improve what we do. If you have any comments or suggestions on how these Modules can be improved, then please contact us. Customer needs are regularly discussed within CEEM and BSI—we'll ensure that your comments reach the right person.

In the meantime, good luck with your quality journey. We look forward to adding value to your organization in the months and years ahead!

Annex 1
Utilization Chart of Management Systems Standards
ISO 9001:2000, ISO 14001:1996 and OHSAS 18001

Clause	ISO 9001:2000	Clause	ISO 14001:1996	Clause	OHSAS 18001:1999
0	**Introduction**		Introduction		Foreword
0.1	General				
0.2	Process approach				
0.3	Relationship with ISO 9004				
0.4	Compatibility with other management systems				
1	**Scope**	1	**Scope**	1	**Scope**
1.1	General				
1.2	Application				
2	**Normative references**	2	**Normative references**	2	**Reference publications**
3	**Terms and definitions**	3	**Definitions**	3	**Terms and definitions**
4	**Quality management system**	4	**Environmental management system requirements**	4	**OH&S management system elements**
4.1	General requirements	4.1	General requirements	4.1	General requirements
4.2	Documentation requirements			4.4.4	Documentation
4.2.1	General	4.4.4	Environmental management system documentation		
4.2.2	Quality manual	4.4.4	Environmental management system documentation		
4.2.3	Control of documents	4.4.5	Document control	4.4.5	Document and data control
4.2.4	Control of records	4.5.3	Records	4.5.3	Records and records management
5	**Management responsibility**	4.4.1	**Structure & responsibility**	4.4.1	**Structure & responsibility**
5.1	Management commitment	4.2	Environmental policy	4.2	OH&S policy
		4.4.1	Structure & responsibility	4.4.1	Structure & responsibility
5.2	Customer focus	4.3.1	Environmental aspects	4.3.2	Legal & other requirements
		4.3.2	Legal & other requirements		
5.3	Quality policy	4.2	Environmental policy	4.2	OH&S policy
5.4	Planning	4.3	Planning	4.3	Planning
5.4.1	Quality objectives	4.3.3	Objectives and targets	4.3	Objectives
5.4.2	Quality management system planning	4.3.4	Environmental management system programme	4.3.4	OH&S management system programme
5.5	Responsibility, authority and communication	4.1	General requirements	4.4.1	Structure & responsibility
		4.4.1	Structure & responsibility		
5.5.1	Responsibility & authority	4.4.1	Structure & responsibility	4.4.1	Structure & responsibility
5.5.2	Management representative	4.4.1	Structure & responsibility	4.4.1	Structure & responsibility
5.5.3	Internal communication	4.4.3	Communication	4.4.3	Consultation and communication
5.6	Management review	4.6	Management review	4.6	Management review
5.6.1	General				
5.6.2	Review input				
5.6.3	Review output				
6	**Resource management**	4.4.1	Structure & responsibility	4.4.1	Structure & responsibility
6.1	Provision of resources				
6.2	Human resources				
6.2.1	General				
6.2.2	Competence, awareness and training	4.4.2	Training, awareness and competence	4.4.2	Training, awareness and competence

Annex 1
Utilization Chart of Management Systems Standards
ISO 9001:2000, ISO 14001:1996 and OHSAS 18001

Clause	ISO 9001:2000	Clause	ISO 14001:1996	Clause	OHSAS 18001:1999
6.3	Infrastructure	4.4.1	Structure & Responsibility	4.4.1	Structure & Responsibility
6.4	Work environment			4.3.1	Planning for hazard identification, risk assessment and risk control
7	**Product realization**	4.4	Implementation & operation	4.4	Implementation & operation
		4.4.6	Operational control	4.4.6	Operational control
7.1	Planning of product realization	4.4.6	Operational control	4.4.6	Operational control
7.2	Customer-related processes				
7.2.1	Determination of requirements related to product	4.3.1 4.3.2 4.4.6	Environmental Aspects Legal & other requirements Operational control	4.3.1 4.4.6	Planning for hazard identification, risk assessment and risk control Operational control
7.2.2	Review of requirements related to the product	4.4.6 4.3.1	Operational control Environmental aspects	4.4.6	Operational control
7.2.3	Customer communication	4.4.3	Communications	4.4.3	Consultation and communication
7.3	Design and development	4.4.6	Operational control	4.4.6	Operational control
7.3.1	Design and development planning				
7.3.2	Design and development inputs				
7.3.3	Design and development outputs				
7.3.4	Design and development review				
7.3.5	Design and development verification				
7.3.6	Design and development validation				
7.3.7	Control of design and development changes				
7.4	Purchasing	4.4.6	Operational control	4.4.6	Operational control
7.4.1	Purchasing process				
7.4.2	Purchasing information				
7.4.3	Verification of purchased product				
7.5	Production and service provision	4.4.6	Operational control	4.4.6	Operational control
7.5.1	Control of production and service provision				
7.5.2	Validation of processes for production and service provision				
7.5.3	Identification & traceability				
7.5.4	Customer property				
7.5.5	Preservation of product				
7.6	Control of monitoring and measuring devices	4.5.1	Monitoring & measurement	4.5.1	Performance measurement and monitoring

Annex 1
Utilization Chart of Management Systems Standards
ISO 9001:2000, ISO 14001:1996 and OHSAS 18001

Clause	ISO 9001:2000	Clause	ISO 14001:1996	Clause	OHSAS 18001:1999
8	**Measurement, analysis and improvement**	4.5	Checking and corrective action	4.5.1	Performance measurement and monitoring
8.1	General	4.5.1	Monitoring & measurement		
8.2	Monitoring & measurement				
8.2.1	Customer satisfaction				
8.2.2	Internal audit	4.5.4	Environmental management system audit	4.5.4	Audit
8.2.3	Monitoring and measurement of processes	4.5.1	Monitoring & measurement	4.5.1	Performance measurement and monitoring
8.2.4	Monitoring and measurement of product				
8.3	Control of nonconforming product	4.5.2	Nonconformance and corrective and preventive action	4.5.2	Accidents, incidents, non-conformances and corrective and preventive action
		4.4.7	Emergency preparedness and response	4.4.7	Emergency preparedness and response
8.4	Analysis of data	4.5.1	Monitoring & measurement	4.5.1	Performance measurement and monitoring
8.5	Improvement	4.2	Environmental policy	4.2	OH&S policy
8.5.1	Continual improvement	4.3.4	Environmental management programme	4.3.3	Objectives
8.5.2	Corrective action	4.5.2	Nonconformance and corrective and preventive action	4.5.2	Accidents, incidents, non-conformances and corrective and preventive action
8.5.3	Preventive action				

Glossary of Terms

Accreditation—procedure by which an authoritative body formally recognizes that a body or person is competent to carry out specific tasks. Accreditation bodies, such as the Registrar Accreditation Board and the United Kingdom Accreditation Service, ensure that registrars are in compliance with Guide 62 and that they meet all of the requirements to be a impartial organization when issuing registrations.

Accreditation Marks—the marks associated with the accreditation bodies that monitor the registrar's activities. These marks can only be used in conjunction with the registrar's.

American Society for Quality (ASQ)—ASQ is a society of individual and organizational members dedicated to the ongoing, development, advancement and promotion of quality concepts, principles and techniques. Visit www.asq.org for more details.

Analysis—resolution or breaking up of something complex into its various simple elements; the exact determination of the elements or components of something complex.

Appendix—supporting sheets to a certificate that define the activities and locations assessed and certified under one quality system.

Audit/assessment—a verification of the effectiveness of the management system operated by a firm through examination of materials, processes, finished product, methods of test, records, systems, services and other activities established by a firm within its management system.

Auditor/assessor (third party)—a qualified industry expert who visits your organization, examines what you do and how it is managed through your quality system.

Audit criteria—set of policies, procedures or requirements used as a reference. (BS EN ISO 9000:2000)

Audit evidence—records, statement of fact or other information that are relevant to the audit criteria and verifiable. (BS EN ISO 9000:2000)

Audit findings—results of the evaluation of the collected audit evidence against audit criteria. (BS EN ISO 9000:2000)

Audit program—set of one or more audits planned for a specific timeframe and directed toward a specific purpose. (BS EN ISO 9000:2000)

Audit report—a formal document prepared by an audit team that contains the recommendation for registration and/or the statement of the situation found by the auditors based on their observations. The report highlights particular areas that require corrective action but does not advise the client on how to correct nonconformities.

Audit team—one or more auditors conducting an audit. (BS EN ISO 9000:2000)

Certificate—awarded following recommendation after a registrar's initial audit.

Characteristic—a distinguishing feature.

Closing meeting—the formal meeting between a client and an audit team at the end of an assessment to discuss the findings and make recommendation for improvement. BSI auditors leave a copy of the audit report with you.

Competence—demonstrated ability to apply knowledge and skills.

Conformance—an affirmative indication or judgment that a product or service has met requirements of the relevant specifications, contract or regulation; the state of meeting requirements; fulfillment of a requirement.

Consultants—people or organizations that help companies implement a management system and achieve registration. They can help design, write and implement a management system in accordance with the standard and provide organizations with immediate assistance.

Continual improvement—According to ISO 9000:2000, continual improvement is the recurring activity to increase an organization's ability to fulfill requirements. The process of establishing objectives and finding opportunities for improvement is a continual process through the use of audit findings and audit conclusions, analysis of data, management reviews or other means and generally leads to corrective action and/or preventive action.

Continuing assessment—the periodic (every six months) visits that registrars make to a company to ensure it is still using its management system effectively. At each visit, registrars generally review 25 percent of the system and certain critical elements are reviewed at each visit. For example, internal audits, customer complaints, management review(s) and corrective action requirements from the previous visit.

Corrective action—short-term action to address a nonconformity.

Customer—organization or person that receives a product.

Customer requirement—a specification issued by an organization that outlines needs and expectations of a product or service.

Customer satisfaction—the customer's perception of the degree to which the customer's requirements have been fulfilled.

Data—facts, especially numerical facts, collected together for reference or information.

Defect—non-fulfillment of a requirement related to an intended or specified use. (BS EN ISO 9000:2000)

Design and development—set of processes that transforms requirements into specified characteristics or into the specification of a product, process or system. (BS EN ISO 9000:2000) Examples include records, specifications, procedures, drawings, reports, standards, etc.

Document—information and its supporting medium. (BS EN ISO 9000:2000)

Documentation—written parts or evidence within a quality management system, which can include documents, guidelines, procedures, a quality manual, a quality plan, records and specifications.

Effectiveness—extent to which planned activities are realized and planned results achieved. (BS EN ISO 9000:2000)

Efficiency—relationship between the result achieved and the resources used. (BS EN ISO 9000:2000

Exclusion—(an instance of) shutting out, debarring, rejecting from consideration, etc.

Environmental Management System (ISO 14001)—a part of the overall management system that includes organizational structure, planning activities, responsibilities, practices, procedures, processes and resources for developing, implementing, achieving, reviewing and maintaining the environmental policy.

Experience—practical acquaintance with facts or events, considered as a source of knowledge.

Implement—put a decision, plan or system into effect.

Improvement—part of quality management focused on increasing the ability to fulfill quality requirements. (BS EN ISO 9000:2000)

Independent—not influenced or affected by others; (of an inquiry, audit, investigator, observer, etc.) outside the organization, unit, process etc., concerned.

Inspection—conformity evaluation by observation and judgment accompanied as appropriate by measurement, testing or gauging. (BS EN ISO 9000:2000)

Interested party—person or group having an interest in the performance or success of an organization.

Internal audit—when a member of your own staff audits the systems and procedures you have in place in your own company. A quality manager may do this regularly to see if the quality system is being used and maintained. The internal audit is a check to ensure you are still operating your system effectively and is required in ISO 9001:2000. You cannot conduct an internal audit on your own responsibilities.

International Standard Organization (ISO)—Geneva-based organization responsible for coordinating and publishing ISO 9000, ISO 14001 and other international standards.

ISO 9000:2000—a generic name given to international standards that provide a framework for a quality management system. ISO 9000:2000 was published in December 2000, after two years of development, and is simpler and more flexible than its 1994 predecessor. The primary difference between the two standards is a shift from procedure to process-based activity, enabling organizations to link business objectives with business effectiveness. Companies registered to ISO 9001, 2 or 3:1994 have 3 years to transfer to ISO 9001:2000.

ISO 19011—a jointly prepared document from experts of TC 176 on quality management and quality assurance and TC 207 on environmental management that will help organizations streamline their auditing practices for management systems; also known as the "common auditing standard." Expected publication in 2002.

Management—coordinated activities to direct and control an organization. (BS EN ISO 9000:2000)

Management System—the manner in which an element of your organization is managed—it could be quality, environment, information security or health and safety. Because they can be systemized, they can be standardized and benchmarked/audited and therefore, reviewed and improved.

Measure—ascertain or determine (a spatial magnitude or quantity) by the application of some object of known size or capacity or by comparison with some fixed unit.

Monitor—measure or test at intervals, especially for the purpose of regulation or control.

Nonconformity—non-fulfillment of a requirement. (BS EN ISO 9000:2000)

Objective—something sought, or aimed for, related to quality. (BS EN ISO 9000:2000)

Objective evidence—data supporting the existence or verity of something. (BS EN ISO 9000:2000) Objective evidence may be obtained through observation, measurement, test or other means.

Observation—verbal or written comments that are made by auditors to clients concerning potential nonconformity or areas of concern. (Note: Observations also can be positive.) Observations are important to resolve, but it's up to the organization or auditee to fix them as appropriate. During a registration audit, observations often are raised as opportunities to improve the business, but it is not required that the organization address them immediately.

Organization—group of people and facilities with an arrangement of responsibilities, authorities and relationships. (BS EN ISO 9000:2000)

Organizational structure—arrangement of responsibilities, authorities and relationships between people. (BS EN ISO 9000:2000)

Perception—state of being or process of becoming aware or conscious of a thing, especially through any of the senses; a degree of customer satisfaction.

Performance—execution, accomplishment, fulfillment, the carrying out of a command, duty, purpose, promise, etc.

Plan—arrange in advance (an action or proposed proceeding); formulation or organized method by which something is to be done.

Plan-Do-Check-Act—the model around which ISO 9001:2000 is designed. A fairly common sense process of planning, doing, checking and then acting to continually improve the quality system.

Policy—course of action or principle adopted or proposed by a government, party, individual, etc.

Pre-assessment—this is an optional service from BSI or other registrars to ensure that you conform to the standard. It is a "dry run" to make sure that there are no major problems that would hinder you from achieving registration. For BSI clients that use this service, the pass rate is 95 percent if all the information supplied to the client is addressed prior to the initial assessment.

Prevention—action of stopping something from happening or making impossible an anticipated event or intended act.

Preventive action—action to eliminate the cause of a potential nonconformity or other undesirable potential situation. There can be more than cause for potential nonconformity. Preventive action is taken to prevent occurrence whereas corrective action is taken to prevent recurrence.

Procedure—specified way to carry out an activity or a process. Procedures can be documented or not. When a procedure is documented, the term "written procedure" or "documented procedure" is frequently used. The document that contains a procedure can be called a "procedure document."

Process—a set of interrelated or interacting activities that transforms inputs into outputs. (BS EN ISO 9000:2000)

Process approach—the application of a system of processes within an organization, together with the identification and interactions of these processes, and their management.

Product—the result of a process.

Product Certification—a process of confirming that a product has been manufactured to a product standard and has been independently tested and certified. This differs from management system certification because the product performance is assessed not just the system through which it was produced.

Quality—degree to which a set of inherent characteristics fulfills requirements. (BS EN ISO 9000:2000)

Quality Control—part of quality management focused on fulfilling quality requirements. (BS EN ISO 9000:2000)

Quality improvement—ISO 9000:2000 Clause 3.2.12 defines quality improvement as part of quality management, focused on increasing the ability to fulfill quality requirements. NOTE: The requirements can be related to any aspect such as effectiveness, efficiency or traceability.

Quality Management System (QMS)—a common sense, well-documented system that ensures consistency and improvement of working practices, including the products and services produced.

Quality Manual—a high level document that outlines an organization's intention to operate in a quality manner. It can be used in many ways that include, marketing, communication, training and/or as a document that allows third parties to understand an organization's business and assess its activities against a particular standard such as ISO 9001.

Quality Objectives—The organization's strategic planning and quality policy provide a framework for the setting of quality objectives. The objectives should be capable of being measured in order to facilitate an effective and efficient review by management. Consideration should be given to current and future needs of the organization. The quality objectives should be communicated so employees can contribute to their achievement.

Quality policy—normally defined by top management and written so that it is appropriate to the purpose of the organization, includes a commitment to comply with requirements and continually improve the effectiveness of the quality management system. Provides a framework for establishing and reviewing quality objectives and is communicated and understood within the organization. It should be reviewed for continuing suitability.

Registrar—an independent body that assesses and verifies how an organization uses its management system and conforms to the requirements of a standard. If the organization conforms to the specified requirements, the registrar issues a certificate that demonstrates conformance.

Registrar Accreditation Board—the primary U.S. accreditation body. (See accreditation body.)

Registration/Certification—what an organization achieves when it passes an audit/assessment. A registrar assesses your quality management system against a standard. BSI uses the term registration, as certification is often misunderstood to refer to each product being guaranteed.

Root Cause—a fundamental deficiency that results in a nonconformance and must be corrected to prevent recurrence of the same or similar nonconformance.

Scope of registration—a precise definition of a client's activities that are the subject of audit/assessment.

Standard—a document produced by an international committee of experts setting the guidelines on how things should be done.

Strategic Review—BSI's twice-yearly review of an organization's entire system and past performance that allows it to retain its certification without having to go through a full re-assessment/certification.

Traceability—ability to trace the history, application or location of that which is under consideration. (BS EN ISO 9000:2000)

Validation—confirmation, through the provision of objective evidence that the requirements for a specific intended use or application have been fulfilled. (BS EN ISO 9000:2000)

Verification—confirmation, through the provision of objective evidence that specified requirements have been fulfilled. (BS EN ISO 9000:2000)

Work Instructions—additional details than what is described in procedures. The complexity of the business helps an organization determine whether it needs detailed work instructions in addition to its procedures. Many businesses include work instructions to aid in training, make it clear how a job is done, to reduce mistakes, an *aide-memoir* for staff, a point of reference for jobs that are not often carried out.

Index

More Information

CEEM Inc.
12110 Sunset Hills Road, Suite 100
Reston, VA 20190-3231
Tel: 800-745-5565; 703-250-5900
Fax: 703-250-5313
E-mail: solutions@ceem.com
Internet: www.ceem.com

BSI Inc.
12110 Sunset Hills Road, Suite 140
Reston, VA 20190-3231
Tel: 800-862-4977
Fax: 703-437-9001
E-mail: inquiry@bsiamericas.com
Internet: www.bsiamericas.com

American National Standards Institute (ANSI)
U.S. Member Body of ISO TC 176 and TC 207
11 West 42nd St.
New York, NY 10036
Tel: 212-642-4900
Fax: 212-642-4969
Internet: www.ansi.org

International Organization for Standardization
1 rue de Varemde
Case postale 56, CH-1211
Geneva 20 Switzerland
Tel: +41-22-749-0111
Fax: +41-22-733-3430
Internet: www.iso.ch

QSU Publishing Co.
Publisher of *Quality Systems Update*
3975 University Drive
Fairfax, VA 22030
Tel: 866-225-3122
Fax: 703-359-8462
Internet: qsuonline.com